MUSIC IN RANGE

FILM+MEDIASTUDIES

Film studies is the critical exploration of cinematic texts as art and entertainment, as well as the industries that produce them and the audiences that consume them. Although a medium barely one hundred years old, film is already transformed through the emergence of new media forms. Media studies is an interdisciplinary field that considers the nature and effects of mass media upon individuals and society and analyzes media content and representations. Despite changing modes of consumption—especially the proliferation of individuated viewing technologies—film has retained its cultural dominance into the 21st century, and it is this transformative moment that the WLU Press Film and Media Studies series addresses.

Our Film and Media Studies series includes topics such as identity, gender, sexuality, class, race, visuality, space, music, new media, aesthetics, genre, youth culture, popular culture, consumer culture, regional/national cinemas, film policy, film theory, and film history.

Wilfrid Laurier University Press invites submissions. For further information, please contact the Series editors, all of whom are in the Department of English and Film Studies at Wilfrid Laurier University:

Dr. Philippa Gates
Email: pgates@wlu.ca

Dr. Russell Kilbourn
Email: rkilbourn@wlu.ca

Dr. Ute Lischke
Email: ulischke@wlu.ca

Department of English and Film Studies
Wilfrid Laurier University
75 University Avenue West
Waterloo, ON N2L 3C5
Canada
Phone: 519-884-0710
Fax: 519-884-8307

MUSIC IN RANGE

The Culture of Canadian Campus Radio

Brian Fauteux

WILFRID LAURIER
UNIVERSITY PRESS

Wilfrid Laurier University Press acknowledges the support of the Canada Council for the Arts for our publishing program. We acknowledge the financial support of the Government of Canada through the Canada Book Fund for our publishing activities. This work was supported by the Research Support Fund.

Library and Archives Canada Cataloguing in Publication

Fauteux, Brian, 1983–, author
   Music in range: the culture of Canadian campus radio / Brian Fauteux.

(Film and media studies)
Includes bibliographical references and index.
Issued in print and electronic formats.
Available in other form: Music in range.
ISBN 978-1-77112-150-7 (pbk.).—ISBN 978-1-77112-151-4 (pdf).—
ISBN 978-1-77112-152-1 (epub)

   1. College radio stations—Canada. 2. Community radio—Canada. 3. Radio and music—Canada. 4. Broadcasting policy—Canada. I. Title. II. Series: Film and media studies series

HE8697.95.C3F38 2015   384.54'530971   C2015-902618-0
                                                        C2015-902619-9

Cover design by Jordan Puopolo. Cover photo by Rafal Mrozek. Text design by Mike Bechthold.

This book is printed on FSC® certified paper and is certified Ecologo. It contains post-consumer fibre, is processed chlorine free, and is manufactured using biogas energy.

Printed in Canada

RECYCLED
Paper made from
recycled material
FSC® C103567

Contents

Acknowledgements

This book on campus radio is inspired by campus radio. From back when I would tune into a weekly night-time punk show on CIUT-FM from the suburbs north of Toronto, campus radio has been part of my day-to-day soundtrack. As an undergraduate student at the University of Western Ontario, I regularly awoke to the sounds of CHRW-FM. By starting my days hearing previously unheard sounds, I became increasingly curious about the relationship between campus radio stations and independent artists. This curiosity eventually sparked a number of research questions that became the foundation of my graduate studies and then this very book.

I am fortunate to have been surrounded by a supportive community of friends and scholars while carrying out this research. Charles Acland and Leslie Shade have been exceptional mentors who have been immensely helpful during the various stages of my academic career. Bill Buxton, Elena Razlogova, Sandra Gabriele, Michele Hilmes, and Line Grenier have offered excellent feedback on earlier versions of this work. Frequent meetings and discussions with David Madden, Jacqueline Wallace, M.E. Luka, Constance Lafontaine, Shirley Roburn, and Samuel Thulin have made the research and writing process all the more enjoyable. As well, I am appreciative of the many conversations I have had with colleagues at conferences such as the Canadian Communication Association, the International Association for the Study of Popular Music (Canada and US), and the Society for Cinema and Media Studies. Thanks to Keir Keightley and Norma Coates for igniting my interest in the study of popular music.

A special thanks to CHMA, CKUW, CiTR, and all of the people who agreed to share their stories and contribute to this project. In no particular order: Pierre Malloy, Sandy Mackay, Pat LePoidevin, Steve Ridlington, Rob Schmidt, Robin Eriksson, Ted Turner, Sarah Michaelson, Stu Reid, Brenda Grunau, Nardwuar the Human Serviette, Janis McKenzie, Bill Baker, and

Cameron Reed. Your passion for independent and local media is both motivating and inspiring.

Jessica Antony and Andrew deWaard provided me with places to stay during my research and took the time to show me around their respective cities. Mark Ambrose Harris has been a second set of eyes for select sections of this work. Candice Bjur at the UBC archives and Tyler Palamar at the CRTC archives helped me locate essential documents for this book. Shena Yoshida at Mint Records, Duncan McHugh, David Barclay, Stylus, and Discorder shared the images featured in Chapter 6 without hesitation. The book's cover is courtesy of the very talented Jordan Puopolo.

Blaire Comacchio, Leslie Macredie, Lisa Quinn, and Rob Kohlmeier at WLU Press have been excellent correspondents, especially for an author who is navigating the process of writing his first book.

This research was financially aided by the Social Sciences and Humanities Research Council of Canada and the Faculty of Arts and Sciences at Concordia, for which I am very grateful. Part of Chapter 4 appeared as "Beyond Campus Borders: Canadian Campus Radio and Community Representation on the FM Dial," in *The Radio Journal: International Studies in Broadcast & Audio Media* 11, number 2.

Finally, thanks go to my family (the Fauteuxs and the Curows) for the ongoing support in all my endeavours. And, of course, to Dallas, my partner in most things, whose unrivalled spirits always keep my spirits up.

1

Introduction

In an unprecedented decision by the Canadian Radio-television and Tele-communications Commission (CRTC), the campus radio station at Ryerson University in Toronto, Ontario, had its broadcast licence revoked on 12 February 2011. The station ceased broadcasting due to a lack of organizational structure and its failure to comply with federal broadcasting regulations as set out by the CRTC, the independent public authority that regulates and supervises Canadian broadcasting and telecommunications. In January 2011 the Toronto-based blog *Torontoist* presented a series of points leading up to the loss of licence, including internal disputes between August 2007 and March 2009 that resulted in the election of competing boards of directors, a staff lockout from March to October 2009, a failure by the station to submit annual returns with the CRTC, the late filing of tapes, logs, and program schedules, and a number of confused and conflicted management and administrative decisions (Kupferman 2011b). The decision was said to be unprecedented since such revocations have always followed a mandatory order or a short-term licence renewal (CRTC 2011a). On 11 September 2012, CKLN's frequency, 88.1 FM, was awarded to Rock 95 Broadcasting Ltd. to launch a commercial indie rock station CIND-FM, or "Indie 88." Some ex-CKLN staff and volunteers were invited to join Radio Regent, an online radio station operated by the Regent Park Focus Youth Media Arts Centre (http://www.radioregent.com). The decision to terminate CKLN's licence raises questions about what constitutes a legitimate campus radio station in Canada and what the limits of "alternative" approaches to radio broadcasting in Canada might be. The fact that this licence revocation came at a time when a number of campus and college radio stations in North America were faced with funding and sustainability issues is noteworthy, as the value of campus radio becomes increasingly important to consider, as does the presence of local, community media outlets in the North American media environment.

In January 2011, KUSF, the college radio station at the University of San Francisco, closed its studio doors after having been on the air since 1963. An entry on the San Francisco–based blog *SF Weekly* profiled the closing, noting that "USF officials abruptly shut the doors to KUSF, the college's well-known indie radio station ... locking out students and DJs with no notice" (Sherbert 2011). The university had "quietly" sold the station to a "classical public radio network," which launched a "noncommercial classical music station." However, KUSF would live on as an online radio station. University officials at USF claimed that the move to the online format "will give the station more capacity to accommodate 'thousands' of listeners as opposed to the 100 listeners it is now limited to, according to the university" (Sherbert 2011). The closing was justified by the assumption that for smaller or "alternative" radio stations, online broadcasting was more viable than local FM broadcasting.

The following summer, WRVU at Vanderbilt University sold its licence to a local public radio station. A *New York Times* opinion piece aptly titled "The Day the Music Died" stated that this sale added Vanderbilt to "a growing list of colleges and universities ... where college radio licenses are being sold off, backed by the assertion that today's well-wired students no longer tune in to the medium" (O'Connell 2011). However, the article's author claimed that this assertion "misses the point: college radio is not only a vital part of the communities it serves, but it is even more essential in the Internet era." WRVU had always encouraged members from the off-campus community to get involved with the station, and it was very much tied to the rich cultural heritage of Nashville. The station had a history of playing traditional bluegrass, world music, and electronic, "to name just a few genres." WRVU was a "cornerstone of the local community," a place where "students learned from veterans, townies got to know Vanderbilt and Nashvillians got access to a chunk of the public commons otherwise dominated by big business: the airwaves." The article described college radio as "free from the demands of profit and playability" and claimed it to be a great source of music at a time when local content was disappearing from the airwaves.

The closing of college radio stations like WRVU and KUSF was anticipated in a *New York Times* article in December 2010, which emphasized the role of college radio stations in playing "a broad swath of music – from undiscovered indie bands and obscure blues acts to '60s garage rock and '80s postpunk," genres and sounds "largely absent" on commercial radio

(Vorwald 2010). At the centre of public debate and discussion surrounding the viability of campus stations is the question of whether or not students are actually tuning in to the universities' FM signals. The following year, another *New York Times* article profiled a number of American college stations that had moved exclusively online, where texting and sending messages to a Facebook page could easily be integrated into programming practices. The article cited Fredonia campus in southwest Buffalo, where a station streams on the Internet and where "tousled-haired disc jockeys in faded band T's are constantly encouraging listeners to check out a rolling supply of podcasts, YouTube clips, photos and campus news on the station's Web site" (Spencer 2011). Students at Yale University's WYBCX referred to the online station as a "global entity" with shows "designed for audiences beyond Yale." A former student programmer at Princeton's WPRB said that the power of college stations "has been diluted because music blogs like Pitchfork and social networking sites ... are offering those same opportunities to discover new music." And while university officials have been emphasizing the feasibility of FM stations moving online, others feel that "the loss of a terrestrial signal will effectively delegitimize" these stations.

Joey Yang, a student at Rice University and station manager for the university's KTRU, said that as "a 50,000-watt station that can be heard all across Houston, there's a sense of responsibility to the community," and when "you lose a terrestrial footprint in Houston – anyone can put out a signal that's on the Internet – it takes away the legitimacy of what [the station is] trying to do" (Vorwald 2010). The student-run KTRU was sold to the University of Houston for use by its public radio network at the price of US$9.5 million. On 28 April 2011, college stations across the United States mourned the loss of the station with a "College Radio Minute of Silence" (Waits 2013). Since the sale, the Houston classical public radio station, KUHA, has laid off full-time staff members and has been "replacing local programming with syndicated classical music content" (Waits 2013).

Many student-run stations still exist within the non-commercial portion of the spectrum in the United States (88.1 to 91.9 MHz), but a trend that began in the 1990s has seen others "driven onto the Web or into oblivion when college administrators have decided to sell their licenses for much-needed cash" (Troop 2011). A number of college radio practitioners and advocates do believe that online broadcasting offers an effective means for smaller stations to reach a large audience and see the potential for programmers to share local sounds with distant listeners. The argument that online broadcasting better reflects a student's daily experience with media and technology is certainly worth considering. Some stations have begun as online radio stations and have worked to cultivate a local audience. Kyle

Barnett, the faculty adviser for Bellarmine's online college station, claims that most of the station's listeners are connected to the university. "We increasingly have the sense that our local focus in an online context has allowed us to reach a variety of listeners with Bellarmine and Louisville ties in far-flung locales, from Belfast to Shanghai" (Barnett 2013). However, this trend of station closures points to the fact that there is an economic barrier preventing smaller stations from remaining on the dial as the value of the FM spectrum increases. Moreover, the broader North American radio landscape is increasingly displaced, reliant on digital technologies and online platforms, and removed from the complexities and distinctions that are tied to a specific locality.

The history of the licensing of the Canadian campus radio sector offers an intriguing juxtaposition and poignant example of how licensed FM campus radio has come to be associated with a commitment to representing the cultural and musical interests within a station's broadcast range. That is, the processes and practices by which campus stations have acquired licences from the CRTC ensure that campus stations do their best to reflect and represent the communities they are licensed within. In Canada, FM regulation has helped campus stations realize their goal of representing their communities; this, in turn, has increased their inclusivity and diversity in operations and programming. A commitment to the "community" is a defining trait that sets Canadian campus stations apart from American college stations. Since 2000, the latter have been licensed as part of the Low Power FM (LPFM) radio service, and this has helped some new low-power college stations to develop. These stations are authorized for non-commercial educational broadcasting, and they must operate with a maximum power of 100 watts with an approximate service range of 5.6 kilometres (FCC 2013). In contrast to Canadian campus stations just north of the border, which are typically higher in range and wattage, a LPFM college station's commitment to broadcasting for the surrounding community is only referenced when there are conflicting applications for a frequency. In these cases, the applicant with a presence in the community for at least two years and a commitment to provide at least eight hours of locally originated programming each day will be granted the permit.

The contemporary relevance of North American campus and college radio broadcasting has been increasingly at the centre of debates and discussions initiated by policy-makers, students, university administrations, and radio practitioners. Student governments and university administrations searching for ways to cut spending have turned their attention to services like student radio. Campus stations without support from the university and without strong leadership have faced issues of sustainability.

Yet at the same time, campus radio stations have been recognized for their long-standing commitment to community-based radio programming and for showcasing innovative and diverse musical genres and styles, as well as spoken-word news and political programming. A weekly program grid at a Canadian campus radio station typically includes a range of shows profiling emerging and independent music, news and spoken-word, folk and country, hip hop, jazz and blues, and content for a variety of ethnic and cultural communities within the station's broadcast range, often in a variety of languages. The music-based programming at a campus radio station reflects a number of musical communities and genres, and programmers tend to promote new and innovative sounds and styles. The Community Radio Fund of Canada (CRFC) – a fund that has a mandate to financially support community and campus stations across the country – was founded in 2007. Astral Media committed $1.4 million over seven years to "help community broadcasters respond to the increasing demands of their communities for independent, local programming" (Kaestner 2008). A press release describing the fund claimed that there had been a decline in programming that reflects local communities in both commercial and public media, and that the establishment of this fund would "help community broadcasting reach its full potential as an independent, diverse, and accessible part of Canadian media" (Kaestner 2008). This fund grew out of a three-year partnership (three years before the launch of this press release) among Canada's three largest community radio associations: the National Campus and Community Radio Association (NCRA/ANREC), l'Alliance des radios communautaires du Canada (l'ARC du Canada), and l'Association des radiodiffuseurs communautaires du Québec (l'ARCQ). As of this writing, the CRFC receives funding and benefits from a number of private broadcasters, including BCE, COGECO, and Rogers, as well as SIRIUS Satellite Radio (http://communityradiofund.org).

CJLO, the campus radio station at Concordia University in Montreal, is one of many examples that point to the contemporary relevance of the campus sector to Canadian culture and music. The station won notable accolades in 2010, having been recognized as the best college station in North America at the annual College Music Journal (CMJ) awards. This recognition landed the station on the Huffington Post's "9 Best College Radio Stations" in 2010, making it the only one representing Canada (Wiener-Bronner 2010). In December 2011, Concordia students voted in favour of increasing the station's fee levy (57 percent voting "Yes"), which added nine cents to the already existing levy of twenty-five cents, applicable to all undergraduate students. CJLO's website hosted a page informing readers that with this increased support the station planned to apply for a small FM frequency in Montreal's downtown core (as of this writing CJLO broadcasts as an AM station and online), purchase recording equipment for students, increase campus and community outreach, and become less dependent on paid advertising to ensure space for free advertising for student clubs and groups ("CJLO Fee Levy ..."). The station was nominated for six CMJ College Radio Awards in 2012, including "Station of the Year," and it ended up winning for "Biggest Champion of the Local Scene." In the same year, CJLO was one of the first recipients of funding from Radiometres, a program offered by the CRFC. The station received $14,500 to pursue a project titled "CJLO's Community Recording Project." The project enabled the station to work with a minimum of five local bands or artists over a period of ten months to help them produce albums.

While some North American campus stations have been facing pressure to surrender their frequencies, others are being recognized for the dynamic and important role they play in the overall broadcasting environment and in the cultural industries. In Canada, CRTC regulation as outlined in a number of policy documents – such as the Broadcasting Act (1991), Campus and Community Radio Policy 2010; (Public Notice CRTC 2010-499), and the earlier Campus Radio Policy (Public Notice CRTC 2000-12) – has in many ways acted as a safety net for the sector, one concerned with ensuring that diversity and a commitment to local programming are maintained in some form within the overall broadcast system. This is not to say that Canadian universities are exempt from the pressures related to financial sustainability, which many student services like campus radio have been facing. CJLO's neighbour, McGill University's CKUT, has been implicated in a dispute over online opt-outs with the university's administration and student government for a number of years. An online opt-out allows students to cancel their financial contribution to the station with the click of a button. At the thirtieth annual National Campus and Community Radio Conference (NCRC) in 2011, hosted by CKDU-FM in Halifax, Nova Scotia, a representative from Radio Laurier spoke about the University of Waterloo's CKMS losing funding from student fee levies. He claimed that students were not aware of the station, or its location on campus, and that the student union used these reasons to hold a referendum that resulted in the loss of fees. Yet as examples such as the vote for CJLO at Concordia have shown, many students are eager to help fund and support campus radio. Furthermore, the CRFC signifies a level of respect for the sector and a willingness to find ways to ensure its sustainability; so do the CRTC public hearings, which have helped formulate campus and community radio policy. The revocation of Ryerson's CKLN is an anomaly, given the support that the campus sector in Canada has generally received, but also suggests there are certain boundaries, both political and historical, that campus stations must be aware of in order to maintain operations.

The ways in which campus radio broadcasting has come to command the attention of popular discourse and policy-making inspire a closer look into the history of the sector in Canada. Moreover, the capacity of Canadian campus radio stations to represent and reflect their campuses, as well as the communities within their broadcast range, is an important topic to consider at a time when localism and diversity in radio broadcasting are often bypassed in favour of more financially sustainable ways of organizing media and communication systems. Campus radio stations represent an important component of the mediascape available to people, one that is often framed as "alternative," "independent," or "local," or as having a responsibility to the "community."

This book argues that Canadian campus radio broadcasting offers a local alternative within a broadcasting system that is increasingly centralized and consolidated. It explores the development of the sector by highlighting the factors that have shaped its close connection to local music and culture. Campus radio broadcasting is a prominent component of the community sector in Canada's single broadcasting system, which also includes the more dominant private and public broadcasting sectors ("single," as determined by the Broadcasting Act 1991, because the system makes use of public airwaves and is regulated by a single public authority, the CRTC).

To assess how and why Canadian campus radio offers a local alternative for media practitioners, radio and music listeners, and cultural producers within Canada's broadcasting system, this book pursues two key questions. First, how significant is federal broadcasting policy in determining the programming, operations, and culture of campus stations, relative to the influence of the specific locality that surrounds a station? Campus radio broadcasting has been discursively and strategically framed throughout its development in Canada, both in policy-making at the federal level and by stations and practitioners through the crafting of mandates and internal policy. In this book, discourses and debates at the level of policy-making are compared and contrasted with the ways in which campus radio stations define themselves. Ideological terms like "alternative," "community," "local," and "independent" have practical applications and construct specific campus radio cultures. How, then, do individual stations navigate broadcasting policy in ways that speak to the specificity of nearby musical and cultural communities?

Second, how does the culture of campus radio extend beyond an individual station into the wider locality, and what connects campus radio to cultural institutions and cultural producers within music scenes and communities that are active in a station's broadcast range? These local connections have the potential to respond to a changing radio landscape in which consolidation and convergence have reduced and limited local radio programming; they also point to alternative methods and values for circulating music.

Section 3(b) of Canada's Broadcasting Act (1991) highlights three elements of the country's single broadcasting system: public, private, and community. Campus stations fall under the "community" element of Canada's broadcasting system. Up until 2010, campus stations were distinguished from community stations and defined by the CRTC as "not-for-profit undertakings associated with institutions of post-secondary education. Campus radio stations rely almost exclusively on volunteers from the campus, and from the community at large, for their programming and operation" (CRTC, 2000c). The 2010 policy for the sector groups campus and community stations together, noting that both cater to their respective communities through key elements such as a high percentage of Canadian content, the broadcasting of local information, and the promotion of local culture, arts, and music, as well as by supporting emerging local talent and local/regional content pertaining to social and community issues (CRTC 2010c). Canadian campus radio stations, therefore, are grouped under the larger category of community broadcasting but are distinguished by the participation of student volunteers in programming and governance, by students and academic administrators sitting on their boards, and by the funding they generate from the academic institution and the student population.

In the United States, stations that broadcast from a university or college are commonly referred to as "college radio" stations, due in part to the use of "college music" or "college radio" to describe a genre paralleling the "alternative music" heard on American college stations during the 1980s and 1990s, and prior to that, rock and folk in the 1960s and 1970s. As Holly Kruse (2003) explains, "college music" became "a relevant term because it could define a genre through the primary medium by which it was disseminated: college radio" (12). Campus stations in Canada often play "alternative" or "indie" music, yet the sector has avoided becoming defined by these genres as a result of its strong commitment to programming various musical genres as well as spoken-word, news, and diverse cultural content. Additionally, regulatory frameworks are a key component in terms of what sets Canadian campus stations apart from American college stations. In Canada, a campus station on the FM dial is regulated in a manner that strongly emphasizes a commitment to Canadian and local programming, as well as community responsibility, much more so than college stations in the United States.

A Radio and TV Station List compiled by the CRTC in 2014 (https://services.crtc.gc.ca/pub/BroadListRad/Default-Defaut.aspx) includes forty-seven community-based campus radio stations (not including instructional stations). This number increases when we add closed-circuit campus stations, high school stations, campus stations that have since become community stations, like Trent University's CFFF-FM in Peterborough, Ontario, and campus stations that only broadcast on the Internet. About nine of these campus stations first hit the airwaves in the 2000s, with most stations establishing themselves throughout the 1970s and 1980s. Many began broadcasting as closed-circuit or cable FM stations, serving a small geographic area located within, or just around, the university or college campus. Throughout the 1990s and into the 2000s, campus stations have grown considerably, increasing in wattage and becoming licensed by the CRTC as AM or FM radio stations.

The policy that regulates Canadian campus and community radio stations was reviewed and revised by the CRTC in July 2010, following a public hearing held in Gatineau, Quebec, in January of that year. Central issues in this review process included spectrum scarcity, sustainability and funding, programming requirements, new media and technology, and new approaches to defining the campus and community sector. During this review, both commercial and campus stations staked claims for spots on the FM band. Some cited the Internet as an important supplement to FM broadcasting, but most advocates of community and campus radio argued that it does not serve as an adequate replacement. Evidently, many of the issues covered by the journalistic pieces cited above are also playing out at the level of federal policy-making. As noted by the CRTC's former vice-chair of broadcasting, Michel Arpin, "there continues to be a strong demand for new FM radio licences, even though the FM dial in many markets has become overcrowded" (Arpin 2010). Inherent within these debates and discourses are ideas as to what role the three broadcasting sectors in Canada should play within the contemporary media environment.

By pursuing a study of campus radio based on its focus on local music and culture, this book repositions radio within a growing body of scholarship that explores the democratic potential for circulating music and culture digitally and online. For instance, Kembrew McLeod (2005) argues that music file sharing has created "an alternative means of music distribution for artists who are often marginalized by the mainstream music industry" (521). As well, changing conceptualizations of communication stemming from the rise of online media forms are now prominent in communication and media studies literature. Henry Jenkins's popular book *Convergence Culture: Where Old and New Media Collide* (2006) presents a number of examples where access to online and digital content is necessary for fully engaging with a television show or popular film. Lisa Nakamura (2009) discusses the place of digital video within cinema studies, arguing that this transitional phase warrants study and that a "challenge that faces cinema and media scholars today is to learn some of the new visual languages that arise from popular digital moving image practices," including online video games and YouTube (155). While these claims and arguments are advancing media and communication studies considerably, there is room to ascertain whether radio, which is considered by many to be a more "traditional" medium, is a vital cultural institution for supporting and sustaining music and culture, especially that which is labelled and described as "alternative" or "independent." Furthermore, there are significant overlaps and interrelated components between digital and visual media and radio broadcasting (Hilmes 2013) that a study of campus radio programming practices helps illustrate.

A goal of this book is to locate the significant sites where Canadian campus radio emerged as well as the key factors that took these stations from university campuses to wider communities. The moments at which campus stations became licensed and regulated by the CRTC are particularly relevant, as licensing sets the terms for how these stations operate. Highlighting the terminology and discursive strategies used in policy is essential for understanding the particular forms and structures that campus stations are to operate under. An understanding of policy should include not only the end result of the processes by which rules and regulations are made but also a close consideration of the discourses and debates among various stakeholders that precede a published policy decision. Acquiring a licence ties a station to a larger regulatory framework, and the discourses and debates implicated in this regulatory process demonstrate the ways in which policy frames campus radio in comparison to commercial (and to a lesser extent, public) radio. The similarities and the differences between policy-making at the federal and local levels illustrate the various commitments that campus stations have, both in regard to the official goals that stations must achieve in order to remain in operation and with respect to the communities and mandates that stations respond to. The geographic environment that a station is situated in and serves – both through programming and in its function as an institutional centre that is home to technical resources, music libraries, volunteers, and community members – is central in determining the operations and culture of campus stations.

Despite a relationship to larger bureaucratic systems of policy-making, campus radio stations approach music-based programming in a way that offers an *alternative* to the music-based programming of commercial radio stations. "Alternative," in this case, refers to programming and operational practices that are decidedly distinct in some ways from private and public broadcasting practices and that have the ultimate goal of circulating and disseminating music that is "local," "independent" (or somewhat independent), or rooted in social or community-based causes. Of course, what constitutes "local" and "independent" differs from station to station, but this book will elucidate what these terms mean and how they function in the programming and operations of campus radio, and most importantly, why a local focus presents an alternative within Canada's single broadcasting system.

This book's focus on music programming by campus radio includes Canada's cultural industries, which are also prone to the influence of media convergence and consolidation. For instance, the predictably successful artists are those most welcomed by commercial radio stations. The Canadian artists who are the most accustomed to writing grants and marketing themselves often become the most frequently programmed on the various music channels and programs under the public radio offerings of the CBC. The field is increasingly difficult for new and independent artists who are without the financial backing of an established label or the accomplishment of having already entered into the public consciousness. How campus stations work with independent artists and styles or genres of music that are not typically represented on commercial radio or public radio, and how these relationships construct our sense of a city or town's music scene, is a central mode of inquiry for this book.

There are numerous reasons why a study of campus radio is pertinent and why it responds to research gaps that present an intriguing and inviting problematic. Canadian communication and media studies have paid close attention to the ways in which public and private broadcasting have developed, emphasizing key points such as the relations of power behind the private sector and whether and how public broadcasting adequately fulfills its democratic, nation-binding potential. In contrast, there has been minimal research on community radio in Canada and even less that focuses specifically on campus radio. Much of the work that has been done looks at community radio in Quebec, where the provincial government was allocating community media funding as early as the late 1960s. Provincial government funding for community media was allotted predominantly to visual media organizations, such as Vidéographe, a Montreal-based centre for independent film production and distribution, but community radio initiatives in

Quebec can be located throughout studies and reports that describe these developments in the province.

A number of studies that locate the role of cities in conceptualizing music scenes are helpful for thinking about campus radio as a local alternative for radio practitioners, music fans, and cultural producers. Sara Cohen (1991) effectively details the social and cultural lifestyle within Liverpool's music scene, a lifestyle that is implicit in musical practices. Her work responds to what she feels to be a lack of ethnographic and microsociological detail in the study of popular music scenes, particularly rock music scenes. Ruth Finnegan (1989) argues that sociability "runs through musical practice" (328). Musicians and listeners are moved not just by their love of music but by the desire to be with friends and peers. Cultural institutions, which include campus radio stations, are social spaces for people to congregate around shared interests such as a particular musical genre, and these connections form pathways within a locality and beyond. Geoff Stahl (2003) claims that there is a notable absence of discussions about the significant role played by cities in shaping the sociomusical experience. He investigates the aspects of the city that motivate music-making, using experiential, materialist, and discursive methodological frameworks, complemented by mapping analyses, diary entries, and interviews. Stahl points to the importance of institutional sites, such as community radio stations, in fostering opportunities for interaction between different "musical worlds" and allowing for local knowledge to be transferred from generation to generation (197). These works situate the role of cultural institutions within their analyses, although campus radio does not figure prominently.

The implications of policy-making on the structure and function of radio broadcasting are outlined by Jody Berland, who argues that as radio airwaves are increasingly subject to the politics behind the privatization of media, radio becomes more popular and structured around music formats (1993). Canadian music, and music not immediately considered economically viable, has moved to the margins, where campus and community radio operate. Radio has the potential to constitute the communities that speak through the media and map local life, Berland argues, but this ability is restricted by the centralization that results from technological rationalization. She illustrates radio's capacity to sustain strong connections to local music and a listening community and explains how commercial radio is tied to regulation and market logic that affects music programming. Her work exposes an area for further inquiry – that of campus and community radio and the constitution of local culture, music, and listening.

Music in Range brings together cultural history, critical policy studies, and popular music and sound studies. Cultural history emphasizes the ways in which everyday relations and processes among individuals largely determine the organization of media forms and systems. As Michele Hilmes argues in her influential study of early American radio, we should regard radio not simply as a technology, a "collection of wires," but as a social practice rooted in everyday life (1997, xiii). Critical policy studies point to the implications of policy and the power dynamics within processes of crafting policy with respect to our experience of media and culture. A study of policy should account for the ways in which policy is made, including the discourses and debates among various stakeholders that are present in public hearings and written submissions that argue for one position or another. So in addition to consulting a number of archived public hearing transcripts, the research behind this book has involved attending public hearings in January 2010 for the campus radio policy that was published that year. This book is also inspired by popular music and sound studies that profile the organizational structure and operations behind the circulation of music and sound; that illustrate the cultural practices of individuals and institutions as they influence our ideas and experiences of music and music scenes; and that unpack the mythologies tied to certain locations where musical activity takes place. As such, the research for this book also involved conducting interviews with campus radio practitioners about the ways in which campus stations have crafted internal policies and station mandates. By putting these approaches in conversation with one another, *Music in Range* profiles the place and role of the campus radio sector within Canada's broadcasting environment and cultural industries.

This book has seven chapters, including the introduction and conclusion. Chapter 2 situates the Canadian campus radio sector within the larger North American media environment. It positions the sector's relationship to public and private broadcasting by drawing on ideas about alternative and community media and the purposes they are to serve. It briefly describes the political economy and cultural context of Canadian radio broadcasting and the changing nature of media regulation in North America, paying particular attention to issues like localism in media and industry consolidation. The development of commercial radio policies that have facilitated consolidation in ownership and programming strategies is outlined here, to serve as an example of the political and economic framework against which campus radio practices work.

Chapter 3 focuses on Canadian campus radio's historical and political background. It describes some of the trends that influenced the development of campus radio in Canada. It begins by tracing the early educational radio broadcasting that took place on a number of university campuses across the country. Analyses of available policy documents, and of monographs and theses that detail aspects of community radio or early educational radio, contribute to this chapter as a background against which to situate the campus radio stations profiled in later chapters. This chapter describes the ways in which social and political activism in community media, and cultural hierarchies in educational radio broadcasting at a number of Canadian universities, eventually came together to shape the development of the Canadian campus radio sector.

Chapter 4 elaborates on the historical background provided in Chapter 3. It includes an investigation of the respective pre-FM histories of three Canadian campus stations (CHMA in Sackville, New Brunswick, CKUW in Winnipeg, Manitoba, and CiTR in Vancouver, British Columbia). These stories illustrate the various paths that campus stations have taken in order to become FM broadcasters. Each points to a particular culture that existed at the station before CRTC licensing and hints at the struggles and tactics used by campus stations to increase their presence and prominence in the wider community. Chapter 4 also examines the programming, structure, and operations of campus radio stations. By emphasizing the discursive strategies of campus radio stations in forming an identity, and in acquiring (a level of) autonomy from broadcasting policy and regulation, this chapter also argues that internal policies specific to a station's locality are the primary means by which a given station operates and crafts its own distinct sound.

Chapter 5 points to two key policy-making moments for campus radio that emphasized the centrality of a community-based mandate for the sector. The comprehensive policy for the Canadian campus and community radio sector was reviewed and revised by the CRTC in 2010. That same year, the CRTC held a public hearing to consider non-compliance issues at Ryerson University's CKLN-FM in Toronto, which resulted in the station losing its broadcasting licence. Both of these significant policy-making moments would set the terms for the role and significance of the campus radio sector in Canada. These policy-making moments also suggest that there are certain organizational and operational guidelines that a campus station must meet in order to sustain a licence to broadcast. A community-based mandate is a key characteristic of Canadian campus stations and grounds a station's role in and involvement with musical and cultural communities in its broadcast range.

Chapter 6 explores the relationships between campus radio stations and local musical activity. Connections to live music venues, record stores, festivals, and the production and distribution of music are all very much a part of the culture of campus stations. This chapter explains the overlap between campus stations and their volunteers and staff members and other communities or aspects of the music scene that are active in a station's broadcast range. A number of cultural products that demonstrate the connections between campus stations and local musical activity are also featured in this chapter. CiTR and CKUW both publish magazines that predate each station's FM licence. These publications offer commentary on each station's development and further situate the station's role within the wider music scene. This chapter draws from interviews and personal observations to highlight the importance of campus stations as institutions that are home to resources and people who are active in producing a music scene. Campus stations do not just program and broadcast music. They are inherently connected to the individuals and cultural institutions within their broadcast range and act as significant institutions housing resources and technology, such as record collections and recording equipment to help educate and train cultural producers – whether radio hosts, musicians, DJs, singers, writers, or producers.

Chapter 7, the concluding chapter, emphasizes the importance of institutions and spaces in the circulation of culture and explores the production of an alternative music culture by campus radio. An alternative music culture is shaped by taste preferences and cultural hierarchies that are tied to and established by the individuals who offer their volunteer labour to campus stations. Thus, there are important issues of inclusion and exclusion to consider within the culture of Canadian campus radio. This concluding chapter argues that the circulation of independent and local music by cultural capital establishes productive and alternative methods for exchanging and sharing music by radio and within a music scene. This chapter also reflects on the current and future role of campus stations in relation to Canadian media and culture and argues for the need to sustain this sector across the interrelated levels of policy-making, listening, and participation.

Music in Range reveals a component of the Canadian broadcasting environment that has yet to be the focus of a major scholarly work. It illustrates the ways that campus stations have been defined both in broadcasting policy and by the stations themselves. The place of policy and regulation, and the role of station mandates, are helpful for situating campus–community stations in their cultural communities and music scenes, particularly when thinking about music or culture that might not be adequately represented by the commercial and public radio sectors. The significant relationships between broadcasting policy, campus stations, and musical activity illustrate the role played by campus FM stations within the cultural and musical sites they serve, as well as within the Canadian broadcasting and cultural landscape as a whole. This book points to the ways in which campus radio stations, through their music-based programming, their operational practices, and the culture under which these structures and processes operate, produce alternative methods and values for circulating local and independent Canadian artists at a time when more ubiquitous media outlets and broadcast forms do exactly the opposite.

2

"Alternative" Radio

Canadian campus radio is aligned with notions of "alternativeness" and "independence." These terms have implications for a broader understanding of the role community media systems play within the contemporary media environment and for the ways in which campus radio is positioned as a local alternative within Canada's single broadcasting system. Predominantly, campus radio is framed as an alternative medium that conceptually and practically responds to the structural effects of the contemporary political and economic influences on Canadian broadcasting, namely media consolidation and a decline in local content. This response has resulted in campus radio being defined as "alternative," often without much consideration as to what this means. For instance, representatives from the Canadian campus and community radio sector have made efforts to explain that their stations offer much more than an "alternative" to public and private broadcasters in a given market. They emphasized this during the public hearings that took place before regulations for the sector were updated in 2010, prioritizing the significant role stations play within their respective communities and arguing that campus stations should be defined by the numerous ways in which the sector reflects and represents its nearby communities.

An emphasis on "the local" demands a close consideration of the community-based focus and mandate of contemporary campus stations (a topic that is taken up in great detail in later chapters). How, then, can a local focus and a diverse range of programmed music effectively offer an alternative within radio markets that are predominately made up of commercial stations that have been shaped by the consolidation and concentration of the radio and music industries? "Alternative" must not vaguely define

17

the campus sector. The term must account for why, when, and how certain broadcasting practices and station–listener relationships are decidedly distinct within Canada's single broadcasting system.

An idealistic reflection on the establishment of North American mass media might highlight the centrality of the freedom and exchange of information and ideas. A "free press" and "freedom of speech" are apparently integral to North American communication systems and are guaranteed by, and reflected in, ubiquitous nation-defining policies such as the First Amendment in the United States and the Charter of Rights and Freedoms in Canada. As Robert W. McChesney and Dan Schiller (2003) explain, "conventional wisdom" suggests that as long as the government does not intervene with media and communications, "the flow of information and ideas will be safe" (2). However, as McChesney and Schiller emphasize, the State has always been an influential factor as well as a "necessary player" in the formation of media systems (2003, 2). And as economic interests increasingly motivate policy-making and the regulation of North American media systems, the result has been that more radio and television stations are owned by fewer companies. Because of these trends, programming between different stations is sounding more and more alike. Of course, the politics of the United States and Canada differ, but similar policies crafted under a neoliberal market ideology have deregulated the broadcasting industry in a manner that has facilitated these changes.

In the United States, the consolidation of media companies has exerted major changes on the structure and content of radio broadcasting. Media and broadcasting policy plays a role in determining the number of radio stations a single company can own and control, and the consolidation of media companies has been greatly aided by the close relationship between corporate interests and policy-making. McChesney is wise to point out that there is nothing inherent in communications technology that requires a shift to neoliberalism, a term that implies "the relaxation or elimination of barriers to commercial exploitation of media, and concentrated media ownership" (2004, 411; 1999, 241). He argues that if society elected to enhance public service media, the technology would certainly allow for that to happen. Thus, the broader economic and political context that surrounds the development of communication technologies largely shapes our experience of media and culture.

Alongside media consolidation is the continued globalization of media and communications. Before the 1980s and 1990s, media companies and cultural industries were largely national and domestically owned. The role of the State is being significantly lessened as globalization accelerates and national borders become more permeable (Cameron and Stein 2002, 141).

Canada has mediated the effects of global market forces more aggressively than the United States. Nevertheless, in a country like Canada (a "globalizing elite"), nationalism has declined as a significant source of identity under an increasingly global political, economic, and technological sphere (Cameron and Stein 2002, 147–48). Reflecting and representing national cultural identity through media and policy has become more complicated as the global marketplace becomes the standard. This is not to proclaim that a decline in nationalism is either entirely negative or positive – a decline in nationalism, it would seem, should enable a plurality and diversity of voices and representations within and throughout media systems – but rather to highlight the shifting relationships between citizens and the State amid structural changes in media and communications.

Policy-making in Canada has been notably aware of the need for public reflection and representation within the country's media and communication systems. There has been a relative tradition of democracy in communication policy-making in Canada, one that is evident in the variety of State bodies and consultation processes (Royal Commissions, task forces, and so forth) that seek public debate and input on communication issues (Barney 2005, 30). The basic fact that the country has maintained a national public broadcasting system since the 1930s is arguably evidence of this. So are inquiries like the 1970 Special Senate Committee on Mass Media and the 1981 Royal Commission on Newspapers, which have investigated media concentration in Canada and even illustrated how it can lead to a narrowing of viewpoints and perspectives within the news media (Skinner and Gasher 2007, 52). That said, the issues and trends outlined above are present in the country's mediascape, and certain policies have allowed for greater flexibility and mobility for economic interests and integration, both vertically and horizontally. Canada has used each broadcasting sector to its advantage, maintaining a relative balance between a national public service, through the CBC, and the realization of profits and revenues through the commercial, or private, sector. Increasingly, the community sector has provided the single broadcasting system with programming diversity and content for local communities, but because the private commercial broadcasting sector dominates the airwaves, it is sensible to question the balance within the system.

In the Canadian radio industry, private commercial broadcasters account for 61 percent of the market, the largest English-language private operators being Astral, Corus, Rogers, BCE, and Newcap. The largest French-language private broadcasters are Astral, Corus, and Cogeco (Shade and Lithgow 2013). An argument that favours a move towards fewer, larger Canadian media corporations is that they are better able to compete with

American media companies, conglomerates that enjoy benefits that include "audience reach, human resources, capital, and technological resources to invest in content" (Skinner and Gasher 2007, 55). This argument is seemingly adequate if market models of global media are taken to be the norm. However, ownership concentration and streamlined programming have broad implications for creativity and culture, marked by factors such as a decline in localism and diversity in both broadcasting and the musical and cultural industries that are connected to, and often supported by, radio broadcasting.

Short-term financial gains to be made from concentration within the radio broadcasting industry have resulted in the reduction of radio services that cater to local communities. Part of the reason for a strong move away from local content has to do with economic trends towards globalization, but moments of economic deficiency have also factored into cuts directed at local content. During the economic recession of the late 1980s and early 1990s, American radio station owners cut back or eliminated local staff and local news operations (Hilliard and Keith 2005, xiii, 65). Canadian media companies, following economic downturns after the turn of the century, have found their convergence strategies to be less lucrative than originally anticipated, resulting in cuts to jobs and content (Shade 2007, 111). In both the United States and Canada, strategic structuring and restructuring dictated by a prioritization of economic gain has driven commercial radio broadcasting away from the localism on which it was originally established.

Radio's migration from localism has also been facilitated by, and reflected in, the introduction and implementation of digital and satellite radio services. In December 2004, during a public hearing, the CRTC acknowledged and discussed three licence applications for subscription or pay radio services that would be distributed by either satellite or terrestrial transmitters. In 2005 the commission approved the three applications by Canadian Satellite Radio Inc. (CSR), SIRIUS Canada Inc. (Sirius Canada), and CHUM Limited (to be established in partnership with Astral). Each application was approved by the CRTC to provide a package of channels for subscribers, who would pay a monthly fee. CHUM, the one applicant that would only use terrestrial transmitters, never launched its services because it had stated "that if the Commission licensed the three services, it would not proceed" (Armstrong 2010, 167). Canadian listeners now had access to content that would be a mix of Canadian-produced and non-Canadian-produced channels. It is important to note that XM Satellite Radio and SIRIUS Satellite Radio, the two services that were launched, have partnerships with American companies. This international partnership involves carrying over a large proportion of the American channels, as well as the use of

American satellites. These two American companies have since merged (in July 2008), as did the Canadian entities in 2011.

Satellite radio is now available in most new automobiles, and since as far back as the 1960s, there has been a marked shift in radio listening in Canada: listening increasingly takes place outside the home, either at work or in an automobile (Armstrong 2010, 57). When searching through the channels offered by satellite radio, one may find a relative range of genres and styles, but these options are the same throughout the nation. Content is centralized, and news, information, and music can be coming from any location in North America. A listener driving along Highway 401 in Ontario could very well be hearing about concerts or events specific to the southern United States. Furthermore, as Alexander Russo and Bill Kirkpatrick explain, satellite technology has also been central to North American terrestrial radio as far back as the 1970s, and has facilitated the centralization and automation of programming (2012, 157).

Given the structure of satellite radio, and with commercial stations focusing less on locally produced content, these broadcasting systems are not adequately serving localities. A broadcasting locality is defined by Thomas McCain and G. Ferrell Lowe as "'a discrete but nonstandardized geographic area corresponding to a relatively unique and commonly shared collection of situationally and/or culturally determined values and interests represented by the people who live there'" (qtd. in McCourt 1999, 103). The consequences of media convergence, according to Leslie Regan Shade, are "particularly significant when it comes to community and regional news and viewpoints, as the autonomy of local community content vanishes" (2007, 108–9). Similar critiques have been launched against the radio giant Clear Channel. When Clear Channel becomes the dominant player in a given market, "it quickly sacks the news reporters, pares down the local deejays, and fills the airwaves with formulaic pap imported by satellite from distant cities" (Fisher 2007, 286). Evidently, there are powerful trends in the radio industry, as well as in the media and communications environment broadly speaking, that are hindering the capacity for North American radio listeners to experience a rich variety of radio programming specific to the locality in which they reside.

Commercial Radio Policy in Canada

The regulation of the Canadian commercial radio sector has facilitated concentration in the radio industry, particularly since the 1990s, when policies for the sector began to emphasize the need for commercial radio to compete with new media forms in order to remain profitable. Moreover, certain policy initiatives that were intended to enhance the level of Canadian music in programming have instead provided incentives for broadcasters to heavily feature popular Canadian artists.

These policies have a significant influence on the range and diversity of local programming available to Canadians, particularly since the private radio sector was tasked with catering to local community interests once the public sector began to prioritize national interests in the late 1940s (Raboy 1990, 97). Canada's Broadcasting Act of 1991 outlines the aims of the CBC, emphasizing its role as a public service that reflects "Canada and its regions to national and regional audiences" and as a contributor "to shared national consciousness and identity."

The regulation of the CBC since the 2000s has involved the commission working to mediate the effects of budget cuts and new media technologies as well as the goal of reflecting regional interests through a national service. In 2000, the CRTC explained in a Public Notice that preceded a comprehensive licence renewal for the CBC's radio and television stations that the "CBC has a very particular role to play as a voice for all Canadians, from every part of the country … Its programs must more effectively reflect all of Canada and the experience of all Canadians" (CRTC 2000b). This valiant but difficult goal of reflecting both national and regional interests has been made all the more challenging as the CBC faces budget cuts. A number of interventions submitted during the licence renewal explained that "listeners and viewers have noticed that there are fewer new episodes on television and more repeat programming on both radio and television. Even news and public affairs have suffered a reduction in the quantity and quality of regional and international coverage" (CRTC 2000b). The CRTC decision that followed the Public Notice echoed this concern: many "people expressed the opinion that programming decisions made in response to budget reductions have resulted in a perceptible reduction in the quality of the CBC's English radio services." Of added concern "was a perception that local programming has suffered" (CRTC 2000a).

A Broadcasting Decision from 2013 that once again renewed the licences for CBC programming services positioned the corporation within a society that was now more dependent on digital technologies. That decision continued to emphasize the CBC's role as a "pan-Canadian service that reflects and serves the needs of all Canadians in both official languages regardless of where they live," while also discussing the CBC's five-year strategic plan, *Strategy 2015: Everyone, Every Way* (CRTC 2013). The strategy involves the CBC increasing its regional presence through multimedia initiatives and by launching new local websites and services. Financial issues facing the CBC were also debated and discussed, with regard to paid national advertising for two of the CBC's radio services, Espace Musique and Radio 2, two stations that feature music by emerging Canadian artists. Many interveners expressed concern that advertising "would disrupt the balance between public and commercial broadcasting" and that the CBC programmers and producers would alter "programming to make the networks more attractive to the mass radio audiences that are currently served by commercial stations" (CRTC 2013). Evidently, Canada's public radio sector was facing financial challenges that were impeding its ability to adequately serve all of Canada's regions, and budget cuts were turning the corporation towards less expensive digital strategies and services (digital media are one of the "three pillars" of *Strategy 2015*). Meanwhile, since the early 1990s, the regulation of the commercial sector has led to increased concentration in the ownership of stations and a reduced range and diversity of local programming options.

"An FM Policy for the Nineties" was crafted for the commercial radio sector in December 1990. The policy accounted for the increasing popularity of the FM band in Canada. FM receivers were much more common in households in 1990, versus 1975 when the prior FM radio policy was enacted, and the new policy reflected the greater number of FM frequencies in a given market. Other dramatic changes for FM radio included increases in revenue and profits even while revenues, profits, and listenership had declined for AM radio. Also, in the years between FM radio policies, the Canadian music industry had expanded considerably, as had the number of private radio networks and program syndicators (CRTC 1990d).

The expansion and maturation of the nation's music industry was reflected not just on commercial radio but also on public and community radio, as the policy made evident, particularly when it came to the importance of diversity over the airwaves. "Strategies to provide diversity are not limited to commercial radio," the commission noted, adding that it "continues to view the diverse and balanced programming of the CBC's radio service as the cornerstone of Canadian radio. In addition, educational, community and campus radio contribute alternative programming and access by local groups" (CRTC 1990d). A divide becomes apparent here: three sectors would share the increasingly popular and profitable FM band. The CBC was a point of national pride, according to the commission, and was still the "cornerstone" of the nation's radio system. Community and campus radio were seen as providing listeners with alternative, or a diversity of, programming choices. So, the commercial sector could focus on increasing audiences for which to sell advertising and could program popular musical selections, both Canadian and non-Canadian.

A key component of the 1990 policy was the removal of format distinctions for popular music stations, primarily the distinction between pop and rock. The commission believed that "competition between broadcasters striving to attract audiences in a multi-station environment will ensure a measure of diversity among stations seeking mass audiences" (CRTC 1990d). Thus, formats that fell within the larger category of popular music were combined into one subcategory, "Pop and Rock." It was thought that after the formats were combined, "competitive forces" would maintain diversity while allowing stations to develop "creative and innovative niche programming." The commission justified this decision by noting that the private sector was somewhat limited in its ability to achieve the desired objective of diversity among commercial rock and pop stations:

> At a certain point, programming becomes so specialized that audience levels become too low to generate the revenues that commercial stations need to survive. Almost all commercial FM stations concentrate on the presentation of popular music. This approach enables them to appeal to the broad general audiences they must attract to generate adequate advertising revenues. However, with the convergence of pop and rock music styles over the years, it has become increasingly difficult to retain the distinctions between stations basing their programming on pop and rock music. The Commission believes that a level of diversity will result as stations differentiate themselves in order to serve different audiences. (CRTC 1990d)

Responding to the elimination of the distinctions between popular music formats, a number of broadcasters expressed concern that the result would be a homogenization of sound and a reduction in diversity on the FM band.

Exempting Canadian musical selections from a regulation on the number of "hits" that a commercial FM station could play in a given week – less than 50 percent of all popular music selections each week – was also argued for, and implemented, on the basis that this would allow the programming of a greater number of "new" Canadian selections. "Hits," then, were redefined in order to "exclude Canadian selections for the 12-month period after they first appear on a Top 40 hit chart" (CRTC 1990d). Although the commission had good intentions when initiating this exemption – it was hoping to remove disincentives for the programming of new Canadian music – that exemption also enabled stations to rely on highly successful Canadian selections to pair with non-Canadian hits. Hence, the now common critique that Canadian content is repetitive and does not adequately represent Canadian music and culture.

In 1998 the CRTC crafted a new Commercial Radio Policy, one that was said to be in line with its vision for managing "a delicate balance between achieving various social and cultural objectives and ensuring an economically strong and competitive communications industry" (CRTC

1998b). The new policy outlined objectives that reflected economic trends toward ownership consolidation. Ensuring a "strong, well-financed radio industry that is better poised to achieve its obligations under the Act and to meet the challenges of the 21st century" was the first objective stated in the document. The commission decided to meet this objective through increased consolidation of ownership; it hoped this would strengthen the sector's overall performance, attract investment, and allow it to compete with other forms of media.

A significant revision to the 1998 policy allowed for the ownership of as many as three stations operating in one language with a maximum of two stations on any one frequency band for markets with fewer than eight commercial stations operating in a given language. Prior to this amendment, a common ownership policy had restricted ownership to a maximum of one AM and one FM undertaking operating in the same language in the same market. In markets with eight or more commercial stations in a given language, one was now permitted to own or control as many as two AM and two FM stations in that language. Representatives of the commercial sector assumed that diversity requirements would be met by ensuring the sector's financial stability and relative competitiveness, as well as by initiatives such as the commission's increase in Canadian content for popular music selections during each broadcast week from 30 to 35 percent. Moreover, ownership concentration had implications for simulcasting, since a 1996 amendment to the 1986 Radio Regulations had permitted broadcasters to simulcast up to forty-two hours of programming during the week on commonly owned AM and FM stations (CRTC 1996). The amendment came as an addition to the already allowed simulcasting that took place between midnight and 6:00 a.m. Thus, an increase in ownership meant that an increase in simulcast content in a given market was possible.

The policy for the commercial radio sector was updated again in 2006. The new policy reiterated the private sector's goal of operating "effectively in an increasingly competitive environment for the delivery of audio programming" (CRTC 2006b). It followed the commission's implementation and licensing of satellite radio in 2005. New methods of distributing audio content, both Canadian and otherwise, were apparent for both policymakers and radio stations at this time. Commercial broadcasters claimed that "there has been a proliferation of alternative technologies for the distribution of music to consumers" and that "a significant effect on listeners' habits is inevitable, and the financial performance of commercial radio stations may well decline as a result" (CRTC 2006b). Statistics pointed to a decrease in weekly listening levels for conventional radio. Those levels had fallen by approximately one hour and twenty-five minutes between 1999 and 2005, and that decrease was most prominent in the teen demographic (12–17) and among adults aged 18 to 34. Despite such concerns, the sector was said to be financially sound, one reason being the 1998 policy – specifically, the increases in the limits on the number of stations a licensee could own in a single market (CRTC 2006b). Localism was stressed as a key factor if commercial stations were to remain relevant in "an environment of rapidly changing technology and consumer behaviour," but few tangible methods for ensuring local relevance were implemented. A suggestion that Canadian content levels for popular music selections be increased was met with claims that "listeners are not seeking more Canadian music" and that such increases would result in listeners embracing "alternative methods of hearing their favourite foreign music, such as CDs, the Internet, satellite radio, iPods, and MP3 players" (CRTC 2006b). Proposals for increasing broadcast selections for "emerging" artists were also, essentially, dismissed in favour of an approach that would assess the situation on a "case-by-case basis taking into account the particular circumstances of each station."

A dissenting opinion of commissioner Stuart Langford critiqued the commission's status quo position on these issues. He argued that commercial broadcasters adhere to "the letter of the law" that 35 percent of all musical selections be Canadian, yet "they do so by playing just a few marquee artists over and over again. That's great for big names like Shania Twain and Avril Lavigne, but not so good for lesser known performers" (CRTC 2006b). Langford added that a "lack of imagination also appears to be the hallmark of the majority's reaction to the plight of Canada's new and emerging artists. Rather than solving the problem by requiring FM licensees to provide airplay opportunities for as many Canadian artists as possible, the majority has decided to duck the problem today and leave it to be solved on a case-by-case basis."

Throughout the 2006 policy for commercial radio, the potential for the community and campus sector to treat issues of localism and cultural diversity with a seriousness not matched by the commercial sector was expressed. A number of intervening parties, including *l'ARC du Québec*, "stressed the unique role that community and ethnic radio play in contributing to diversity in the radio sector as a whole." *L'ARC du Québec* recommended the creation of a fund for community broadcasting, in light of the "crucial role" it was playing in broadcasting a diversity of voices, formats, genres, and artists. In 2007, shortly after this policy, the Community Radio Fund of Canada was established. From a policy perspective, it seemed that regulations to ensure the financial feasibility of commercial radio had trumped issues of localism and diversity. Meanwhile, services to the community and the overall diversity of Canada's radio broadcasting system had been left to the community radio sector, under which campus radio falls.

These political, economic, and technological trends have implications for the ways in which programming and content are received by listeners, as well as for the types of content being distributed. A major criticism of music-based radio content that caters to mass audiences is that it is generally based on a limited repertoire of songs that have established themselves as "hits" – a repertoire that is similar from station to station (Lewis and Booth 1989, 5). Similarities among stations increase as fewer entities control more stations. For Canadian radio listeners, an added concern is that oftentimes the mass programming they encounter is generated from south of the border. Content that originates in Canada is subject to regulation that mandates a certain level of Canadian content, whereas radio signals that migrate north from the United States "know no such constraint" (Barney 2005, 12). Additionally, since the start of the twenty-first century, the majority of cultural products circulating throughout Canada have originated from American sources (Barney 2005, 73; Skinner and Gasher 2007, 51). The American entertainment industry, which "constitutes a special case not found in any other country," produces "an enormous quantity of music, television programs, theatrical feature films, and Internet content, whose costs are largely amortized in the huge U.S. domestic market that serves more than 300 million people" (Armstrong 2010, 225). American cultural products and services, "whose basic costs have been covered in the U.S. market, can then be exported to other nations, including Canada, at low prices that cannot be matched by producers in these countries" (Armstrong 2010, 225). Considering globalizing politics, economics, and the technologies that have facilitated such changes, and given the fact that it is largely an American model of media production, circulation, and regulation that is being exported throughout the world, the distinction between Canadian and American content can easily be lost on listeners.

The Canadian music and radio industries have taken shape in relation to the more dominant American radio and cultural industries. Globalization and media concentration have greatly altered the cultural industries, and the Canadian music industry has both taken advantage of large American and/or global recording and distribution companies and been restrained by them. Will Straw, commenting on the Canadian music industry in the early 1990s, noted that some excitement was being generated among Canadian musicians regarding the major-label representatives who were "combing the bars [in cities like] Halifax in search of new alternative rock groups to sign" (1996, 96). Such opportunities came in the wake of high international record sales from prominent Canadian acts like Céline Dion and the Crash

Test Dummies (Straw 1996, 95). Straw explains that over "the reporting year 1993–94, the dollar value of all sound recordings sold in Canada had grown at an annual rate of 16.5 per cent, reaching a 10-year high of $738 million" (1996, 95–96). The situation was not so rosy for Canadian independent record labels, which complained that they could not compete with the worldwide release plans proposed by the major labels and that "their own place within the Canadian industry had become even more fragile" (1996, 96). Even the handful of "alternative" or "independent" labels in Canada that achieved a relative level of success in the early 2000s had to rely on larger multinational companies. Arts & Crafts, the label behind bands like Broken Social Scene and Feist, signed with EMI Music Canada, while Last Gang (Metric, Death From Above 1979) signed with Warner (Edwardson 2009, 218). This bodes well for the artists signed to these smaller labels, for it potentially increases their income and exposure, but it also raises significant questions about the business models and practices that so-called independent or small labels are to maintain under the watch of a multinational company. Are there implications for the types of artists these labels can then sign and promote, and is the creative autonomy of the label subject to the parent company? There is likely a different answer for each particular case, but these concerns are well founded given the circumstances and historical trends in the music and radio industries.

Canadian content regulations for Canadian broadcasting have developed in response to concerns over the prevalence of American cultural products and services. Before the Broadcasting Act of 1958, "the notion of the regulatory agency placing Canadian content requirements on private broadcasters was largely absent and, in any case, the CBC's regulations, applicable to both radio and television, were sometimes unenforced" (Armstrong 2010, 36). The 1958 Broadcasting Act declared that Canadian broadcasting should be "basically Canadian in content and character," yet this declaration did not result in successful implementation of Canadian content requirements. Following the Broadcasting Act of 1968, the CRTC would implement "a new series of Canadian content requirements for radio and television broadcasting by means of regulations and policies," starting in 1970. A press release from May 1970 announced the commission's intention to enforce a 30 percent Canadian content requirement for AM radio (Armstrong 2010, 43–44). Commercial stations airing popular music now have to ensure that at least 35 percent of all musical selections programmed between 6:00 a.m. and 6:00 p.m. Monday to Friday are Canadian and that a minimum of 35 percent of all musical selections throughout the entire broadcast week are Canadian. For musical selections, Canadian content is determined by the MAPL system. To qualify as Canadian, a musical selection must fulfill at least two of the MAPL categories, with "M" refer-ring to the composition of the music (i.e., Was the composer of the music Canadian?), "A" to the nationality of the artist, "P" to the location of the recorded performance or a live performance that is being broadcasted, and, "L" to the nationality of the person who wrote the lyrics.

These regulations are enforced under the assumption that they enhance the availability of Canadian music on the radio. However, as the commer-cial radio policies outlined above suggest, as well as the larger political and economic trends that have shaped the radio and music industries, Cana-dian content regulations for commercial radio often result in the repetitive and predictable programming of successful Canadian artists.

The potential for greater success and exposure in an industry mov-ing towards reliance on international distribution does provide financial and promotional benefits for Canadian artists, but mainly for those select few who have acquired representation by a major label. Top-selling artists tend to end up fulfilling most of the Canadian content requirements for Canadian radio stations, leaving less-established bands and artists to fend for themselves. According to Straw, the support for local music talent in Canada by commercial radio stations has historically been "more gestural than genuine" (1996, 106). And one might argue that with a "survival of the fittest" scenario for Canadian bands or artists, the most economically viable does not always equate with the most diverse, experimental, or cre-ative sounding. If anything, a logic that favours the prestige of international exposure over the new or the local makes it difficult for experimental and innovative artists to establish themselves, should they wish to do so.

Discourses of "Alternative"

Canada's community broadcasting sector is one of the three recognized sectors in the overall broadcast system as defined by the Broadcasting Act (1991). Community radio strives for local relevance by providing program-ming for nearby communities; it also enables non-professional groups and individuals to produce programming. Campus radio falls within the com-munity broadcasting sector and is the most dynamic component of the Canadian community radio sector when it comes to musical programming. Campus stations must meet high Canadian content quotas, and Canadian content rules ensure that broadcasters air a certain percentage of content that was either fully or partly created by Canadians. On ideological, struc-tural, and practical levels, the campus radio sector offers an effective chal-lenge to the political, economic, and technological trends that have shaped the commercial radio sector's move away from localism. Campus radio stations typically construct a mandate that emphasizes "alternativeness" as a means to ground a community-based focus. Music and culture that embraces "independence" from the commercial or mainstream cultural industries is also a prominent characteristic of campus radio.

Terms like "alternative," "independent," and "community" have particular meanings in relation to certain moments in history, during which specific issues and concerns become central to discourses and debates surrounding the radio and music industries. Lisa Gitelman (2008) argues that a history of sound recording and of the technologies and practices associated with it makes visible the ways "media emerge as local anomalies that are also deeply embedded within the ongoing discursive formations of their day, within the what, who, how, and why of public memory, public knowledge, and public life" (29). Early radio in Canada focused largely on how Canadian broadcasting could be an *alternative* to American radio broadcasting and culture. Terms like "alternative," "independent," and "community" are also used to label and define musical styles. Commercial and cultural processes shape the construction and boundaries of musical genres (Frith 1996, 89); terms like "alternative" and "independent," by their very essence, work to oppose commercial or mainstream music and are very much a part of the culture of campus radio. However, these terms have also been used by major record labels to market commerically successful artists, highlighting the porous borders of "alternative" and "independent" music.

Apprehension about the mass production of culture and the commercial nature of broadcasting has been evident ever since it became apparent that broadcasting technology could freely and easily reach "mass" audiences. It is through this apprehension that a basic understanding of the rhetorical function of terms like "alternative" and "independent" can be applied. Critical assessments of a music industry that treats music as a mass-produced commodity assert that under the laws of the political economy, music "and the musician essentially become either objects of consumption like everything else, recuperators of subversion, or meaningless noise" (Attali 1985, 8). French economist Jacques Attali claimed that, around the middle of the twentieth century, the purpose of music became fulfillment of "the economic requirements of accumulation" (1985, 88). A "degraded, censored, artificial music took centre stage," a "mass music for an anesthetized market" (1985, 105). Thus, under a system that prioritizes profits, music is less about creativity or originality and more about appealing to basic human desires in order to sell it efficiently. In transitioning between a discussion of the "representation" and the "repeating" stages of music production, Attali described radio as a technology that "made representation free" and that promoted, along with the phonograph record, the repetition of music (84). Theodor Adorno, a committed critic of the cultural industries (or *culture industry*, to use his term, which emphasized the similarities he perceived between industries), echoed this sentiment, arguing that the mass production of music converts listeners into nothing more than "the acquiescent purchaser" (1938/1991, 32). Adorno claimed that the "counterpart to the fetishism of music is the regression of listening," which is "tied to production by the machinery of distribution, and particularly by advertising" (1938/1991, 46–47). In other words, the process of listening, or consuming, is determined by the industrial and economic systems that produce music en masse. Music produced under these circumstances must have mass appeal. Adorno also argued that the radio both wears out music and overexposes it (1938/1991, 47, 52). Such concerns are partly rooted in the fact that the radio era brought forth the idea of media reaching a large group of people at any one time. As radio developed into the 1930s, its power to sell records and make stars "came with the shift in the commodity status of music" (Thornton 1996, 36). These arguments are worth debating, especially given a more contemporary context in which the variety of cultural creation and production is much more pronounced than it was in the late 1930s. Nevertheless, these are important critiques to consider, particularly in an era when neoliberal market strategies have motivated structural changes to North American cultural industries and the media environment. Furthermore, these critiques illustrate the ways in which the radio and music industries operate in a similar fashion under a political and economic system that prioritizes profit.

Campus radio's focus on localism presents listeners, cultural producers, and radio practitioners with alternative methods for engaging with media production, circulation, and reception. We can tailor the term "alternative" for thinking about campus radio by examining its historical use within Canadian broadcasting discourses. "Alternative" appears in Canadian political debates over broadcasting as far back as the 1920s. Marc Raboy (1990) has noted that "the late 1920s was a time of strong nationalist sentiment in English Canada and the Aird report (1929) confirmed what most thoughtful Canadians apparently felt: that the only viable alternative to American domination of the Canadian airwaves was a national public enterprise" (29) and this resulted in the establishment of the Canadian Radio Broadcasting Company. In this instance, Canadian national broadcasting was framed as an alternative to the more dominant forces of American commercial radio. However, the term has also been used to argue strategically for private broadcasting. Throughout the late 1950s and into the 1960s, a case was made for an alternative to national public broadcasting. Private broadcasters claimed that "a strong alternative service operated by the private element would only be good" (Raboy 1990, 149). A similar use of "alternative" can be found in American broadcasting discourses. In debates about deregulation, those individuals lobbying in favour of it (typically the same "as those who wish to do business with radio") often use terms like "freedom" and "independence," maintaining "that such terms are attractive alternatives to the values of regulated, public-service broadcasting" (Wallis and Malm 1993, 158).

But "alternative" also figures into debates about broadcasting that stake claims for community media and for media that do not fit within the market model of commercial broadcasting or the nationalist ideology of public broadcasting. In Canada during the late 1960s, arguments were made for broadcasting that was distinct from both commercial and State-sponsored public broadcasting. According to Raboy, "because the idea of 'public' media was so ineluctably associated with the centralized, state-owned, hierarchized model, the new approaches were often labeled ... 'alternative' or 'community' media" (1990, 12). A similar use of "alternative" was central in a 1979 report for the Telecommunications Research Group; that report highlighted a reaction against the "big" and "centralized" government and government policies of the 1960s. According to the report, these reactions set the foundations for the development of community and campus radio in Canada (McNulty 1979, 57).

The terms "independent" and "alternative" share many characteristics; in particular, both insist on discursively distancing a medium like radio from mainstream or commercial broadcasting and popular music. Yet again, political and economic elites have used the former term to argue for State-sponsored or commercial broadcasting. "Independent" was used in the 1920s by Canadians arguing for a national broadcaster that was "independent" from the United States. At the time of early radio broadcasting in Canada, a national public broadcasting service was thought of as both alternative to and independent from American radio broadcasting. Interestingly, as years went on, the term "independent" was used by advocates for Canadian private broadcasting to define a system that was independent from the national public service. Independence in that sense referred to independent ownership. In the late 1940s, the Canadian Association of Broadcasters "presented the same basic position it had held since the early 1940s, with some semantic refinements. It then described its membership as a system of 'independently-owned community stations'" that thought of themselves as alternatives to the national system (Raboy 1990, 84). "Independent," then, has served the rhetorical function of arguing for the establishment of the public *and* private broadcasting sectors.

"Independent" has also been used to define broadcasting practices that challenge the notion that media deregulation increases broadcaster's "independence" and listeners' "choice" (Bennett et al., 1993, 102). For American micro and pirate radio advocates and practitioners, demonstrating independent broadcasting techniques meant broadcasting illegally, outside of sanctioned licensing by the FCC (Opel 2004, 38). Simon Frith makes a similar point about the ideology of "independence," claiming that it means "challenging the usual rules of public provision and acquiescent consumption, and developing a do-it-yourself infrastructure of unofficial (and often illegal) sales and promotion – pirate radio, 'blues,' bootleg tapes, sampled records, and so on" (1993, 19). There is a continuum of "independence" and autonomy along which different types of radio can be placed. For example, pirate radio emphasizes freedom from the "restrictive rules and regulations of the CRTC" (Nopper 2010, 66), whereas campus or community stations are indeed regulated by the CRTC. There are also dynamic processes between various levels of power and the challenges posed by different cultural forces determined by different levels of independence.

Finally, "community" is an especially relevant term because it defines the overall broadcasting sector that Canadian campus radio falls within and highlights radio's ability to connect listeners through a shared listening experience. Historically, as with "alternative" and "independent," "community" has justified broadcasting that is both commercial and non-commercial. The purpose of Canadian private broadcasting has historically been to serve local, community interests. In the late 1940s, the CBC "conceded local community interests to the private sector and equated the public interest with the national interest – or, more precisely, with the interest of the national system" (Raboy 1990, 97). However, as private broadcasting has prioritized profits over service to local communities, the term "community" has become more appropriately associated with broadcasting practices that enable participative and accessible media production. Radio technology is able to constitute a sense of community, allowing the community to speak through the medium even while forming that community through structures, selections, and strategies. This ability to shape communities is part of radio's cultural history. According to John Hartley, as early as the late 1920s, "radio was envisaged as a means for community-building, collective communication and dramatic imagination" (2000, 155). "Community" applies to the ways in which listeners might be constituted through radio technology within a given geographic space. As a number of community and student radio stations were licensed throughout the 1970s, the term "community" came to reflect accessible and decentralized broadcasting practices imbued with specific sets of values or political and social aspirations.

Despite the fact that the terms "alternative," "independent," and "community" have been embedded in dominant power systems and used by those with political and economic power to argue for deregulation and private broadcasting, they have also been prominent in establishing broadcasting practices that challenge more mainstream and commercial broadcasting systems. As the remainder of this book will highlight, these terms have been significant for constituting ideas about local radio and local cultural production.

A Local Alternative

Radio broadcasting constitutes space. Sound waves, which are dependent on such factors as frequency and wattage, cover a geographic locality. Through radio, according to Jody Berland, "music mediates our interactions with space and our contradictory senses of belonging. Each spatial organization and scale of locality – the city, the nation, the ancestral home, and the space between ears – is organized by cultural technologies of space, and each offers its imprimatur to the mix" (2009, 191). The study of cultural technologies "helps to reveal how these 'relationships among sites' are produced," and music "has played a special role in this process, for its dominance of the media soundscape enables listeners to find a sense of belonging in the midst of widely dispersed situations" (2009, 186). Of course, the constitution of space by communication technologies, and the ways in which listeners are connected through sound, are dependent on the particular social, cultural, political, and historical characteristics of a given space (2009, 186). So it is necessary to acknowledge such site-specific factors when exploring the relationship between a radio station and its broadcast range. Canadian broadcasting policy is tied to issues of space and geography. As Berland argues, "communication technologies mediate the social relations of a particular society by setting the limits and boundaries within which power and knowledge operate" (2009, 69). Within the broadcast range of a given campus radio station, what sorts of connections are made between the listeners and the station? And between those listeners and the institutional sites that are integral to the musical and cultural community? How do these connections and intricacies offer an alternative for listeners, media practitioners, and musicians, in the face of contemporary power dynamics between political and economic systems that shape the radio and music industries in Canada?

The campus radio sector's attention to reflecting a diversity of local musical and cultural expressions is a strategic reaction to the contemporary political economy of broadcasting in Canada. Certain normative practices that are part of commercial radio logic are no doubt going to have some influence on community radio practices. But normative practices present significant gaps or blind spots where alternative practices can be fostered.

Thus, an economic logic that has facilitated a move away from localism offers space for local alternatives, ones that involve programming diverse and varied local cultural and musical content while nurturing connections between radio practitioners, musicians, and listeners. "Alternative," "independent," and "community" have become integral terms and concepts for social movements and formations tied to community radio broadcasting, and they are manifest in systems that seek to increase diversity, access, and participation, in media and communication.

Within Canada's regulatory system for radio broadcasting, local programming has commanded attention as a key factor for measuring the diversity of voices and sounds heard over the airwaves. "Diversity of voices," according to the CRTC's Diversity of Voices policy (2008), refers to the common objective of ensuring "the provision of a diversity of viewpoints either through ownership regulations or by means of programming obligations" (CRTC 2008). Diversity can refer to the availability of a variety of genres and formats or to the programming of content created by a variety of producers. Regulations that shape both the structure and the sound of a given radio market are factors in assessing its diversity, and the commission is aware of the role of community stations in ensuring diversity within the single broadcasting system. "Canada has played a central role in the development of community media," according to the CRTC, "and it is considered by many to be the birthplace of community broadcasting" (CRTC 2008). The commission has emphasized that the "community element was developed to provide local groups with access to the broadcasting system. Community broadcasting, which is local, volunteer-based and largely not-for-profit, is often able to broadcast a diverse range of voices, alternative points of view, and innovative programming ideas" (CRTC 2008).

A shortcoming of the CRTC's assessment of diversity within local radio programming is the lack of attention given to music. For instance, the CRTC has defined a local radio station as "a commercial radio station licensed to operate in a market where the licensee is expected to provide local news and information" (CRTC 2008). Prior to the Commission's Diversity of Voices policy, in its 2003 report *Our Cultural Sovereignty*, the Standing Committee on Canadian Heritage pointed out the relative non-existence of local non-news programming. Concerns that "community, local and regional broadcasting services have become endangered species, and that many parts of Canada are being underserved," were raised by the committee (Canada 2003, 13). Moreover, the report claimed that "private broadcasters go where they can make a profit and the CBC has, in reality, retreated from many localities and even from entire parts of the country" (13). The fact that assessments of local programming rarely take into account the presence of non-news content is compelling. As the committee dramatically explained, "an entire layer of Canadian life and experience is missing from the screen and the airwaves – and these forms of expression are arguably the places where the Canadian experience is the most original and vibrant, where the country discovers and defines itself" (13). A major goal of the upcoming chapters is to assess the ways a locality or a music scene is connected to a campus radio station. How effective is the campus radio broadcasting sector in its response to neoliberal and globalizing trends in the contemporary political economy of Canadian broadcasting and cultural industries – trends that pull radio broadcasting away from local communities and towards centralized and standardized programming?

The following chapter describes the development of Canadian campus radio broadcasting, introducing the technological, cultural, economic, and political factors that helped establish the sector. An integral part of this history are the policies that have developed over the years alongside significant technological changes, both at the federal level and in more local, specific instances. Other factors that have shaped the campus sector include the presence of cultural hierarchies in early educational radio and the social and political activist traditions that were expressed through community media initiatives in the 1960s and 1970s. Situating campus radio within a historical framework that foregrounds policy is helpful for understanding the ways in which discourses and traditions that have used concepts like "alternative," "independent," and "community" have been central in establishing its ongoing role in local musical and cultural communities.

3

The Canadian Campus Radio Sector Takes Shape

The Canadian campus radio sector spans the nation from east to west, with stations as far north as Prince George, British Columbia, and Edmonton, Alberta, and as far east as St. John's, Newfoundland. Campus stations broadcast a wide variety of musical selections and spoken-word programs to students and members of the surrounding community from morning to night, and often around the clock. Section 2 of the Broadcasting Act of 1968 stated that the Canadian broadcasting system was comprised of public and private elements and that its regulations would attempt to strike a balance between these two sectors. In the 1991 act, the community element was added, to recognize and reflect the development and expansion of community media in Canada.

A policy to regulate the campus and community sector was updated in January 2010. That policy emphasized a commitment to local content and recommended increases in Canadian musical content. New funding strategies were implemented to help sustain the sector. The commission also integrated sound art and turntablism (the art of using one or more turntables and mixers to produce sounds) into the policy, demonstrating that it was aware of innovative musical styles and genres. However, many radio stations existed on university campuses prior to CRTC licensing and regulation. It was not until the mid-1970s that FM campus radio stations were *officially* licensed and recognized by the CRTC, despite many radio clubs and on-campus broadcasters operating for decades before this. The broad trends and traditions that influenced the development of campus radio in

Canada, and its related policy, include the development and growth of community media initiatives and various educational radio experiments that increasingly enabled individual personalities, musical tastes, and interests to shape and structure programming.

Social Responsibility and Cultural Hierarchies in the Development of Campus Radio

Canadian radio communication began at the turn of the twentieth century. In 1901, two federal government radio installations operated across the Strait of Belle Isle in northern Newfoundland. That same year, Guglielmo Marconi conducted his radio experiments between Poldhu, Cornwall, and St. John's, Newfoundland. In these early years, debate focused on what sort of broadcasting system Canada should develop, taking into consideration the establishment of commercial radio in the United States and public radio in Britain. In the 1920s and 1930s, a consensus emerged that public broadcasting was the system best suited to the national objectives of Canadian broadcasting (Raboy 1990, 48). Extensive accounts of the early days of Canadian radio broadcasting can be found in thorough works such as Franks Peers's *The Politics of Canadian Broadcasting, 1920–1951* (1969) and *The Public Eye: Television and the Politics of Canadian Broadcasting, 1952–1968* (1979), Mary Vipond's *Listening In: The First Decade of Canadian Broadcasting, 1922–1932* (1992), and Marc Raboy's *Missed Opportunities* (1990). Because the development of the campus sector predominantly occurred after the chronological scope of most of these books, much of its history has been left relatively unexplored. The focus of this chapter, then, is to call attention to significant historical moments that illustrate how and why the Canadian campus sector has taken its current form and structure.

The development of the campus radio sector in Canada has been greatly influenced by two interrelated paths. The first is early educational radio; the second, numerous experiments with community media in the 1960s and 1970s. In Canada, one way in which community radio has developed is through community access to the CBC's low-power radio transmitters (LPRTs), particularly in northern Aboriginal communities. Growth in community radio in more densely populated urban areas in the South followed development in the North, most significantly in francophone communities in Quebec and on university and college campuses across the country (Fairchild 2001, 137–38). Before the mid-1970s, when the CRTC began developing a licensing framework for campus broadcasting, radio existed on a number of Canadian college and university campuses, primarily as sites of technical training for students interested in media production, or as efforts in university extension for rural populations and for promoting the university to the wider community. These stations operated at a very low wattage with a very limited range, having just enough power to serve the campus community (Wilkinson 1988, 18). There are many similarities between contemporary non-campus community radio stations and campus radio stations that serve their community (commonly referred to as community-based campus stations, or as campus–community stations), although with campus–community radio, a university, a university-based corporation, or a student society or government may hold the licence. Also, campus–community stations receive money from student fees and levies, or general funding from the college or university. Campus–community stations are invested in involving and reflecting the respective city or community that the university or college is near, but the campus stations licensed by the CRTC in the mid-1970s catered primarily to the campus and their broadcast range was still fairly contained within campus boundaries (McNulty 1979, 116). Nevertheless, since the early to mid-1970s, campus–community broadcasting has continued to expand its range and prominence and has become the dominant form of public access radio across the country (Fairchild 2001, 151).

There were three types of radio licences granted in the 1920s: private commercial, public commercial, and amateur. The amateur licences were given to university stations and radio clubs for low-power broadcasting. The American universities of Wisconsin and Minnesota, and the Latter-Day Saints University in Salt Lake City, had "pioneered the concept of university-owned radio stations in 1922 – a year that ultimately saw seventy-three American educational institutions receive radio licences" (Walters 2002, 13). Prominent university or educational stations that emerged in the 1920s in Canada included CFRC at Queen's University (1922) and CKUA at the University of Alberta (1927), although before the First World War, Dr. Augustin Frigon held a licence for a college station on behalf of the École Polytechnique in Montreal. CFRC and CKUA both still exist, the former as a campus–community station, the latter as part of the not-for-profit network, CKUA Radio Foundation, which generates most of its funding through listener donations (Fairchild 2001, 132; Ogilvie 1983, 10). These early university stations served rural areas that were without access to other radio services.

C-calls for radio licences were first published in Canada in August 1922. At this time, there were no college stations on the list, and licensees were mainly electric and telephone companies, radio stores, and newspapers. There were, however, four experimental licences issued to educational institutions. These included Acadia University (9AT), the University of Alberta's Physics Department in Edmonton (9AU), Queen's University (9BT), and

Sprott-Shaw School in Vancouver (9AX) (Zimmerman 1991, 165). In 1923, two college stations were given C-calls: CFRC at Queen's University and CFUC at the University of Montreal (which was not renewed in 1924). In 1924, the University of Toronto was granted a 9-call, 9BZ; in 1927, the University of Alberta's 9AU became CKUA; and in 1933, CKIC was granted to Acadia (Zimmerman 1991, 165). By the late 1920s, a number of other Canadian universities either rented or were granted time on other local stations; these included Dalhousie University, McGill University, the University of Manitoba, the University of Saskatchewan, and the University of British Columbia (Faris 1975, 81).

CKUA at the University of Alberta began operating in 1927, a culmination of radio broadcasting and adult education. Marylu Walters's *CKUA: Radio Worth Fighting For* (2002) provides a comprehensive history of the station, amalgamating two prior historical booklets (published on the station's fortieth and sixtieth anniversaries). Walters explains that like "newspaper owners, educators and religious evangelists immediately grasped radio's power to reach people" (2002, 8). Closely following the development of radio technology were William Aberhart, a Calgary high school teacher and Baptist preacher, and Albert Ottewell and H.P. Brown, two members of the University of Alberta's Department of Extension (Walters 2002, 8). Walters claims that "[it] didn't take long for Brown to see the superiority of radio over mules and Model Ts in the dead of winter for taking the university to the people" (2002, 12). Before the establishment of CKUA, Ottewell set up an arrangement with Edmonton's first private commercial station, CJCA, which had the extension department broadcasting Monday evening lectures as of late 1925. In 1926, the university's Division of Visual Instruction constructed a rudimentary studio and increased its involvement with CJCA to broadcast over two hours a week, with programming consisting of "songs, poetry and stories by English, Scottish, Irish, Welsh, French and Ukrainian artists for homesick newcomers" (Walters 2002, 12). In early May 1927, Ottewell and Dr. Edward Annand Corbett (more commonly referred to as Ned, or E.A.), a pioneer of Canadian adult education, fronted a committee on university broadcasting and decided that the university should build its own radio station. The station was ready for broadcast as of 21 November 1927 (Walters 2002, 14, 18). The station concentrated on programming for rural audiences, not only because there was a greater need for rural programming, but also because, in Corbett's words, "'people who live in the country are more disposed and have more time, particularly in the long winter evenings, to listen to programs of a sound educational character'" (Walters 2002, 21). Evidently, early educational broadcasting by CKUA was focused on providing content that had educational value for those listeners who resided outside the urban area, but also for new Canadians with British or European backgrounds. By 1932, the station was running three days a week, offering informative programs and lectures, such as "What You Should Know Concerning Mouth Hygiene," programmed during *Homemakers' Hour* (Walters 2002, 22).

Another prominent university radio station during the early years of Canadian broadcasting, and one of North America's oldest, is CFRC at Queen's University. As with CKUA, a full-length monograph details CFRC's history: Arthur Eric Zimmerman's *In the Shadow of the Shield* (1991), which dates back to the university's work with wireless telegraphy before the establishment of the radio station. A professor by the name of James William L. Bain was put in charge of the station in 1924. His vision for the station was to promote the university, as well as its rugby and football teams (355). In March 1924, the station broadcasted its first lectures on "Canadian Poetry" in conjunction with University Extension. The lectures, however, were never used as credit courses for off-campus students, and the station's educational projects were under pressure to consider commercial possibilities, a sentiment that would increase between the mid-1920s and mid-1930s (359, 403).

In 1929, the Aird Commission famously recommended the nationalization of radio broadcasting and created the Canadian Radio Broadcasting Commission (CRBC), which was responsible for creating a cross-country network of high-power radio stations and was launched in 1932. Although many individuals were in strong favour of establishing a national system, some criticized the idea. The *Toronto Telegram* was one newspaper that was quite skeptical of the Aird Commission's plans, claiming that the commission was not representative of popular opinion and arguing that "'when Parliament united to pass the Act which created the Radio Broadcasting Commission, it was without regard to the considerable body of protest which came from many parts of the country'" (Fortner 2005, 147). Nevertheless, in 1936 the CRBC was replaced with the Canadian Broadcasting Corporation, which would dominate Canadian broadcasting throughout the 1930s and 1940s, promoting "a centralized vision of Canada" (Raboy 1990, 8). The CBC was also involved in community-based broadcasting in some areas. For instance, the Canadian Association for Adult Education (CAAE) "formed a bridge between the CBC and mass-membership organizations" in order to develop two program series. One of these called itself the *Farm Forum* and "reached an *organized* listening audience of about thirty thousand, meeting weekly in groups of ten to twenty" throughout the 1940s and 1950s (Raboy 1990, 75). The other series, *Citizen's Forum*, broadcasted in 1943 and was modelled after the farm program. The people behind these programs were attempting to foster public participation in radio broadcasting – the same impetus or philosophy behind community and campus broadcasting today.

In 1934, CKUA was looking to extend its broadcast range in order to meet new standards imposed by the CRBC. The station collaborated with CFAC in Calgary and CJOC in Lethbridge establishing the Foothills Network. The network was used to broadcast lectures and news reports related to agriculture that were prepared by the Alberta government. CKUA took advantage of this new connection to create a citizen's forum called the *Round Table*, the first program of its type and the forerunner of the CBC's *Citizens' Forum* (Walters 2002, 53). Following this, CKUA established a *Farm Radio Forum* that brought together 108 different listening groups with a combined 1,500 members. This "pioneering concept" predated the CBC's farm forum, which began in 1941 (54). The CBC series was co-sponsored by the Canadian Association for Adult Education (CAAE), of which Corbett was the first director for fifteen years, and the Canadian Federation of Agriculture. The forum was produced by the CBC and was immediately considered by many to be quite successful (Faris 1975, 23, 30–31). Reflecting on these Canadian forum broadcasts, Charles Fairchild claims they represented "the first successful attempts by any broadcasting institution in North America to pursue the ideals of two-way communication and democratic participation in media" (2001, 136). In many instances, early educational broadcasters advocated for social responsibility and activism. The CAAE's operating manifesto was evidence of this; it emphasized its "efficient service to the community," and it championed "neither the old individualism nor the newer mass-collectivism but a relationship of voluntary co-operation, which balances rights with responsibilities" (Faris 1975, 156). The CBC *Farm Radio Forum*'s operating slogan of "Read. Listen. Discuss. Act." illustrates the centrality of radio broadcasting in organizing and informing community members in a manner that had individuals participating in the production process, an ideological pillar of contemporary community radio. The forum exemplifies the multimedia nature of early educational radio, wherein broadcasting is combined with reading, discussion, and education.

Both CKUA and CFRC were susceptible to the tensions and struggles that come with operating an educational or non-commercial station that does not receive considerable revenue from the sale of on-air advertising. An educational mandate often meant reduced fees for university stations, but it also restricted their ability to generate funds through advertising. In 1927, CKUA transferred to a private commercial licence but paid a reduced fee because of its educational purposes (Walters 2002, 63). However, toward the end of the 1930s, educational programming was decreasing in popularity, and Alberta's premier, William Aberhart, offered to provide funds for the station if it operated on a semi-commercial basis and if the government took control of the station (63–64). CKUA found itself with a joint board that included members from the government. It increased its wattage to one thousand.

The station's licence was renewed in 1941; however, the CBC's board of governors now stipulated that it was not to operate on a commercial basis at all (Walters 2002, 74). The station's "Programme Principles" dated 24 June 1943 emphasized its distinction from other stations in range: for example, "the service should be unique, not merely a duplication of service afforded by other stations in Edmonton," and "Swing music, crooning, and 'thriller' plays have no place in our programmes. These may be quite legitimate forms of entertainment but they are already available in abundance on existing stations" (85).

The tension between operating a university station with an educational mandate and pursuing a commercial radio licence for increased range or funding was also an issue for CFRC in Kingston. In 1935, CFRC was essentially an experimental operation of the Electrical Engineering Department, providing a few feeds to the CRBC station and receiving a few as well. The Queen's administration was primarily interested in a "non-commercial community service broadcasting role" for the station, yet as Zimmerman explains, the "expenses involved made this project impossible" (1991, 435). Shortly thereafter, CFRC partnered with a local newspaper, the *Whig-Standard*, to bring Kingston a daily radio service that was described as both "commercial and cultural" (447). The station's licence was amended to authorize a private commercial broadcasting service, and the station was remodelled technically according to CRBC specifications. In 1941, talks about increasing reception for the area surfaced, but this would require an increase in revenue for the station. Many people believed that Queen's was not in a position to sustain a competitive commercial radio operation and that if it was to be taxed on any profits generated by the station, there might be further clashes between "the needs of a commercial operation and the main purposes of a university" (439, 509). In June of that year, it was reported that the CBC board would not grant the station a licence if Queen's operated the station. It was stated that "a university should not be involved in commercial radio." The university discontinued commercial operations, and the *Whig-Standard* commenced full operations of the commercial station, CKWS. The university could no longer carry any programs that originated outside of Kingston (509–10).

After the Alberta government gained control of CKUA in the mid-1940s, Walter Blake, a man with experience in commercial radio, took over as manager. Blake pointed out that two-thirds of the population of northern Alberta lived in the country, and he stated that CKUA intended to program for the country audience more than other Edmonton-based stations CFRN or CJCA had been doing. He proclaimed that "'there is a wealth of musical talent in Northern Alberta' and CKUA intended to 'develop and polish this talent and if possible originate the talent when ready, to the CBC'" (Walters 2002, 96). An emphasis on local music and culture was an important direction for the station, one that stemmed both from the university's promotion of "educational" programming and from the station's inability to be granted a commercial licence.

During the late 1940s, CKUA began to foreground "quality" music programming, which was often live and local. There was a "live-talent policy," as well as an "Alberta Talent Program," which aimed to help many young musicians in the area. The Alberta Talent Program was extended to Calgary and Medicine Hat, forming "a Provincial Network to widen the scope of the Alberta Talent Program" (Walters 2002, 106). Live remote broadcasts were also a feature of CKUA programming at the time. Station manager John Langdon's future wife, Nelda Faulkner, was an accomplished musician with Canada's Young Artists Series, and she "presented a weekly program of popular and classical organ solos from a downtown music store" (118). This commitment to involving the community and other local institutions in the station's programming was reflected in the cultural and musical programming the station focused on. In 1946, the station introduced *Continental Musicale*, a radio show that played European music to cater to the great influx of post–Second World War immigrants. Walters describes the show as "a mixed bag of folk, pop and classical music from [the host's] private collection, which eventually numbered more than fifty thousand records" (120). The show's host, Gaby Haas, had immigrated to Canada from Czechoslovakia in 1939. Individuals involved with CKUA throughout its development, like Haas, were central to shaping its musical programming. Arthur Craig, a transmitter operator in 1939, did not really enjoy the station's music programming at the time. He considered it too "high-brow," appropriate for the "suitably old." To remedy this, he brought one of his own records to play at the station (62). Over time, the station would continue to develop its music programming, in terms of programming for various cultural groups and for those who appreciated music that was not being played on commercial stations in the same area. In 1948, CKUA was granted an FM licence to broadcast on the frequency 98.1.

These examples demonstrate the growing presence of early university radio stations within their own localities. They also begin to tease out the taste hierarchies and value judgments present both in a station's listenership and in its approach to programming. Tommy Banks, the host of a teen radio show in the late 1940s at CKUA, explained that he first got involved with the station after realizing that it "'played really good music that other radio stations didn't play'" (Walters 2002, 115). CKUA's listeners were drawn to this music programming of a "higher quality" and became "very possessive" of the station. Walters explains that because of "the station's emphasis on classical music, its listeners were different from those of other stations" (125). Alongside a discourse of distinction from the commercial stations, then, is a discourse of elitism. A broadcasting "alternative" paid attention to communities that could benefit from the service, as exemplified by the farm and citizen forums; at the same time, the music programming considered to be "alternative" was distinct from or of a "higher quality" than the mass programming offered by the commercial stations at the time. Both strategies of distinction would become even more apparent as the private broadcasting sector increased its presence across the nation.

Community Media and Its Response to the Rise of Private Broadcasting

Between 1958 and 1963 the Canadian television and radio broadcasting environment underwent significant changes as private broadcasters established themselves as dominant content providers. These developments followed in the wake of a final report by the Royal Commission on Broadcasting, chaired by Robert M. Fowler, published in March 1957. Many of the report's recommendations appeared in a new Broadcasting Act of 1958, legislated by John Diefenbaker's Conservative government. New recommendations "included the inclusion of private broadcasting networks (CTV and TVA), the establishment of an independent regulator (the Board of Broadcast Governors), and the implementation of 'Canadian content' quotas for Canadian television and radio" (Wagman 2006, 205–6). In 1963, the Liberal government replaced the Conservatives, leaving private broadcasting to "enjoy its new spoils," and began working to re-establish the political function of the Canadian broadcasting system (Raboy 1990, 137). The Report of the Committee on Broadcasting (Fowler Committee) (1965) highlighted the increasing dominance of private broadcasting at the time but also emphasized the need to restore the role and prominence of public broadcasting. Private broadcasters were encouraged to "achieve a greater degree of common purpose" and to "participate in the national objectives of the Canadian broadcasting system to which they belong." The report reinforced the role of private broadcasters as rendering local services to individual communities, suggesting this as a key objective for the sector (Canada 1965, 12). At this time, private broadcasters were positioned as complementing the nationwide service goals of the public sector, though their focus on local programming would eventually deteriorate, especially following media consolidation and new commercial radio policies throughout the 1990s and 2000s (as discussed in the previous chapter). The report labelled the CBC as a dominant force for fostering national cultural identity and ideology, arguing that "the simple fact – the crucial fact – which must be clearly understood is that the CBC is the *essential* element of the Canadian broadcasting system and the most important single instrument available for the development and maintenance of the unity of Canada" (12).

In response to the increasing dominance of the private broadcasting sector in Canada, numerous social, cultural, political, and technological changes began to incite community media movements throughout the country. Social and community-based media experiments would eventually influence the CRTC's recognition of community and campus radio in broadcasting policy. As the campus sector increased its range, developmental focal points in terms of structure and ideological practices were caught up with strategies of distinction. Programming practices were distinctly local, and proponents of educational and campus radio considered its content to be of a higher quality, or cultural worth, than what was programmed for a mass audience.

In 1968, a number of changes to television and radio broadcasting policy were outlined in a new Broadcasting Act. As noted retrospectively in 1986 by the Report of the Task Force on Broadcasting Policy, the 1968 act had been generated at a time when broadcasting was expanding, as was the country. The 1986 report noted that a "large postwar influx of people into the cities from the country, together with the baby boom and heavy immigration, was transforming urban Canada, creating an environment in which mass media flourished" (Canada 1986, 14–15). The relevance of the act, however, has been questioned. For instance, Marc Raboy argues that by "the time it was adopted in 1968, the new broadcasting policy was already insufficient to deal with the technological and political climate" (Raboy 1990, 180). Ease of access to technology and the inability of public and commercial broadcasting to cater to the vast number of voices and opinions present across Canada required further changes in broadcasting policy to allocate spectrum to smaller-scale radio operations.

A report conducted by Jean McNulty in 1979 – researched under contract for the now-defunct Federal Department of Communications – examined the political, technological, and cultural factors contributing to the development of community radio in Canada in the late 1960s and early 1970s. The report, titled *Other Voices in Broadcasting*, argued that "the origins and ideas for the development of new forms of local programming in Canada stem from ideas about social change and the democratization of society which were prevalent in the 1960s" (1979, viii). McNulty found that a reaction against "big" and centralized government in the 1960s was central in setting the foundations for the development of community radio in Canada (57). McNulty's report emphasized how a variety of community media initiatives were instigated by individuals at the local level. Local broadcasting and programming was responding to "a lack of service at the local level in broadcasting or in all media" and "a need for alternative media programming to counter-balance the commercial media" (viii). The 1960s were a decade of proliferating notions of participatory democracy and social change, especially among young and educated Canadians. The idea of participatory democracy was central to the emergence of new, community-based initiatives, such as the Company of Young Canadians (a group whose mandate was to develop programs for social, economic, and community development) (Wilkinson 1988, 7). Government multicultural policy of the 1970s has also been cited as contributing to an increased desire for media that reflected a variety of cultural communities in a locality. According to Jean Ogilvie, a more "liberal (rather than conserving and preserving the nationalist vision alone) view of Canadian 'diversity'" may have been "spearheaded by new government initiatives and policy on multiculturalism" (Ogilvie, cited in Monk 1997, 53). In 1971, the federal government's multiculturalism policy established various programs to help cultural groups preserve their heritage. This policy helped plant "the seeds of a national cultural identity that differed from the American concept of the melting pot," although it still left many of Quebec's political and cultural concerns unsettled (more on this shortly) (Thomas 1992). Government multicultural policy was less focused on catering to a single, all-encompassing nation, as cultural policy had been in the past; rather, it acknowledged Canadian multiculturalism and anticipated local and community media initiatives across the nation.

These cultural and political shifts were reflected in a change of direction at the provincial educational station CKUA in Edmonton. Between 1956 and 1972, "CKUA reinvented itself, taking on the eclecticism and intellectual playfulness that would become its trademark. In the process it began to attract announcers who saw CKUA as a home for their creative temperament rather than a gateway to greener pastures" (Walters 2002, 131). A move towards eclecticism in programming was in large part due to the individuals involved in the station, individuals immersed in the cultural "feeling" of the time. A shift away from the "popular" was tied to the hiring of announcers with a passion for music who were knowledgeable about what they were playing and who were immersed in the "social, politi-cal and musical revolution that was happening at the time" (133). Walters notes that an "attitude of benign neglect on the part of management from the top down, starting with the Alberta government," also aided in creating an atmosphere of creative freedom at CKUA (134). Although the govern-ment was less involved in determining the limits of the station's freedom, listeners were implicated in setting such boundaries. Listeners expressed appreciation for the "exciting new influences in music that they wouldn't hear on commercial stations till later, if ever," but they kept things from getting too out of control, voicing concerns and providing "checks and balances" if things got too "experimental" (143–44). The role of listeners in providing the programmers and hosts with feedback is reflective of the radio station's role within the cultural and musical communities it served. In the 1960s, CKUA played a central role in cultural and intellectual activi-ties in Edmonton. Musicians visiting the city, including Stan Kenton and the Smothers Brothers, often came to the station to give interviews (150). The station's move toward eclecticism and programming that reflected the personal tastes of its programmers was also marked by an awareness of the station's *and* the university's role as a prominent cultural and educational institution in the city.

A similar direction was taken by CFRC at Queen's University. Into the early 1960s, the station's service to both the university and the community was becoming recognized and broadcasting was increased to a full fifty-two weeks a year (Zimmerman 1991, 613). In 1968, Margaret Angus, the direc-tor of radio, retired; she was replaced by Andrew Marshall, who had joined the station as a student in 1962. Under his "regime the station began to change in direction. He introduced a new image, moving toward the kind of music he felt that students enjoy, like rock and folk-rock, plus a dinner hour show featuring high quality pops" (616). This approach was significantly different than a few years earlier, when the station had a policy of playing 50 percent "popular music and good quality jazz" and 50 percent "classi-cal records" (614). Although the inclusion of genres like jazz and classi-cal certainly signified a programming approach that was distinct and "high quality," the music that "students enjoy" was no doubt distinct in its own way, given the levels of cultural and educational capital required to attend university.

Throughout the 1960s, many university radio stations began to move away from a strict focus on educational or "enriching" content and started programming music and spoken-word that reflected the interests and expertise of the individuals running these stations, as well as the cultural and musical communities nearby. Other experiments in community media around the same time also focused on the interests of community members, but with a strong focus on social and cultural activism.

Canadian Community Radio in the 1970s

The 1970s saw growth in community media initiatives across the country. As it turned out, this preceded the eventual expansion and heightened sophistication of on-campus broadcasting. The community radio model has inspired campus stations to take on a local, community-based focus and to extend its range and coverage beyond the campus and into surrounding communities. Thus, an overview of the development of community radio in Canada illustrates key aspects of Canadian campus radio history as well as the ideological and practical aims of campus stations.

Canadian community radio has primarily northern roots. It began with a variety of radio production efforts by various First Nations communications societies, mostly in Yukon and the Northwest Territories, but also in northern areas of Quebec, Ontario, and the Western provinces (McNulty 1979, 112–13; see also Bredin 2012). Attempts at using radio communications with Native groups were prominent in mid-1960s, when the Indian–Eskimo Association hired a sociologist named Alex Sim, who proposed radio experiments influenced by the *Farm Radio Forum* (Ogilvie 1983, 27). Community radio experiments in northern Canada did much to legitimize the community radio broadcasting sector in policy and in urban and rural spaces. Many of the earliest community radio stations were in the Northwest Territories; their purpose was to provide radio services to connect people out on the land who were hunting or travelling to those in the villages (McNulty 1979, 112–13). Also, northern community radio services grew alongside two policy initiatives unique to Canada: the attempted integration of regional differences; and the goal of total cross-country coverage (Fairchild 2001, 141).

In 1972 and 1973, the Canadian Department of Communications installed community radio stations in the Keewatin District of the Northwest Territories and in Northern Ontario. The stations were to be run by local people, who were organized into communication societies with the goal of improving communications in remote areas (McNulty 1979, 80). Another early community radio experiment in northern Ontario was Radio Kenomadiwam, created by a group of university students in 1969 under the Company for Young Canadians. They taught the basics of radio production to the Ojibway of Ontario's Longlac region. Some of the staff would later be involved in Vancouver's Co-op Radio, beginning in 1973

(142). There was also CHRQ-FM, a 50-watt station in Listuguj, Quebec, licensed to the Gespegewag Communications Society. That station's mandate was to develop Mi'kmaq language and educational media in the region (144). Community broadcasting in northern communities was often born out of ideas about local cultural development and about producing services that were not available through commercial or public broadcasting.

Many northern community radio projects brought together community development practices and the use of social animators, who were often put in place by the CBC. Their role was to encourage participation in local media by people in the community (McNulty 1979, 81). In 1972, a community radio experiment in Espanola, Ontario, a small pulp-and-paper town, sought to test possibilities for local individuals to participate in production at the local CBC station. The outcome of this collaboration was the establishment of a small studio attached to the CBC rebroadcast transmitter, where people could produce informational programming to supplement CBC network services (83). However, once the CBC's professional animator left the area, community involvement "dwindled to nothing" (Ogilvie 1983, 23), indicating that this sort of partnership was not always successful or in the community's best interests.

The CBC established the Office of Community Radio in order to coordinate these developments (Ogilvie 1983, 84). That office operated out of Toronto from 1972 until 1978, when it was disbanded due to budget cuts; in 1977, it published a catalogue of community radio operations. The catalogue noted that there were forty-three stations broadcasting community programming. Twelve of these were owned by the CBC; another twelve were in the Northwest Territories and in northern Quebec and were unlicensed by the CRTC. Of the remaining nineteen, two were student stations, five were urban, and the rest were located in rural areas (McNulty 1979, 113). Shortly after the catalogue was published, between 1977 and 1979, thirty-four community-based licences were issued, most of which were granted to Native communications societies in Ontario and Manitoba. Of the remaining nine, two were student stations, one was a college station, four involved community access arrangements with the CBC, and two were for community organizations in small communities (113). In the 1970s, policy-making began to account for the increased cultural role of university stations in their surrounding communities, as well as for the increased social activist and developmental goals of community radio stations. The province of Quebec played a central role in establishing community radio by advocating for local interests that were not necessarily recognized or supported by a national broadcaster. Of course, the politics of community media developments in Quebec are much more complicated than the description offered in this chapter; that said, the process by which community radio was distinguished from commercial and public broadcasting offers insight into the history of policy-making for the community sector.

During the 1960s and early 1970s, the idea of alternative media in Quebec was closely tied to provincial political movements that were notably distinct from the federal agenda. In 1968, Marcel Pepin, the president of the Confederation of National Trade Unions, "denounced the commercial media for placing profit above the public interest, and called on the union movement and its supporters to create independent vehicles for 'people's' or 'popular' information" (Raboy 1990, 200). The late 1960s in Quebec were also years of social and cultural change, with "a new middle class and new elites, a rising standard of living, widespread secularism, and higher levels of education among the French-speaking population" (Stiles and Lachance 1988, 11). The province of Quebec, in the political and cultural climate in the late 1960s, developed community media to help remedy the fact that much of the province did not feel adequately served and represented by nationalist public broadcasting or by private broadcasting, which was detached from local interests.

A 1971 report titled *Toward a Québec Communications Policy*, by Jean-Paul L'Allier, the communications minister in the Bourassa government, outlined some of the political and cultural reasons for Quebec's desire to control media in the province. The report argued that it was "up to Québec to set up an overall communications policy," and although it "must be coordinated with those of the other governments and consistent with the North American milieu, it must first of all be integrated to Québec's priorities" (1971, 2). Later in the report, the centrality of local programming was stressed. First, the report referenced page four of the 1969 Report of the Task Force on Federal Government Information, which stated that the "'lack of clear information available to all those who wish to participate in the democratic process is fast becoming one of the greatest tragedies of our time'" (46). Second, the report included, as an appendix, "Québec's Policy on Community Cables" from May 1971, which claimed that it was "essential to promote local programming. It is at this level that public opinion is heard, that the daily rhythm of life is perceived and that the concerns of real life are dealt with. This is where the freedom of expression takes shape" (Appendix 12).

The development of community media in Quebec was also tied to the establishment of the *Ministère des Communications du Québec* (MCQ; Quebec Ministry of Communications) in 1969. The MCQ's mandate was to create and implement communications policies, oversee broadcasting in Quebec, and establish communication services for government departments in the province (Stiles and Lachance 1988). Instrumental in "bringing community media under provincial control," it established in 1972 the *Service du développement des media*, which "made an inventory of community media projects and brought project staff together for two meetings to discuss their work" (12–13). As well, in 1973, Quebec's Treasury Board put forth a subsidy program for community media. Its first-year budget was about $390,000, of which half was given to Vidéographe, a group in Montreal that used video to promote social activism (13). Most of the projects funded by the program were television-based, for MCQ thought that television had greater potential than radio. Reflecting the MCQ's interest in television, some of the first instances of community radio in Quebec began without financial support from the province. Examples are CKRL-FM, a station with a non-commercial licence that operated with funding from the Laval University community, and CINQ-FM, a multilingual community station in Montreal that began broadcasting in 1972 in collaboration with McGill's station, Radio McGill (13–14).

CINQ-FM, also known as Radio Centre-Ville, was established after a difficult struggle with the CRTC for a licence (Radio Centre-Ville 1992, 51). Activists involved in the social changes transforming Quebec society throughout the 1970s were part of the station's foundation. The station was eventually licensed as an "experiment" by the CRTC (as was CFRO-FM Co-op Radio in Vancouver, developing around the same time) (51). A licence was granted to CINQ-FM on 27 February 1975, and it became an official station on the FM band, broadcasting with 7.2 watts of power. Once established, Radio Centre-Ville began tailoring its content to Montreal's multilingual communities in an effort to reflect "the coexistence of individuals and different cultures within Québec society" (49). The station was able to provide relevant content for particular segments of the city without promoting a nationalist ideology (something done by the public sector), and without being bound by the demands of advertisers (as were many stations in the private sector). However, some sponsorship from the local community and from not-for-profits was permitted on CINQ-FM. The licensing of Radio Centre-Ville was a significant step for Canadian community radio. The station helped lay the foundations for other, similar developments in Quebec and across the country.

North of Quebec City, in the Saugenay region, community radio stations began operating in the neighbouring towns of Chicoutimi and Jonquière. McNulty wrote that in the 1960s, Chicoutimi–Jonquière was a "distinct geographic, economic and social region, physically isolated ... from the main centres of population in the province" (1979, 202). The services provided by Canada's national public broadcaster were not prominent in the Saugenay, nor were they relevant – the region was too unique in Canada. Moreover, in Chicoutimi, citizens had access to only one FM station. In 1973, interest in FM radio for the region increased, and a group of professors and staff from the Université du Québec à Chicoutimi, along with journalists, businesspeople, and union members, began preliminary planning for the station that would become CHUT-FM (207–8). The station began broadcasting in June 1975 after receiving CRTC approval the previous year. At this time, notably early in the licensing of Canadian community radio, the CRTC made it a requirement that the station utilize advertising revenue in order to support itself (207). This stipulation would contribute to the downfall of the Chicoutimi-based station, highlighting, again, the tension between commercial advertising and the mandate of many community radio stations.

As CHUT-FM continued to develop, it became increasingly confused regarding how best to serve and relate to its local community, becoming first and foremost a music station with a heavy emphasis on rock music (McNulty 1979, 209). The station had difficulty maintaining the "20% community programming" that it claimed it would provide, and it struggled to keep a full staff. Meanwhile, tensions arose between station staff and sponsors. The former were heard criticizing sponsors on the air, and some sponsors believed the station's programming to be "ill-organized and ill-prepared." The result was a drop in sponsorship revenue (208, 210). In August 1977 the station was informed that the MCQ would not be providing a grant for the following year; its licence was soon surrendered to the CRTC (211). While the community media developments in Jonquière were much more successful, the Chicoutimi example highlights problems faced by local and community media developers in the early 1970s – namely, the need to balance funding and advertising with community-based programming.

These examples of community media developments in Quebec illustrate how a particular cultural and political climate sparked alternative forms of media. As well, they point to experiments and operations that brought together universities and their respective communities, sometimes successfully and other times not. Urban areas across the nation began to instigate community radio programs in the mid- to late 1970s. While a number of official institutions and organizations were involved in many of these developments, it was individuals and groups invested in media reform who were the prominent force in eventually establishing a policy framework for campus and community radio.

Regulating the Campus Radio Sector

Throughout the 1960s and 1970s, educational radio stations like CKUA in Alberta continued to face developmental complications; meanwhile, community and student radio stations were established throughout the country with more clearly defined mandates. In 1970 the federal government decided that broadcasting licences could not be granted to provincial governments or educational institutions, and this affected CKUA as well as stations at Queen's, Ryerson, and the University of Saskatchewan. The federal government was apprehensive about granting licences to these entities because of the political climate in both Quebec and Alberta: separatism in the former and the Social Credit party in the latter. CKUA was embroiled in this debate, voicing a desire for provinces to have more control over broadcasting. Educational stations were an intriguing case, for "while education was a provincial responsibility, Ottawa insisted broadcasting was a federal affair" (Walters 2002, 172). Shortly after this 1970 decision, the federal government issued an Order in Council that made amendments allowing for a licence to be granted to an "independent corporation" that was not directly controlled by the provincial government. The licensee, however, would be required to offer programming that could be defined as "educational" (180). This enabled CKUA to remain in operation, although its licence would become property of AECC, the Alberta Educational Communications Corporation (later known as ACCESS). At this time, it was increasingly difficult for CKUA to justify its programming as "educational," although a case was made that the mere task of "taking music seriously" indeed reflected this mandate. The station argued that its listeners possessed an "understanding" about music, not just a simple "liking" (190). But by the late 1980s, CKUA could no longer succeed in claiming an "educational purpose." Years of fighting to keep the station alive would lead it to take on various forms under different owners and ownership models until the station became a not-for-profit broadcaster under the CKUA Radio Foundation in 1994.

In January 1975 the CRTC published a report titled *FM Radio in Canada: A Policy to Ensure a Varied and Comprehensive Radio Service*. The report focused on the FM radio band and how it could best be utilized to diversify Canada's broadcasting system in a way that would be more in sync with the Broadcasting Act of the time. FM broadcasting was the focus of this particular report because, as the commission stated, "since the opening of the FM band in the 1930s there has been a widespread expectation that FM would provide an alternate radio service of higher quality" (CRTC 1975c, 11). In the mid-1970s, the AM spectrum had become "increasingly congested and prone to interference." With the superior sound transmission of the FM band, it was considered to be well suited for the development of new approaches to radio – "both by large metropolitan licenses and by broadcasters who want to exploit its potential for economical coverage of smaller areas" (11). The report highlighted a fundamental and recurring problem, which was how each type of broadcasting could distinctively contribute to fulfilling the Broadcasting Act's objective of providing diverse programming with Canadian resources. A number of applications for new FM stations had been denied in previous years, the report stated, because the applications had not outlined the ways in which they would provide new or different programming opportunities to surrounding communities. Yet at the same time that these commercial FM licences were being refused, with no new stations of this type being licensed until the development of a new FM policy, the commission was approving a number of non-commercial "community FM" stations, including for Kitchener in 1973, for Vancouver, Montreal, and Chicoutimi in 1974, and for a "student FM" station in Quebec City in 1972 (2).

The report also pointed to a number of complaints that were being made against the commercial radio sector, including loud and strident radio, trivial and uninteresting content that was limited in scope, and radio personalities who were not involved in program development. It was argued that FM radio should be working toward offering content that lent itself to the "discovery and appreciation of a greater spectrum of music and the spoken word" (CRTC 1975c, 4, 6). The report stressed the importance of diversity with respect to Canadian cultural heritage and linked diversity to the richness of a society's culture. "In radio," the report proclaimed, "the size of a record library and the usage patterns of recordings within a variety of formats are among the more important aspects of the cultural functioning of that medium" (6). As well, the report connected "diversity" to the notion of "community." New applicants for FM licences would need to specify the hours during the week that would be available for locally produced programming, as well as programming provided by community groups. The report did not explicitly state what the commission claimed a "community group" to be, but it offered its own definition of "community": it was "the entire complex constituency covered by a broadcast transmitter. It is more than a statistic for rating purposes. A community provides an almost limitless resource for program material that can be developed into various participatory formats" (28). Even though the commission considered community and student radio to be experimental at this time, the FM band was beginning to be discussed in terms that would eventually result in more space for campus and community radio on the FM dial. Similarly in the United States, FM radio offered a space for underground and public radio stations in the 1960s and 1970s (see Sterling and Keith 2008). Terms like "community," "participatory," and "diversity" were clearly significant with regard to how the commission envisioned radio broadcasting developing in the mid-1970s. Soon after this report on FM radio was published, the CRTC would take further steps toward legitimizing campus radio in its policy and regulatory framework.

On 27 June 1975, the CRTC licensed two Canadian "student" radio stations as Special FM licences. The 1975 policy decision outlined the sort of service that student stations were to provide. First, a campus station in Winnipeg was licensed, having been applied for by Jim Rogers on behalf of the Radio Operations Committee, "a non-profit corporation without share capital" controlled by voting members comprising mainly students at the University of Manitoba (CRTC 1975b, 7–8). The second application was made by the Carleton University Student's Association for a station in Ottawa. Both applications were for English-language FM broadcast licences. The CRTC explained that "many of the different sectors of social life cannot find a place on the national service or the private commercial outlets." It was for this reason that the commission had developed "new models for different voices" (3). The decision defined student radio stations as "broadcasting undertakings whose structure provides for membership, direction, management, operation and programming primarily by students as members of a post-secondary academic community" (2). At this time, the licensing of student radio was a new endeavour, as made evident by the fact that the CRTC was careful to include working definitions and stipulations in its decision. These stipulations contributed to the distinctiveness or "alternativeness" of campus radio, for they outlined a mandate that was decidedly distinct from that of public or commercial broadcasting.

The 1975 decision also outlined the intended role of campus radio stations within their respective communities. It noted that "an intervention to the Ottawa application asked if the Commission would be prepared to license two or more student FM stations in the same locality." To this it responded: "The public interest at this time will be best served if only one such channel is used for student broadcasting" (CRTC 1975b, 2–3). If the English and French languages both were present, the CRTC refined its previous statement: where "there are both English-speaking and French-speaking post-secondary educational institutions and a sufficient number of frequencies is available in a locality, the Commission may issue two licences, one in each language, in that locality" (3). Each station was to provide a service based on certain characteristics specific to its locality. Particular care was taken to ensure that different stations in a radio market were distinct from one another, a point that reflected the FM radio report from earlier that year. Ideas about new roles for FM radio broadcasting went hand in hand with the legitimization and expanded operations of campus radio broadcasting.

Further stipulations of the 1975 decision included the need for stations to acknowledge community issues in their programming. There was also a requirement that would allow off-campus community groups to have a voice on the station (CRTC 1975b, 6). Non-campus communities were integrated into the CRTC's policy on campus radio advertising. The decision stated that "the Commission is of the opinion that truly *alternative* forms of programming can best be achieved and maintained through financing other than from the sale of air time" (4; emphasis added). Even so, the decision recognized how difficult it was to find funding for alternative broadcasting. Because of that, it allowed for promotional announcements limited to four minutes and six times per clock hour. Promotional announcements were to be regulated in the same way as had been outlined for CINQ-FM in Montreal; this would allow for the inclusion of the sponsor's name, business address, and business hours, as well as a brief description of the product or service, but without mentioning or referencing brand names. Preferred sponsors were to include members of the local community, and promotions could "not refer to price, quality, convenience, durability, or desirability, or contain other comparative or competitive references" (5). The CRTC decision of 27 June 1975 was a significant step in the development of what has now become campus–community radio, and it signified the CRTC's recognition of student radio broadcasting. The decision also anticipated the eventual formulation of a coherent set of stipulations and requirements for the campus and community radio sector.

McNulty's 1979 report explained that according to the CRTC, student radio stations would serve four purposes. The first was to communicate with students beyond the reach of carrier current or closed-circuit stations operated by the academic institution. The second was to reach students not belonging to the college or university that was broadcasting. Third, the student station was to communicate the "concerns, interests and activities" of the campus to the public, and fourth, it was to provide the "general public" with "innovative" and "alternative" programming that made use of the university or college's resources (McNulty 1979, 194). McNulty's report also argued that local programming is best understood in relation to the local society where it has been developed. Three main advantages of local programming were pointed out: the involvement of individuals other than professionals; the dissemination of local information from alternative sources; and opportunities for musicians and artists to reach a local audience (237). The first instances of licensing student stations illustrate the coming together of a strong emphasis on local content that was community-oriented and participative.

The CRTC's recognition of campus radio through policy-making was the result of community media movements launched by many individuals and organizations, including Aboriginal groups, local media activists, and students. Policy would continue to specify and set the basic terms for how community and campus radio would operate. In 1985, as a response to the sector's growth, the National Campus and Community Radio Association (NCRA) was formed by member stations in order to "provide a support and information sharing network" (Monk 1997, 3). Also in 1985, the CRTC issued a public notice reviewing community radio. This review continued to define the characteristics of community radio as determined by the commission. Community radio was to "provide broadly-based programming and a forum for community expression" (CRTC 1985c, 1). Also, community stations were to require community ownership, which meant community participation in programming decisions. Furthermore, the community sector would need to outline "specific programming criteria designed to ensure that the programming be authentically community-oriented, that community participation exist[s] at all levels, and that the programming be different from that of other stations within a given market" (CRTC 1985c, 9). In its summary of this report, the CRTC defined a community station as:

> characterized by its ownership, programming and the market it is called to serve. It is owned and controlled by a non-profit organization whose structure provides for membership, management, operation, and programming primarily by members of the community at large. Its programming should be based on community access and should reflect the interests and special needs of the listeners it is licensed to serve. (CRTC 1985c, 9)

Community stations were grouped together with institutional (which included student) stations and educational radio stations under the licence category "Special FM." The commission explained that all subsequent Special FM licenses would need to meet the criteria set out in this public notice. Another requirement of this policy was that stations should continue to broadcast live shows and concerts by local artists and musicians and encourage other forms of local and regional artistic expression.

Following the 1985 review of community radio, a public notice published in 1987 addressed educational and institutional radio. The notice stated that an institutional station was any station "other than an educational station, which is owned or controlled by a non-profit organization associated with an institution of post-secondary education. This included 'student FM stations'" (CRTC 1987b). However, the Commission decided that the twenty-one student FM stations licensed at the time would not be included in this review because of their "special and reasonably well-defined mandate that is different from Educational and other Institutional stations" (CRTC 1987b). This document again defined the Special FM licence class, as licences other than CBC FM licences in which the number, duration, and type of commercial messages broadcast were restricted by a condition of licence. The document also distinguished between educational, institutional, and community stations, while also highlighting problems with this "definitional scheme." The first problem was that student FM stations were grouped under "institutional" although they already had a policy for which to operate, while other types of institutional stations did not. This "lack of precision" resulted in individuals making submissions to the CRTC that confused educational stations (those operated by provincial independent corporations) with institutional stations (student FM stations). Because of this, the commission altered its definitions so that the distinction between stations was clearer. First, "educational" was changed to "provincial educational." Second, student radio stations were distinguished from stations that merely had some level of association with an institution of post-secondary education. A student station was then defined as "that which is owned or controlled by a non-profit organization and has a structure providing for membership, direction, management, operation and programming primarily by students of the institution of post-secondary education with which it is associated" (CRTC 1987b). According to these two public notices from 1985 and 1987, student stations, which would eventually become the campus radio sector, were becoming their own entity, with increasing distinctiveness and clear internal policies for governance and operations.

In 2000, an extensive policy was created for the campus radio sector. This policy had its background in, and evolved out of, prior policy documents published throughout the 1990s. The 2000 policy replaced Public Notice CRTC 1992-38, Policies for Community and Campus Radio, which had been in effect since 1992. Community and campus stations were grouped together within the goals of the 1992 community and campus radio policy. The commission stated that "there are many similarities between the two" and that a major goal in the development of this policy, "which will apply to community and campus stations operating on both the AM and FM bands, has been to ensure that community and campus stations have the necessary flexibility to respond to the needs of listeners in their communities while ensuring ... a programming alternative" (CRTC 1992a). Community and campus radio stations were defined separately in this document, and their respective roles were carefully outlined. Campus radio was defined after community radio, with the subdefinitions of "campus station," "campus/

community," and "instructional." At the time of this policy, a "campus station" was considered to be a station "owned or controlled by a not-for-profit organization associated with a post-secondary educational institution." A "campus/community station" had programming "produced by volunteers who are either students or members of the community at large," while an "instructional" station had "the training of professional broadcasters as its primary objective."

In 1997 the CRTC initiated a review of its policies for campus radio (CRTC 1997), instigated in "light of the evolving communications environment" (CRTC 2000c). The review would culminate in the 2000 policy for the sector. The commission stated that a "consultative process" involving campus broadcasters (as well as commercial radio, other types of not-for-profit radio, and the CBC) would help determine the new policy for the sector. This consultative process was completed in the fall of 1998. A total of forty-three comments were made to the CRTC regarding the proposed policies for campus radio. Comments were submitted by groups such as the NCRA, the Canadian Association of Broadcasters (CAB), the Society of Composers, Authors and Music Publishers of Canada (SOCAN), and various other interested parties and individuals. Most of these comments were "generally supportive" of the proposed policies; several parties addressed the commission's proposed policies in areas such as the structure of the boards of directors of campus stations and the Canadian content requirements in genres with fewer available Canadian musical selections (CRTC 1999). A major goal of the revised policy was "to ensure diversity within the broadcasting system, while providing greater flexibility to the campus radio sector through the introduction of streamlined regulatory and administrative requirements" (CRTC 2000c).

The proposed policy revisions that altered the licensing and structure of campus radio stations were numerous. Many of them dealt with the programming structure of all campus stations. For instance, the revised policy stated that at least 25 percent of weekly broadcast programming must be spoken-word programming. Also, for English-language community-based campus stations, no more than 10 percent of weekly musical selections should be hits (no more than 30 percent for instructional stations). For French-language stations, however, "in the absence of effective tools to define French-language hits," the commission would not restrict the number of hits such stations could broadcast per week (CRTC 2000c). The revised regulations and proposed amendments also mentioned key initiatives related to the following: means to ensure that the programming of campus stations would offer an alternative to other types of stations; Canadian music and local talent development; the structure of the boards of directors; and finally, policies for advertising (CRTC 2000c). Furthermore, the policy granted campus stations increased flexibility by streamlining the various regulatory and administrative requirements to which they would be subject (CRTC 2000c). These stipulations, including the restriction on the number of "hits" that an English-language station could program, are key examples of how "alternativeness" can be reaffirmed through policy, although much of this operating ethos was present throughout the sector before a comprehensive policy was developed. Apparently, the commission was concerned about how the radio spectrum was to be allocated, so it ensured that licensed campus stations would not compete with commercial radio stations. Commercial "hits" could not be prominently programmed; "alternatives" would be required.

Throughout Campus Radio Policy, the relationship between campus radio stations and "alternative" programming was reflected in guidelines that addressed Canadian content regulations as well as programming directed at "culturally diverse" listeners. The commission believed that a "healthy and vibrant not-for-profit sector is essential to fulfill the goals of the Act" and that "campus stations play a unique and valuable role in the communities they serve" (CRTC 2000c). The document pointed to the cultural diversity that was evident in many Canadian communities, claiming that "campus stations serving those centres [are] in a position to make a strong contribution to the reflection of that cultural diversity, especially by providing exposure to new and developing artists from minority cultural groups" (CRTC 2000c). Campus stations in areas without an already existing ethnic station were allowed to provide up to 40 percent third-language programming without the commission's approval. For all campus and community licence applications, the commission examined "closely the applicant's plans to provide programming that would increase diversity in the market" (CRTC 2000c). Emphasizing "diversity in the market" is a recurring aspect of campus radio policy that is central to the commission's idea of how the "alternativeness" of campus broadcasting should function.

The new policy also increased the total minimum percentage of category 2 music that a station must play in a broadcast week from 30 to 35 percent (CRTC 2000c). And for category 3 music, the commission amended the regulations to increase the minimum level of Canadian content from 10 to 12 percent over the broadcast week (CRTC 2000c). Category 2 is "Popular Music," which includes pop, rock, and dance; country and country-oriented; acoustic; and easy listening. Category 3 is "Special Interest Music," which includes concert; folk and folk-oriented; World beat and international; jazz and blues; and, non-classic religious. These categories enable the commission to group genres based on notions of popularity and listenership, whereby more popular genres are separated from less popular genres. When campus stations are asked to program a greater number of non-Canadian category 3 musical selections, competition with commercial stations becomes less of an issue, for the genres in this category are hardly heard on commercial radio. As well, a higher Canadian content quota for category 2 music ensures that any "Popular Music" genres are largely Canadian.

The comments that were submitted to the commission during the consultative process provide an interesting perspective on how the revised policy influenced different parties. The NCRA expressed support for an increase in Canadian content, category 2, to 35 percent, but it did not support the proposed increase in category 3 music because "many small stations have real difficulty getting enough servicing in this area to fulfill even the current requirements" (Cote 1999, 1–2). The Society of Composers, Authors and Music Publishers of Canada (SOCAN) also supported the proposal to increase minimum levels of Canadian content in category 2 from 30 to 35 percent, but unlike the NCRA, it also supported an increase in category 3 from 10 to 12 percent. As a representative of the Canadian performing rights of musicians and publishers, SOCAN was obviously in favour of increasing Canadian content quotas for campus radio programming. SOCAN said it did not agree that "'campus stations *appear* to have difficulty finding Canadian material in certain genres,'" arguing that "further empirical study of this issue is required" (Rock 1999, 2; emphasis original). The Canadian Association of Broadcasters also supported the increase in Canadian content for both category 2 and category 3 musical selections (CAB Radio Board 1999, 3). It seems that most parties are in favour of maintaining or increasing Canadian content for campus radio, which should not surprise, for many of them represent the interests of Canadian artists. High Canadian content quotas help ensure that campus radio remains devoted to local music; it also keeps stations from competing with commercial broadcasters by restricting their ability to program widely popular hits. Thus, Canadian groups and artists constitute a significant component of campus and community radio programming, and this bodes well for Canadian artists but also for groups and organizations that represent the interests of Canadian groups and artists, such as SOCAN.

The structure of boards of directors for campus stations was also addressed in the proposed policy amendments. While the former policy "generally expected that a majority of the board of directors of a campus station would come from the student body, faculty, administration and other groups closely associated with the educational institution," the revised policy promoted a balanced representation from the student body, as well as members from the associated college or university, station volunteers, and the community at large (CRTC 2000c). Campus stations licensed to serve the community, therefore, had to recognize and reflect the role and significance of community members in their maintenance and operations. Furthermore, the revised policy encouraged members of the board to hold positions with terms of more than one year. The commission pointed out that a station would need to confirm that its board complied with this structure at the time of licence renewal; if it did not, the station would need to provide detailed plans regarding how it would conform to the policy.

The NCRA expressed dissatisfaction with the proposed restructuring of boards of directors. It argued that board members should come from "organizations whose specific mandate is to hold and operate a licence," and it stated that "radio societies should be autonomous; no outside organization (such as a student union or university administration) should hold a controlling interest in the radio society through appointed board members" (Cote 1999, 5). The Canadian Association of Broadcasters was more supportive of the commission's proposals, noting that it supported a structure with balanced board representation (CAB Radio Board 1999, 4). The NCRA's concerns did not alter the commission's proposed amendments to restructure the board of directors for campus radio stations; those concerns did, however, highlight a notable tension in campus broadcasting policy. Organizations such as a student union can be helpful in providing necessary resources to the station, but, as NCRA argued, this also risks reducing the station's autonomy.

Other significant revisions in the 2000 policy concerned advertising, local talent development, and the commission's streamlined regulatory approach. The policy removed all stipulations regarding "restricted" advertising and stated that campus stations would henceforth be permitted to broadcast 504 minutes of advertising per week with a maximum of four minutes of advertising in any hour (CRTC 2000c). The commission's reasoning for this revision was that it felt it would help campus stations increase funding. Additionally the commission made note of Canadian local talent initiatives, stating that these initiatives "are expected, and should be described in licence applications" (CRTC 2000c). Regarding the streamlined regulatory approach, the need for applicants to complete a Promise of Performance was removed, but applicants were asked to submit a proposed program schedule. Such components of this regulatory approach contributed to the primary goal of the campus radio policy after 2000, which was to create "simple, effective and easily-measured requirements" in order "to ensure diversity within the broadcasting system, while providing greater flexibility to the campus radio sector" (CRTC 2000c). While this overview of Campus

Radio Policy does certainly not include mention of each and every policy revision and proposed amendment included in Public Notice 2000-12, it does refer to the policy revisions and proposals that were reflected in subsequent licences and licence renewals of campus radio stations. These specific revisions and proposals are also those that have had the most influence in the areas that contribute to the ways listeners perceive a campus station, including the type of programming a station must broadcast. Initiatives such as a streamlined regulatory process help reduce the amount of work a station is required to do, while other stipulations, such as Canadian content quotas, require attention to detail and administrative tasks.

This historical overview illustrates how Canadian campus radio broadcasting has been shaped by trends, traditions, and broadcasting experiments over the past century. Early educational radio involved universities experimenting with broadcasting technology to establish connections with nearby communities. These stations provided listeners with programming that often strived to be of high quality, whether musical or otherwise. Early educational stations like CKUA advocated for bringing radio to rural communities and to listeners who were beyond the range of other stations. Many community radio stations in Canada worked toward increasing community involvement with the medium and were tied to important social activist movements, particularly during in the 1960s, but also earlier, as was apparent in farm and rural radio broadcasting for and by agricultural communities. The campus radio sector has resulted from the blending of these practices and initiatives. Contemporary campus radio broadcasting is now a vibrant and musically innovative component of the community radio sector in the country, one that amalgamates the "high-quality" trends of educational radio, in terms of how stations treat their music-based programming, and the social activist mandate of community stations from rural and northern communities and from the urban stations that took root during countercultural political movements of the 1960s. The significant contributions of radio activists, students, and cultural producers were the driving force behind the recognition and legitimization of campus and community radio broadcasting in broadcasting policy. However, the establishment of a comprehensive policy for the sector also means that there are rules that can be broken, and consequences for not complying with regulations. The following chapter continues to examine the relationship between campus radio stations and policy, looking closely at the operations and structure of three Canadian campus radio stations, both before and after being licensed by the CRTC as FM broadcasters.

4

From Campus Borders to Communities

Campus Radio in Three Canadian Localities

Alongside the expansion of the Canadian campus radio sector has been the formation of a policy framework for regulating it. That framework has dealt with numerous issues, including specific programming requirements, the ways that campus stations are collectively defined, and funding and sustainability. Cultural distinctiveness, taste cultures, and value judgments about music have been ongoing characteristics of campus radio broadcasting, as have the political and social issues that have inspired community media initiatives.

This chapter explores the development of the Canadian campus radio sector with greater specificity by focusing on three Canadian campus radio stations. It details the pre-FM operations of CHMA in Sackville, New Brunswick, CKUW in Winnipeg, Manitoba, and CiTR in Vancouver, British Columbia, and how these stations acquired their FM licences from the CRTC to broadcast beyond campus borders and into their respective communities. Locally produced station mandates and program grids are juxtaposed with centralized CRTC policy in order to examine the levels of autonomy present at individual stations, as well as stations' ability to structure their operations in a manner that responds to the communities and music scenes within their broadcast range. Individual station mandates and philosophies are significant documents that determine a station's role within local cultural and musical communities and that also emphasize a commitment to providing media practitioners, DJs, listeners, and musicians with a local radio alternative.

The Canadian campus radio sector is large, but the nation's non-campus community radio sector is even larger, extending far north and filling in numerous rural areas that are distant from any college or university campus. These three campus stations were chosen to represent a large metropolis, a medium-sized city, and a small town. They are also somewhat geographically representative of the country, as much as they can be, given the country's vast size.

CHMA is in Sackville, New Brunswick, a town of only 5,500 people, just over 2,000 of them students at Mount Allison University ("Mount A"). In 2008, the city was designated the "cultural capital of Canada" by the Department of Canadian Heritage. CKUW is the campus station at the University of Winnipeg ("U of W"). Winnipeg has a long and significant history of contributing to Canadian popular music and culture, yet it very rarely figures into discussions of either, having been left at the wayside by sites like Montreal and Toronto. The city is fairly isolated in terms of proximity to other large cities (the closest being Minneapolis, approximately an eight-hour drive south). As of the 2011 Canadian Census, Winnipeg is the seventh-largest municipality in Canada with a population of 730,018. The University of Winnipeg, an inner-city school, has about 10,000 students. The university's moderate size and the city's central location make for an interesting research site, as does the fact that the campus is located right in the downtown core. CiTR at the University of British Columbia (UBC) in Vancouver is a station housed within a big university that serves a large metropolitan centre and surrounding area. Greater Vancouver is the third most populous metropolitan area in Canada, according to the aforementioned census, with a population of over 2 million. And while the city proper is slightly smaller than Winnipeg (it is Canada's eighth-largest municipality), the station serves a large portion of Greater Vancouver, making the population for this site considerably larger. Furthermore, UBC has an incredibly large student population of over 50,000 (both Vancouver and Okanagan campuses combined, with most at Vancouver). The main Vancouver campus, where CiTR is located, is about 10 kilometres from the downtown core, on Point Grey, just west of the Kitsilano neighbourhood.

Broadcasting policy and station mandates discursively frame the structure, operations, and programming of campus stations, but these three stations were operating in various formats under the direction of, or from, different organizations or institutions before becoming licensed by the CRTC. Writing about these pre-licensing stories is somewhat difficult because historical records of varying completeness and comprehensiveness have been kept and maintained by each station or the host university. UBC, for instance, has been comparatively more diligent about keeping archival documents pertaining to its Radio Society, largely due to its connection with the Alma Mater Society. Nevertheless, the archival and policy documents, local cultural publications (some that have been produced by campus stations), and interviews with station practitioners and cultural producers provide a telling account of the developmental paths that campus stations followed before being granted a licence by the CRTC.

Most importantly, the processes by which CHMA, CKUW, and CiTR acquired FM licences and crafted mandates that reflect and represent their communities illustrate the particular characteristics of campus stations that are both compliant with CRTC regulations and distinct and autonomous from other campus stations. An FM band licence has helped campus stations realize their goal of community representation by increasing their reach and relevance; this in turn has increased inclusivity and diversity in operations and programming. A commitment to the "community" element of Canada's radio broadcast sector is a defining trait of Canadian campus stations. Furthermore, the processes by which Canadian campus stations acquired FM licences shed light on what can be lost when stations move to an entirely online format, or if the Internet is assumed to be the most viable means of distributing alternative and community radio.

Pre-FM Radio Broadcasting at Three Canadian Universities

CHMA-FM is located in the Wallace McCain Student Centre on York Street, one of the larger buildings on the relatively contained and modestly sized Mount Allison campus in Sackville. The station space is large, clean, and impressive. The windows in the front offices (where the program director and station manager work) enable one to see into other areas of the station space. The station's main room is large and inviting. A foosball table and video games suggest that this is a comfortable and fun space for volunteers and staff to spend time. Chairs and couches are dispersed throughout. Towards the back of the station are the broadcast booth, the production studio, and the music library, which is a well-sized room with CDs and vinyl records stacked from floor to ceiling.

In the 1960s, before CHMA began broadcasting from the student centre, it followed a developmental path that involved some experimental, or "pirate," radio broadcasting from a student dorm room. Steve Ridlington, who arrived on campus in the fall of 1972, was involved with the station in its infancy. At that time, the carrier current station was transmitted by wire running through the campus's heating tunnels, connecting student residences to what at the time was the student centre. Ridlington would remember that Stewart Walker – a physics major and the station's first engineer – was the "man behind the myth of the pirate station" (Ridlington, email correspondence, 4 December 2012). On one occasion, Walker constructed a small FM transmitter and tested it. Soon after, the CRTC shut the transmitter down.

Station manager Pierre Malloy became involved with CHMA in spring of 1995, after moving to Sackville the previous year. Prior to this, in the early 1980s, he had worked at CHSR in Fredericton, New Brunswick; he also had a radio show in the Northwest Territories during the late 1980s and early 1990s. Malloy provided some insight into the station's operations in the 1960s. During the 1960s, "Mount A had one of the premier Engineering programs in the country" (Malloy, personal interview, 6 June 2011). A lot of "bright young guys" were at the university studying engineering, "mostly guys, because it was the 60s," Malloy added. These students had access to all kinds of brand new equipment provided by the university, so they built their own station and played music that fell within their tastes. According to Malloy, "their idea of the station was basically electronics and music." He was careful to stress that the station is much more than this now.

In a CRTC decision dated 10 April 1975, Attic Broadcasting Co. was granted a licence for "an English language AM (carrier current) radio station at Sackville, N.B. on the frequency 670 kHz with a power of 20 watts day-time and night-time" (CRTC 1975a). The decision referenced a public announcement from May 1972, in which the commission stated "that it expects student carrier current radio stations 'to reflect the interests and activities of the total university or college community in which they operate; to schedule a consistently high proportion of Canadian material; and, above all, to promote innovative programming which will explore and enlarge student interests'" (CRTC 1975a). The emphasis here was primarily on the student culture and the campus community. As of the mid-1970s, campus radio broadcasting in Sackville was licensed and regulated by the CRTC, and it would move onto the FM dial in a decade. A letter to the editor written by alumnus Lorey Miller in Mount Allison's *The Argosy* recalled CHMA during the 1970s, when it would "spin" vinyl "in a tiny but adequate studio at the top floor of the Memorial Library building" (Miller 2011).

In 1980, Geoff Ritcey, CHMA's station manager, circulated a report that communicated information he had received while visiting the CRTC offices in Halifax to inquire about setting up an FM transmitter. His tone was optimistic, and he noted that because there were no commercial stations in Sackville, a campus FM station would be under less restriction. He said that the usual thing the commission watches for "is a campus station following the same basic programming as a nearby professional station" (Ritcey

1980, 1). This would not apply to CHMA, given the lack of a Sackville-based commercial station, but the campus station would still regard itself "as an alternative to the area's commercial stations" (1). Ritcey also noted that CHMA would initiate a "Community Bulletin Board" that would run for five minutes and would air three or four times a day. Committing to community programming would, according to Ritcey, assure the station of the "undying affection of the Commission, at least until the first four-letter word emerged from someone's radio!" (1980, 2–3).

Ritcey, as it turned out, was a bit too optimistic. The station soon learned that many more resources – financial, technical, and otherwise – would be required for a successful FM licence application. In March 1982, Ian Hanomansing addressed members of the Student Administrative Council on the status of CHMA. He told them that up "until November 1981, we've had an unrealistically optimistic view of an FM transition. Since late last year, the CHMA executive have reviewed the plans and hammered out what we feel is a feasible application" (Hanomansing 1982, 1). He circulated a five-phase plan to refocus and approach the FM transition; it included appointing key positions like the president and the station's board, as well as taking an approach to programming as if the AM carrier current station was already an FM station.

In 1984, efforts to transition to FM broadcasting intensified. At a meeting of the Students' Administrative Council in October 1984, the council "unanimously voiced its support for the drive to convert CHMA Radio from AM carrier current to FM Broadcasting" (MacDonald 1984). In a letter addressed to G. Harvey Gilmour, the secretary to the executive committee of the board of regents at Mount Allison University, Andrew MacDonald emphasized a number of studies completed by "those most closely involved with the station" that had shown "the feasibility of conversion to FM broadcasting" (MacDonald 1984). He called for the university's support for the final stages of the application process. In a document titled "CHMA-FM Capital Equipment Purchase, Delivery, and Installation Timetable," the specific requirements for the FM station were carefully outlined. For CHMA-FM to operate as a "quality" low-power FM station, new equipment would be required. These requirements were broken down into four categories: equipment required for studio use, equipment for transmitting the studio signal, equipment for operating a mobile dance sound system, and a "list of various other items required to complete the package," such as furniture and filing cabinets. The document also explained that "through years of neglect," the music department library had "not been well stocked with a complete coverage of recorded music" and that "CHMA-FM must be given the record and book resource library necessary for indepth programming in very diverse musical directions." On 12 August 1985, the station was approved for FM broadcasting at 106.9 MHz.

CKUW-FM in Winnipeg is located in an annex above the fourth floor in Centennial Hall. The station space is narrow, with rooms connected to the right of a walkway. To the left are the program director's and station manager's cubicles, followed by a comfortable couch and table, and separated areas that store the station's music collection. Concert and event posters decorate the walls, with the gaps in between covered by stickers for local bands and record labels. The station space feels lived-in and comfortable and conveys a feeling not unlike being in a music venue or record store. The university campus runs alongside Portage Avenue, on the west side of the city's downtown core. It is a fairly small campus that blends in with the city, although a few new buildings of impressive size and design are nearing completion. This is an inner-city campus, and all the characteristics associated with a city are evident in and around the campus grounds – a striking contrast to both Mount Allison and UBC.

Before residing in Centennial Hall, CKUW began as CJUC in 1963, a station started by David Shilliday and Ron Riddell, a physics professor. The call letters were changed to CKUW in 1968 to mark the founding of the University of Winnipeg (formerly United College). At this time, CKUW was a closed-circuit station operating out of the basement and broadcasting to various spaces in the building, including the lounges in Lockhart Hall, the Buffeteria, and the Bulman Students' Centre. In an interview in *Stylus* magazine in October 1998, station manager Rob Schmidt explained to Anna Gilfillan that at that time, speakers were set up in Lockhart cafeteria, and they had individual volume controls so that people could turn them down if the music was not appealing to listeners (Gilfillan 1998, 6). Ted Turner, a long-time station volunteer, periodic staff member, and current station outreach and sponsorship coordinator (as of July 2011), recalled getting involved with the station in 1990 during his second year as a student at the university. Turner remembers always hearing about the station, this place he always knew about that did not broadcast beyond the campus, but rather just through speakers in certain areas on-campus. He and a friend eventually visited the station. "And it was a big deal to go in there," he reflected, "because you were intimidated, because there were a bunch of cool people in there ... And the door was always closed, and there's all this cigarette smoke coming out. You're only nineteen, twenty years old, so how do you walk in there and be like 'Hi, I'd like to be one of you'?" (Turner, personal interview, 7 July 2011). But after attending his first meeting, Turner felt at ease. He found that the station was a friendly space, and right away he felt excited to be involved. He began hosting a radio show, and by the following year he was the station manager.

Throughout the 1990s, Turner recalled, the "idea of going FM was always what was there, it was always the goal that was put out there." For him, getting the station on the FM dial was like a "group of fishermen" working together to get a boat – both "triumphant" and "hilarious." He also mentioned wondering what would have happened if the station had not begun broadcasting on the FM band. He attributed this interest to the simple fact that the station did indeed acquire an FM licence. But his emphasis on a group of people or on a certain energy that existed in the pre-FM days reflected the "feeling" that was there at the time. For Turner, and certainly for others involved with the station at the time, CKUW was "more of a hiding place, and this place where these amazing records would come from Chicago and other places." Records would "just show up," Turner explained. "Somehow [the station] had this magical mailbox where these really amazing underground records would show up and you could play them to a group of people of which maybe a handful were ever listening" (Turner 2011).

For the station to eventually receive its FM licence from the CRTC, a number of factors had to coalesce, including mobilization towards better organization and planning. Turner recalled that the station had to lose its connotation as a "boys' club," especially in the eyes of the university's student association and administration, where "this scary music came from where people were smoking and swearing and probably doing other things" (Turner 2011). The station was shut down a few times throughout the 1990s due to issues like noise complaints. In 1992, Nicole Firlotte became the first woman to be hired as station manager. Turner explained that her hiring was a critical point during the years leading up to CKUW's FM licence. Another major development during the pre-FM years was CKUW's sibling publication, *Stylus*. Turner said that *Stylus* was the station's "transmitter" before becoming licensed; through it, the activity and culture of CKUW was disseminated across the city. "And," Turner said, "it was really well put together, with great writing, great editing, and great leadership." Turner was careful to state that Firlotte was "a lot more than just the first woman to manage the station"; in her role as manager she helped dismantle the station's image as a boys' club and, more importantly, the insular practices that had generated the boys' club image. She "brought a whole different energy, and a sense of organization and professionalism," to the station at the time.

In the mid-1990s, CKUW moved from its basement studio to the annex in Centennial Hall while still operating as a closed-circuit station. A levy campaign was launched in order to line up revenues and hire a full-time manager who could, according to Turner, "look at what it would really mean to go FM." Rob Schmidt was hired as manager, a position he still held as of July 2011. Turner had applied for the manager position after accumulating a lot of experience with the station, and he was "crushed" when he did not get the position. Yet it very soon was clear to him that "it was for the best" because "Rob came in with this whole different skill set" that "no one else had in the city," including prior experience at an FM station. Rob had a real sense for the technical side and "he just came into it with all sorts of energy and worked super hard." Turner also mentioned the hiring of Steve Bates as the first full-time program director as another important contribution to the energy that was moving the station forward, towards the goal of acquiring an FM licence. He referred to Bates as a talented, community-minded guy who "really, *really* got what the potential of this thing could be, because he had been around the culture of CKUW for so long" (Turner 2011). The station "came out of the gate in '99 with this incredible scale, this incredible quality and depth in programming, and diversity" (Turner 2011). The FM station was able to draw from the strengths of the already existing closed-circuit station and of the people who were involved in it for ten to fifteen years.

Rob Schmidt was from northeastern Ontario. He moved to Winnipeg after attending McMaster University in Hamilton and working at the McMaster campus station CFMU. Schmidt emphasized the importance of moving past some of the stigma associated with campus or college radio during its formative years: "I think that in the '60s and the '70s, it really was just students playing records between classes. University was so different back then (Schmidt, personal interview, 5 July 2011). "And then, in the 70s and the 80s," he added,

> I think you had the tail end of the hippy movement and the radical movement and campus radio was a place where people could drink a bottle of wine and play some folk music. And it was sort of a counter-cultural thing, not that that has changed. It's still counter-cultural, largely, but just the organization behind it, you know? I think a lot of our stations really take our mandate *very* seriously now, and act in a more professional and more organized way than it was fifteen years ago.

Schmidt recalled that dealing with policy issues was fairly easy during the first few years of FM broadcasting, because the small-scale closed-circuit station had such a tight-knit group of people working together. A lot of the volunteers knew one another and it was easy to communicate and deal with issues together as a group. As the station developed in the wake of acquiring its FM licence, there were "more and more people that didn't know each other, that didn't have a history," so the station needed a few more rules in place and clearer ways of dealing with things (Schmidt 2011). As the station added more individuals who did not all share the same values, it became necessary to establish internal policies to negotiate differences.

In the September 1994 issue of *Stylus*, editor Jill Wilson admitted that she was "more than a bit miffed when it was suggested to [her] that *Stylus* should work harder at promoting CKUW"; after all, "CKUW is just a closed-circuit, dinky station that most people don't even know exists" (1994, 2). However, a trip to the National Campus/Community Radio Conference changed her feelings about the "dinkiness" of the station: "Those of us who attended the conference came back with a strong sense of purpose; to turn what had originally been dismissed as a pipe dream into reality. CKUW has the potential to bring campus radio to Winnipeg, and that has a level of importance that should transcend any petty squabbles or ego trips" (2). Wilson's initial comment suggests that the desire to broadcast as an FM station was not a unanimously shared goal, or a priority among all the students and individuals who were involved with the pre-FM station. It is very likely that at all three stations profiled in this chapter, some individuals did not feel the need to broadcast on the FM dial, and Turner's noted interest in the alternative history of CKUW (that is, if it had not become an FM station) could also be evidence of this sentiment. However, most of the comments generated in reference to each station's pursuit of an FM licence, both in cultural publications and in interviews, illustrate that the full potential of these stations was not being realized when contained by campus borders. For instance, in the same 1994 issue of *Stylus*, this outlook was emphasized by Alec Stuart in an article titled "Catching a Radio Wave." Stuart asked, "How does it feel to know that Winnipeg is the largest city in Canada without a campus radio station?" (1994, 5). He continued, "Seriously though, Winnipeg sorely needs a campus radio station. The [University of Manitoba] used to have one a number of years ago, but student politics killed that one, and their current financial troubles make a radio station there an unlikely prospect." This article reflects the turn in perspective that would drive the station towards an FM licence. Stuart claimed that "the ball is rolling. We've started to work towards eventual broadcasting, but we need help" (5). He continued that financial donations were greatly appreciated and that the station had started to sell memberships. Stuart implored readers who did not have the "cash to toss around," even for a "worthy cause," to come and see one of the many shows the station had organized that year. "If you own a business," he said, "or work in some such place, write us a letter of support. We need a whole pile of letters to hand in to the CRTC when we finish the application. Most importantly, support the local scene. These are people who are helping us out a lot" (5).

By December 1998, it was evident that the four years prior had been spent preparing for the station to launch its FM service. Station manager Rob Schmidt made this point in an article titled "Launching an FM Radio Station Isn't as Easy as You Might Imagine." In it, he explained that a "CRTC license is only one of the components needed for a successful radio station, and we've been working hard to get the other parts together. Equipment, volunteers, and training all have to be in place before we can even hope to begin broadcasting to the community" (1998, 7). The licence application was approved in October of that year; in the application, CKUW "promised to create programming that is diverse musically and yet has a strong focus on urban issues and concerns. At least half the music [listeners will hear on] 95.9 FM will be coming from the genres of folk, jazz and experimental music." One-quarter would be spoken-word (Schmidt 1998, 7). Schmidt added that gathering equipment "was one of the easiest tasks, but even that had to be done carefully, keeping within budget and remembering [the station's] goals of self-sufficiency and ease-of-use." The studios would be set up before Christmas, with the transmitter installed by the end of January. Schmidt ended by saying that there was still a lot to do, but the station hoped to be on air by February, although "any number of delays could happen between now and then."

CiTR in Vancouver is on the second floor of UBC's Student Union Building. The station space consists of a long hallway that turns right and left, with large rooms and offices on both sides. The first office belongs to the station manager; it is followed by a large music library full of CDs and a lounge of considerable size with numerous places to sit. The office of the station's sibling publication *Discorder* is farther down the hall, along with a production studio, some storage rooms, and, finally, the broadcast booth. Informational documents for prospective volunteers are available in slots fastened to the wall, and promotional posters for local bands and concerts are pinned to the walls. The Student Union Building is just one of many large buildings on UBC's expansive and picturesque campus, which overlooks the Pacific and sits on the University Endowment Lands. The campus is a significant commute from the downtown core and feels self-contained – a very different environment from both Mount Allison and the University of Winnipeg, but especially the latter.

In October 1987, the Alma Mater Society and the Student Radio Society of UBC published a fifteen-page booklet titled "Fifty Years of UBC Radio: 1937–1987," which was researched and written by Alma Mater Society archivist Iolanda Weisz and then–station manager Harry Hertscheg. According to this booklet, in 1937, a Students' Council meeting led to an investigation regarding the possibility of forming a UBC radio program, following a period during which the university was suffering from a lack of funding and facilities. Various proposals were being considered to help generate a publicity campaign in support of the university. The radio program was one of these. In September of the same year, the Alma Mater Society began *Varsity Time*, a weekly radio program that ran for a half-hour on Vancouver-based CJOR (which is now a commercial rock music station, CKPK, or The Peak). The show's purpose was to connect the on-campus students to people in Vancouver and the province of British Columbia, under the supervision of the University's Department of Extension. Starting in October 1937, the Radio Society would broadcast a daily five-minute radio program consisting of farm news on Canadian Broadcasting Radio (CBR), Vancouver's CBC station.

During the second year of UBC radio broadcasting, the Radio Society greatly improved and gained a reputation as one of the most active on-campus clubs. The club changed its name to the University Radio Society (URS), and *Varsity Time* became two separate weekly programs. On Fridays, *News of the Campus* would report on sports and general news, and on Sundays, dramas were aired on CJOR. Over the years, more shows were developed, and in 1944, it was determined that the club's location in the basement of the Agriculture Building was less than ideal. In 1945 a new studio was opened. The opening of this studio, in the South Basement of Brock Hall, coincided with postwar growth in radio club volunteers. After many returning soldiers joined the Radio Society, the general membership doubled to one hundred. By the late 1940s, the club had constructed new studios, and a number of shows were providing students with opportunities to develop their acting, singing, and performing skills.

A fire in Brock Hall in 1954 caused the Radio Society difficulties in terms of maintaining operations, but the studio was later remodelled and broadcasting continued. By 1956, the club was broadcasting as a closed-circuit station for eighteen hours a week. Heading into the 1960s, the Radio Society had a membership of seventy-five and was broadcasting forty hours per week. New programming policies were put in place to allow for entertainment shows like *Playboy Jazz* and *Works of the Masters*. Letters to the editor in the UBC publication *The Ubyssey* suggest what the programming was like at the station at this time. One dated 10 November 1959 asked the station to eliminate *The Works of the Masters* because it was broadcast from 11:00 a.m. until noon, when most non-classical music fans are arriving in Brock after morning classes. The "Two Hopeful Students" who wrote the letter felt that students "do not want to listen to classical music. It can be heard anytime of the day by tuning into a Canadian Radio Station. Popular music, or even music of a livelier type, is much more appreciated by the majority of students as it tends to awaken them" ("Two Hopeful Students" 1959). Similarly, a letter from 3 November of the same year defended rock 'n' roll by citing "the liberal tastes of students in the musical field" (Henderson 1959). Author Ralph Henderson argued that "we are living in a democratic country" and if "the majority of students want to harken to the enchanting strains of 'Mack the Knife' or 'Teen Beat,' then by all means let them!" (Henderson 1959).

In 1964, UBC Radio began working towards increasing listenership and broadcasting to student residences. In 1969, the station moved from the Brock Studios to the Student Union Building and the Radio Society became known as CYVR – UBC Radio. In January of 1973, CYVR was shut down for operating without a licence after the CRTC altered its regulations for closed-circuit stations. However, in July of the following year, CYVR was approved for a licence and the station reopened as Thunderbird Radio (the "TR" in CiTR). In 1975, the station was distributed through cablevision FM on the condition that it would air no commercial content. The following year, a struggle over the musical direction of the station was reported in *The Ubyssey*. Chris Gainor wrote an article titled "Squabble Splits CITR Hacks" in which he claimed that then president Richard Saxton would be challenged by "musical director Mark Forrest, who hinted in an interview ... that he would like to see CITR take a more progressive musical direction." The article continued that "many members are unhappy over the way Saxton has run the station," making it "his station" and insisting that "CITR follow a commercial AM format" (Gainor 1976, 1). Despite these critiques, Saxton was re-elected on 11 March of that year. In 1978, the station filed a formal application to the CRTC for an FM licence, but the federal Department of Communications had put a hold on the last FM channel in the city.

In early 1980, an article in *The Ubyssey* titled "CITR Spreads Waves over Public" clearly anticipated the FM licence that would allow CiTR to expand. Author Steve McClure claimed that the station had "attained a degree of professionalism unknown in past years when only a select company of [Student Union Building] janitors and insomniac students ever bothered to listen to CITR" (1980, 4). However, McClure stressed that the station has its share of problems, including the power of its transmitter, at the time "confined to a carrier current system that allows only 28 per cent of UBC residences to pick up CITR." Furthermore, the "vast majority of Vancouver radio listeners still don't even know of the station's existence." The article mentioned that a promotional campaign to reach out to Vancouver listeners had been initiated and that an application had been made to the CRTC for a low-power FM licence so that the station could reach all of Vancouver "west of Granville Street" (4). At this time, the station also proposed hiring a full-time manager. Some people disapproved of the idea to hire a full-time

manager, because of the costs it would incur and because they were apprehensive that a manager might "wield a greater degree of influence than is
desirable in a student club." Some also felt that hiring a full-time manager
might take the focus away from campus issues and students. However, station members saw the potential for the station to grow and provide a link
between "a UBC that is often too insular and self-absorbed and a city that is
out of contact with western Canada's largest educational institution" (4). An
FM licence would increase the station's broadcast range and its relevance in
the city.

On 11 September 1980, the then president of CiTR Hilary Stout wrote
a "Perspectives" piece in *The Ubyssey* that urged students to give the station a chance and either listen to it or get involved. Stout said that a "hefty
percentage of the students of UBC are surprised to learn they own a radio
station. Not just any old station, but one that's been recognized as a major
influence on Vancouver's music." Stout explained that the station did not
care if people joined it or not but that it cared about whether or not students
gave the station a chance. "I constantly hear people complaining about the
massive number of ads that break up the music on regular AM and FM
radio ... Well, we don't have ads. The same goes with overplaying hit songs,
and the practice of playing only the single from an album. We don't over-
play anything." Stout ended by asking listeners to give the station a chance
and to listen "at 690 AM in the residences or 88.9 on CABLE FM." That
same year, the Alma Mater Society designated CiTR a service organization,
rather than just a club; this granted the station more resources, which were
helpful for making a successful application for an FM licence in 1981.

CiTR had to compete for the frequency with another station, CJAZ, but
ended up winning 101.9 MHz. On April Fool's Day of 1982, music director
Dave McDonagh introduced the new FM broadcaster by playing "Danc-
ing in the Streets" by Martha and the Vandellas. Shortly after, in February of 1983, *Discorder* (at this time subtitled "A Guide to CiTR FM 102
Cable 100") was launched by founding editors Michael Mines and Jennifer
Fahrni. The magazine would promote the station and its playlists, working
towards improving communications between the station and its listeners.
According to the fifty-year celebratory booklet, CiTR's notoriety in the late
1980s came from "the music it plays." The decade before the booklet's publication had "seen a focus on alternative music by non-mainstream, independent artists – particularly local, underground bands – who do not receive
airplay on commercial Top 40 stations" (Weisz and Hertscheg 1987, 14). By
expanding beyond the campus borders, the station was able to better reflect
the musical and cultural activities of the city of Vancouver and provide listeners with a diverse array of musical programming.

Canadian Campus Radio and Community Representation on the FM Dial

On Canada's east coast during the 1960s and 1970s, students had experimented with amateur radio, briefly setting up a pirate radio station in a dormitory on the campus of Mount Allison University. In Winnipeg, students at the University of Winnipeg operated a closed-circuit radio station from a small basement studio, spawning stories of cigarette smoke and rare records that could be heard on speakers in select campus spaces, much to the dismay of many students and the university administration. At UBC, just west of Vancouver's downtown core, a student radio society was launched in the 1930s, and it grew in membership following the Second World War. What these stations have in common is the collective drive of students and community members, who at a particular point felt it was time for the campus station to expand beyond the campus and reach more listeners. These were public efforts, with students and radio practitioners justifying their stations to other students and to university administrators, asking for support that ranged from financial contributions to simply asking other students to tune in and give the station a chance. There came a time in each station's history when the scale and scope of volunteers could not be contained by a low-range broadcaster and when students felt the need to activate their links to the wider cultural and musical communities of their city or town. The move to FM broadcasting required hard work and organization by the majority of those involved with these stations to ensure that they were ready to broadcast to the wider community.

In some instances, the unlicensed nature of these campus stations limited the diversity and inclusivity of campus radio. In part, this was a function of the expertise and technological adeptness that the students who first began working with radio equipment at universities needed to have. University engineering departments and early departments of extension were often behind the development of on-campus radio broadcasting, and more often than not, given the times in which these stations developed, the departments and the students working on these projects were predominately male. The development of early university radio stations, like the one at UBC, and (much later) like the dorm room pirate station at Mount Allison, was largely the result of radio enthusiasts or hobbyists, not unlike the amateur DXers whom Susan Douglas describes in *Listening In: Radio and the American Imagination*. Douglas writes, referring to amateur radio in the late 1910s and early 1920s:, "Trapped between the legacy of genteel culture and the pull of the primitivism so popularized in the new mass culture, and certainly trapped between the need to conform and the desire to break out, many boys and men reclaimed a sense of mastery, indeed of masculinity itself, through the control of technology" (1999, 68). As these on-campus stations developed and as more individuals became involved in campus broadcasting, technical mastery over radio equipment seemed to transform itself into a cultural mastery or elitism in terms of musical tastes and the valorization of extensive record collections. This culture, which Ted Turner describes as a "boys' club," is part of a larger issue in which "authentic" music is often felt to be somewhat rare or distinct, like the records that ended up at CKUW from Chicago.

The valorization of authentic and rare music, or the discovery of rare and culturally rich or diverse music, is often viewed as, and written about as, a male realm. A number of works have focused on authenticity and masculinity in popular music. In "Sizing Up Record Collections: Gender and Connoisseurship in Rock Music Culture," Will Straw notes that "record collecting, within Anglo-American cultures at least, is among the more predictably male-dominated of music-related practices" (1997, 4). Turner described the feeling of the basement studio of CKUW as a place of escape; in this vein, Straw writes that record collections, "like sports statistics, provide the raw materials around which the rituals of homosocial interaction take shape," creating "a shared universe of critical judgment" (5). A small, secluded closed-circuit station tucked away in a basement can act as a private space for individuals to hide away and play records, especially if very few people are listening or paying attention. However, as stations worked toward the goal of going FM and broadcasting to a wider listenership, the private/public ratio had to be renegotiated.

CiTR board member Janis McKenzie is also a former CiTR volunteer and *Discorder* writer. She joined the station in the mid-1980s after listening to CiTR since the time of the station's first FM licence. McKenzie reflected on her early days at the station and shared her thoughts on the renegotiation of private versus public space in relation to the station's efforts at recruiting more women after being granted an FM licence. At that time, "there were very, very few women on the air at CiTR. I think at one point, and this is just a really rough estimate, that there were about forty-two slots on the air, and probably three or four of them were filled by women" (McKenzie, personal interview, 12 July 2011). However, "there was a real desire, even then, to try to make sure we had more women on the air." Women still had to operate under the same standards as male programmers, but if women students were interested in having a show, it "might have been a little easier to get on the air even with standard indie rock programming."

McKenzie's sentiments echo the stories about CKUW as it neared an FM licence. CKUW worked to dismantle the boys' club, both in reputation and in operations; it also fostered a more inclusive space that reached a larger public. As each station became licensed by the CRTC, the negotiation of private and public space continued. Stations retained their specialized knowledge of music and culture, but now that knowledge was becoming available to more people as more diverse programs and programmers became part of the station's musical and cultural fabric, and as more listeners tuned in. Stations increased their presence in the communities within their broadcast range; meanwhile, the CRTC established a national policy to regulate the sector. This policy followed in the wake of campaigns by the pre-FM stations that had made strong efforts to grow themselves beyond the campus borders. Volunteers, students, staff members, and radio practitioners achieved the goal of broadcasting to a wider audience on the FM band, while emphasizing the significant role of campus radio as a participatory and accessible medium that reflected and circulated local music and culture.

On 14 September 1981, CiTR was the first of these three campus stations to be granted an FM radio licence by the CRTC. The commission approved the application "for a broadcasting licence to carry on a low-power, non-commercial English language student FM radio station" that would serve the university campus and surrounding Vancouver area, on 101.9 MHz, with an effective radiated power of 19 watts (CRTC 1981a, 1). However, the licence was set to expire on 30 September 1984 so that the commission could consider its renewal alongside those of other stations in the region. The station's commitment to the wider community was outlined in the decision: it was expected "to continue to be actively involved in the development and promotion of local talent on campus and in the community." Three hours per week were designated for community access programming, including two hours for the use of other post-secondary schools in the city (CRTC 1981a, 2). A Promise of Performance, submitted by the station in advance of the decision, stated that CiTR would not broadcast any advertisements. At the public hearing preceding the licence, the station reaffirmed that "funding for the operation of the station was assured through subsidies from the University Student Council and through the rental of its mobile sound service" (CRTC 1981a, 3). The decision ended with the CRTC "reminding" CiTR that "the frequency approved by this decision is an unprotected frequency. In the event that optimum utilization of the broadcasting spectrum demands that this low-power station change to another frequency, the licensee must either agree to do so or cease operation" (CRTC 1981a, 4). This reminder hints at the precariousness of allocating spectrum to a campus radio station in a busy radio market at this time.

Ten years after Attic Broadcasting acquired an AM licence from the CRTC, the station at Mount Allison University was granted an FM licence on 106.9, upgrading the previous carrier current power of 20 watts to an effective radiated power of 50 watts. On 12 August 1985, the CRTC issued an FM licence that would expire on 31 March 1990 (CRTC 1985a). The decision referenced the 1975 student radio decision that licensed stations in Ottawa and Winnipeg, reiterating that the purpose of student broadcasting was primarily "to communicate the concerns, interests and activities of the campus as well as of the academic environment to the public, and to offer to the general public innovative and alternative programming fare which makes use of the many resources available to the academic institution" (CRTC 1985a). Interestingly, the station was the first to be licensed to serve Sackville, and CHMA recognized this unique role by creating such objectives as to provide "innovative programming based on the resources of both the Mount Allison and Sackville communities" and to develop and promote local arts, besides encouraging "interest among individuals to learn broadcasting skills." The decision also emphasized the relationship between the university and the local community; for example, it stipulated that CHMA was to ensure that newscasts included content that was 25 percent local or regional. Students from Sackville's Tantramar Regional High School were granted the opportunity to produce a weekly news program to air on CHMA that covered high school activities and events.

Regarding music-based programming, CHMA stated that its emphasis would "be placed on selections from small label artists, new artists and the non-hit musical material from established artists." Also, the station "proposed to enhance its musical diversity through a range of special music shows that will feature 'classical, jazz, experimental, folk and traditional, country, bluegrass/traditional country, reggae, blues, soul, contemporary religious and various combinations of these limited only by the programmer's creativity.'" The station committed $500 for the production and programming of tapes provided by local artists, and it opened its studio space to local theatre groups. Regarding advertising and sponsorship, the station was permitted to broadcast statements of sponsorship that identified a sponsor of the station or of a specific program. These statements, however, were not to "contain language which attempts to persuade consumers to purchase and thus must not contain references to convenience, durability or desirability or contain other comparative or competitive references" (CRTC 1985a). The station would have to generate most of its sponsors from the area in which it broadcast, and it was not to use pre-produced national advertisements.

CKUW was the last of these three radio stations to be granted an FM licence, on 5 October 1998. The licence placed CKUW on the frequency 95.9 MHz with an effective radiated power of 450 watts (CRTC 1998a). The

licence was set to expire on 31 August 2005 and was granted under the stipulations of Public Notice CRTC 1992-38, which outlined the regulations
for community and campus radio at this time. The decision referenced this
policy, stating that campus radio stations must provide a service that complemented what was offered by other local, commercial radio stations and
any other campus station in the market. CKUW stated that it would offer
diverse musical programming that was heavy on "'new music and styles not
represented on commercial radio stations'"; spoken-word content would
centre on downtown community issues, student life, and activism. A commitment to nearby communities included 105 hours of local programming
each week, a two-hour weekly program consisting of interviews with artists performing in the Winnipeg area, and an hour-long program featuring
interviews and the latest releases from Manitoba artists. One commitment
that set CKUW's FM licence apart from those granted to CiTR and CHMA
involved "a maximum repeat factor of 7 and a maximum percentage of hits
selections of 5%" (CRTC 1998a). Limiting the number of times a certain
song could be played during the week was an effort to ensure a diversity of
musical selections by the station; so was controlling the number of songs
played that were concurrently listed on a major Top 40 chart. As well, a
minimum of 20 percent of total music programming on the station would
be from category 3, which included the Traditional and Special Interest
genres. This decision also reminded the station that the chief executive officer and no less than 80 percent of the board of directors must be Canadian.
Because the station was licensed after Public Notice CRTC 1993-38, a document that set out a policy for advertising on campus stations, the station
could broadcast no more than 504 minutes of advertising per week, with a
maximum of four minutes per hour. Of the weekly total, a maximum of 126
minutes might be conventional advertising; the remainder would need to
conform to the CRTC's definition of "restricted advertising" (CRTC 1993c).
The decision ended with a final stipulation that this licence would only be
issued once the station had completed its construction undertaking, and
once it was prepared to commence operations.

These three FM licences span the better part of two decades, yet a number of factors are common to each. Most importantly, each licence committed the station to expand its operations from catering content to the campus
to reaching listeners in the surrounding community. Each licence was also
specific to the geographic space surrounding the station, so certain differences are apparent. For instance, in Sackville, local theatre groups were
mentioned, invoking the notion of a small town from radio's early days,
when live theatre was regularly disseminated over radio waves. CKUW, in
contrast, referred to its inner-city location and confirmed its commitment

to downtown life and activism. Over this twenty-year period, a few significant trends illustrated the changing radio broadcasting environment and its
related regulatory routine. For one, the wattage of each licence grew considerably larger as time went on, beginning with the 19 watts given to CiTR
at the beginning of the 1980s, then rising to the 450 watts given to CKUW
just before the turn of the century. The power of CiTR would increase as
well over this twenty-year period. Moreover, with each succeeding licence,
a station's ability to use advertising to fund its activities became less complicated. CiTR promised no advertising; by the time CKUW hit the FM airwaves, a carefully crafted advertising policy for campus radio was in place.
This relaxation of advertising restrictions reflected the realities of operating
an FM radio station that served not just the campus but the surrounding
communities as well. Given that there are regulations restricting the types
of advertisements campus radio stations can air and that the campus sector
maintains a commitment to local culture, most advertisements are for local
businesses and student groups. Examining the subsequent licence renewals
for each station will shed further light on these discourses and the regulatory trends that have emerged.

The CRTC decisions that approved the licence renewals for each station
following its initial FM licence are fairly brief and lacklustre. Their primary
purpose was to ensure that the stations were aligned with other federal regulatory frameworks. Only very briefly did they give a sense of the structure
and operations of these individual stations. In 1990, CiTR and CHMA had
their licences renewed, and at this point the CRTC outlined a number of
provisions on which the licences were dependent. Decision CRTC 90-379,
dated 18 April 1990, renewed CiTR until 31 August 1995. The decision
explained that a condition of this licence was that the station would retain
"full control over all decisions concerning the management and programming of this station and that the majority of directors be students." As well,
"the chairman or other presiding officer and each of the directors or other
similar officers of the licensee must be Canadian citizens" (CRTC 1990a).
The same statements were repeated in CHMA's licence renewal of that same
year (CRTC 1990c), as well as in its 1993 renewal (CRTC 1993a). Shortly
after CHMA's 1993 renewal, a second decision followed that applied a cor-
rection to the first licence. The decision, dated 21 October 1993, corrected a
condition of licence that outlined the structure of the board of directors. It
replaced the phrase "the majority of directors be students" with "representatives of the student body, faculty, alumni or administration representatives
of the university or college with which the station is associated, considered together, form the majority of the board of directors" (CRTC 1993b).
The decision stated that this language was in line with the commission's

campus radio policies in Public Notice 1992-38. This same text is found in CKUW's renewal in 2006 (CRTC 2006a). CKUW's renewal specified that "the chair and not less than 80% of the members of the board of directors must be Canadians ordinarily resident in Canada" (CRTC 2006a). The language of CKUW's 2006 renewal also reflected the fact that the chair could be a woman or a man, as opposed to the use of "chairman" by the CRTC in CiTR's 1990 renewal.

Evidently, these licence renewals ensured that Canadian campus radio stations would be controlled mainly by students and that they would operate with as much involvement from the university as possible. A second major trend inherent in these licence renewals is that the CRTC was beginning to align campus station licences with other centralized policies pertaining to the radio broadcasting system as a whole. CiTR's first renewal was very brief, dated 11 January 1984. It renewed the station for only one year, due to a Review of Radio that had been conducted by the commission and upcoming amendments to the Radio (FM) Broadcasting Regulations that would require licensees to review their Promise of Performance (CRTC 1984). In the Review of Radio of 1983, the commission expanded "its definition of 'restricted' commercial activity to permit the inclusion of price, name and brand name of a product in messages broadcast by community stations, but continued to disallow references to convenience, durability or other comparative or competitive references" (CRTC 1985c). In CiTR's 1990 renewal, other policies were referenced and enforced through conditions of licences that stated that the station must adhere to the Canadian Association of Broadcasters's "self-regulatory guidelines on sex-role stereotyping," as well as its Broadcast Code for Advertising to Children (CRTC 1990a). CHMA's renewal from the same year also mentioned these CAB codes, as well as the broader principles outlined in the Broadcasting Act and Radio Regulations of 1986 (CRTC 1990c). Strangely, these decisions made it sound as if the CRTC was renewing commercial radio stations. There was not much that really drove home the unique purpose of a campus radio station. However, these renewals came before the 1992 policy for campus and community radio, so their briefness and reliance on codes created by the CAB can be attributed to this fact. That said, minimal reference was made to the 1992 campus and community radio policy for licence renewals that followed in its wake. This is because the 1992 policy served to temporarily regulate the campus and community sectors until the commission could formulate a broader, more comprehensive policy for campus radio. CiTR's 1995 renewal stated that the renewal was for a term less than the maximum of seven years that were allowed by the Broadcasting Act, because the commission wanted to "consider the next license renewal of this undertaking in accordance with the Commission's regional plan for campus/community radio undertakings across Canada and to better distribute the Commission's workload" (CRTC 1995a). In 2000, the CRTC issued its comprehensive campus radio policy, which subsequent renewals would follow.

Licence renewals after the year 2000 were in accordance with the commission's policy for campus radio. Another policy document referenced after the year 2000 was Public Notice CRTC 2000-156, New License Form for Campus Radio Stations. CiTR and CHMA's renewals from 2001 stated that they were now following the renewal procedure put in place by this notice. The goal of the notice was to "simplify and harmonize" the renewal process and "lighten the administrative burden and increase efficiency" (CRTC 2000d). This involved eliminating the need to submit a Promise of Performance. Also, all conditions of licence that generally applied to campus radio stations were now on the licence form itself. CiTR and CHMA were again renewed in 2007 (CRTC 2007), and their new licences cited the comprehensive Campus Radio Policy from 2000. The same was the case for CKUW's 2006 renewal. These efforts at streamlining the licence renewal process allowed the commission to outline the basic mandate of Canadian campus stations through a centralized policy; this in turn increased efficiency when it came to subsequent licence renewals for individual stations. Any issue specific to a certain station could then be dealt with at the time of an individual station's renewal.

In addition to these broad policy alignments, wherein campus stations were to meet the requirements set out in public notices and codes, a few lines in certain licence renewals were devoted to describing the role that campus stations were to play in terms of programming and developing Canadian music. CiTR's 1990 renewal stated that the CRTC noted "the annual budgets and the initiatives undertaken by the licensee in respect of Canadian talent development" (CRTC 1990a). CHMA's 1993 renewal also emphasized the importance of developing Canadian talent and noted that CHMA-FM would continue broadcasting new Canadian music and interviews with Canadian artists (CRTC 1993a). The station's 2001 renewal expected the station to implement the initiatives laid out in its plan for Canadian talent development, to establish measures that encouraged volunteer participation, and to demonstrate a commitment to Canadian programming.

Before a licence is granted or denied in a CRTC decision, a discursive process may first take place at the level of the station or of the CRTC, or both. Depending on the licence, this may be an in-depth process involving a lengthy discussion that takes place at a public hearing, as well as student surveys or administrative discussions at the university level. Or, the process might be brief, with little or no debate or discussion. These discourses provide more detailed background information about the licensing process and highlight the role of campus radio practitioners during the regulatory process.

CiTR was granted its FM licence after competing for a frequency with another station, CJAZ. Because of this, a substantial presentation was required at a public hearing in Vancouver on 30 April 1981. Presenting on behalf of CiTR, station manager Hilary Louise Stout pleaded the station's case: "I have a letter up here signed by 29 student radio stations from across the country, supporting our request to hold the only student FM license west of Ontario" (CRTC 1981b). Stout hoped that the station would be "the first of many Western Canadian student radio stations." CiTR's presentation stressed the importance of connecting the university to wider communities: "UBC should be a familiar part of the whole community, not a remote and mysterious fortress. Our goal is to promote greater interaction between the University and the community." In response to an intervention by Vancouver community station Co-op radio, which claimed that students were a "special interest group," Stout argued: "We have incredible diversity of interests on campus. The more than one hundred clubs that are flourishing on campus prove that" (CRTC 1981b). CiTR used the hearing to explain that the station was prepared to begin FM broadcasting and to demonstrate the importance of connecting the university to the city of Vancouver.

In September 1988, another decision involving CiTR was issued, but it was not a licence renewal. Rather, it was to approve a significant power increase from 19 watts to 390 watts (CRTC 1988). Minimal details are provided in the CRTC decision itself, but some of the documents generated by the station are descriptive, including the application submitted by the station, a number of letters of support from listeners, and the results of "The High Power Hi-Test Questionnaire." The application asked questions that were in line with the typical conditions and stipulations of licences and renewals. The CRTC asked the station whether it would promote live and recorded Canadian music on air; CiTR replied that it "regularly interviews local bands and plays demonstration tapes produced by Canadian bands during mosaic programs" (CiTR 1985). The application also asked whether CiTR would broadcast station-produced programs featuring other forms of Canadian cultural expression. CiTR explained that its magazine, *Discorder*, programmed feature reviews of local arts productions and regularly featured local arts and artists.

In one of the many letters supporting CiTR's high-power application submitted to Fernand Belisle, the secretary general of the CRTC at that time, Charles J. Campbell wrote that

> CITR offers a unique service to many people who cannot otherwise find outlets for their music and ideas as well as to the community, which is provided with a bold, different view of the world, not available to it through the mainstream media. The station is one of a handful of radio stations that offer alternatives to programming that ... is controlled by a few rich and powerful men. (Campbell 1985)

In addition, the results of a questionnaire completed by eighteen individuals helped the High Power Working Group pursue increased broadcast power for the station. The top reasons cited for having the station increase its power included an increase in signal strength, expanded reception to other areas of the city, increased audience, and the expansion of the university's image into the wider community. The questionnaire also asked where the station should put its energy in terms of increasing the amount of public affairs and spoken-word programming. Respondents were mostly in favour of featuring university researchers and community events and groups.

These station-generated documents communicated a sense of what an increased community service and listenership would mean for the station, much more so than what could be gleaned from the brief CRTC licence renewals. There was more descriptive content in the discussions surrounding these licence renewals than in the licence renewals themselves. Actually, very little from the comments, interventions, and letters of support found its way into the official decisions and licences, even though they were central to the overall renewal process. If the final CRTC-generated licence renewal documents are indicative of anything, it is that the commission paid only moderate attention to the specific circumstances of each station, including its locality (which was more likely to be a factor at the time the station was granted its first licence). Instead, the commission acted as a mediator between more substantial, centralized policy documents and each station's licence renewal. Time and effort had been put into crafting documents such as Public Notice 2000-12, Campus Radio Policy, and the Campus and Community Radio Policy outlined in CRTC 2010-499. These were lengthy accounts of how campus stations would ensure that their programming was distinct from the private and public sectors. These policies also outlined how campus stations would make strong contributions to the cultural diversity of the surrounding locality (CRTC 2000c). The lack of station-specific stipulations in each licence renewal can be attributed to the efficiency the renewal process enabled: the commission simply referred to a number of documents and regulations in order to facilitate a quick renewal process. In other words, as long as these stations were meeting their basic requirements as set out in centralized broadcasting policy and their original conditions of licence, everything would be fine come renewal time. Furthermore, the CRTC typically operates on a "by complaint only" basis, which means that it only looks at licence infractions if enough complaints are generated by listeners. If certain infractions go unnoticed or not reported, they are not likely to figure into the renewal process.

According to the NCRA/ANREC, this streamlined approach was also appreciated by representatives of the sector. Writing in favour of CiTR and CHMA's 2007 licence renewal (as well as those of ten other member stations), then NCRA/ANREC President Chad Saunders said that "the sector welcomes streamlined and simplified processes, as we often lack the resources to support each station individually, and stations themselves benefit from opportunities to work together to help understand the requirements and paperwork involved in regulatory processes" (Saunders 2007). From Saunders's perspective, the sector welcomed the commission's increased understanding and flexibility, given especially the "complex nature of many regulatory processes and the fact that most volunteers and staff in our sector are inexperienced with these processes" (Saunders 2007). According to the NCRA, this streamlined and centralized approach allows stations to focus most of their time on day-to-day operations and station-specific issues, as opposed to spending limited time and resources on the regulatory process. Thus, both organizations benefited from this system. This regulatory process enabled a certain level of openness or autonomy for each station in terms of how they chose to fit within the necessary requirements that must be met to ensure licence renewal.

Reflecting on the CRTC's comments on FM radio in 1975 (discussed in Chapter 3), the FM radio band was re-examined in terms of how it might diversify radio broadcasting. Shortly after, the CRTC began licensing campus radio stations, and by the time the national policy from 2000 was established, it appeared as though the commission had left the sector to operate with a relative level of autonomy, except for a few basic yet essential regulations. Perhaps this was an efficient way for the Canadian broadcasting environment to appear diverse and in tune with local communities, by ensuring there was a small but vibrant radio sector that had local programming at the core of its mandate. Meanwhile, the commercial sector could become more centralized and determined by political and economic trends, and the public sector could focus on remaining competitive enough financially to sustain itself, while also serving its role as a national broadcaster and curator of Canadian "cultural identity." A skeptical look at this situation may cite power dynamics in the media industries and in policy-making, as discussed in Chapter 2. There is market logic at work, one that allows the commercial broadcasting sector to increase profits by a variety of means, including by centralizing programming and playlists, so long as localities are reflected somewhere within the single broadcasting system. Increasingly, this important service is being carried out by the campus and community sector. Therefore, a policy is updated every ten years or so (1992, 2000, and 2010) to ensure that the campus and community sector is "alternative," "diverse," "community-oriented," and "local," insofar as it maintains practical and philosophical distance from commercial and public radio stations.

This analysis of FM licensing, and the licence renewal process, explains why renewals are brief and short on specifics. For the most part, the CRTC licence renewals give little detail as to how stations might actually be distinct from one another, regardless of the centralized policy that regulates the sector. CRTC policy for the campus sector appears to afford stations a level of freedom to craft their own internal policies. Mandates and station philosophies allow a campus station to specify its own role as a community media outlet and to outline its own rules and procedures. As the pre-FM histories of each station suggest, as do the comments, interventions, and letters of support crafted during moments within larger regulatory processes, individual stations negotiate their responsibilities to both the CRTC and their communities in distinct ways.

Mandates and Philosophies

Individual campus radio stations establish and abide by an operating mandate or a set of rules and regulations, which can be distributed to volunteers and staff members. A clear and specific description of the role of campus radio is conveyed by these documents. CHMA, for instance, does not have an explicit mandate listed on its website, but it provides a general introduction to the station in an "About Us" section. The station also publicizes its extensive training documents and policies online. CHMA's "About Us" section highlights the not-for-profit status of the organization and claims to provide members "with an opportunity to create innovative, educational and alternative community-based programming." The station describes its schedule as including "open format and specialty music shows, spoken word programs on a variety of topics as well as audio art programming that explores the limits of this thing we call radio." CHMA is careful to project its inclusivity, stating that a membership gives volunteers an opportunity to get involved with the station on a number of levels and that most of the station's members begin with no experience in broadcasting. The section ends quite persuasively, stating that "If you are interested in independent media and the power of community radio, now is the time to get involved" ("About Us").

CHMA's training manuals demonstrate the ways in which the station negotiates broadcasting policy; they also provide staff and volunteers with specific rules and regulations. The first of four manuals is subtitled "Orientation & Station Tour." This document provides all the necessary background information on the station, including brief descriptions of each staff position, as well as information about related organizations like the CRTC, SOCAN, and the NCRA (CHMA 2005a). This is followed by a number of station rules that add to those enforced by the CRTC. Examples of CHMA station rules include maintaining a certain level of professionalism (essentially, not "behaving like an idiot"), not stealing music or resources, not discriminating against others (here is included CHMA's written policy on sexual harassment), and maintaining station security (CHMA 2005a). These rules are followed by a section on volunteer rights and responsibilities. More precise is a list of "Rules and Regulations," which is meant to help volunteer programmers avoid fines and legal problems and comply with federal policies; however, the language of this list is more in line with the station's culture. These rules touch on personal issues – for example, "If you are suddenly injured or become ill or your boyfriend or girlfriend dumped you and you feel you cannot make your show, you must still inform the Programming Director." They also explain what should or should not be said on the air (CHMA 2005b). Things to avoid include free advertising, discussing station policy on the air, and making false statements ("You're listening to CHMA News and Coca Cola has purchased Mount Allison University").

The "Radio Regulations" section integrates CRTC policy with the station's own guidelines. It states that the station's main objective "is to provide alternative programming such as music, especially Canadian music, not generally heard on commercial stations." The section goes into great detail about profanity, slander, defamation, and sex role stereotyping (CHMA 2005b). The manual outlines the various types and categories of music, as determined by the CRTC, as well as copyright issues and emergency procedures. The last two manuals (CHMA 2005c; CHMA 2005d) describe the technical training that volunteers undergo in greater detail, providing readers with information about programming and hosting their first show.

CKUW shares its philosophy on its website, which proudly proclaims that the station is a "true Community/Campus radio station" ("About CKUW"). The philosophy begins by stating that campus community radio is "a reflection of the community that owns and creates the programs – not a preprogrammed infomercial for big business." CKUW is "people driven not profit driven," continues the philosophy, and "the programming is a reflection of the true interests and concerns of the volunteers and the local community." The mandate then comments on the sector on a larger scale, stating that campus radio has the freedom to circulate music and ideas that are not present in mass media. CKUW airs alternative viewpoints, and local musicians take priority over "top 40 jingles." The station also highlights the fact that local cultural programming is integral to its schedule and that its spoken-word programming covers local news, local entertainment, and community-based social justice issues ("About CKUW"). CKUW's philosophy comes across more ardently than CHMA's; it takes jabs at mass programming and dismisses commercial programming as big-business infomercials. It also emphasizes the station's focus on social justice and an awareness of local cultural communities and music scenes.

CKUW is guided by a station policy titled "The Winnipeg Campus/ Community Radio Society By-Laws." The by-laws commence with definitions for the terms used throughout the document, including the station's definition of the community it caters to. According to CKUW, the "community" is simply that which is within the city limits. The definition simply labels the community as "the community of Winnipeg," including "all areas within the city limits" (CKUW 2008). CKUW's by-laws also set out the types of meetings the radio society holds. This includes information on voting procedures and methods for electing – and removing – officers. The document continues, describing other positions, and ends with a brief paragraph on copyright. CKUW's by-laws are more technical and formal than CHMA's training manual and seem to serve more as a policy for ensuring that each individual holding a staff or board position is aware of her or his role.

CiTR's mandate is "to serve, instruct and inform the UBC and Greater Vancouver Community through radio broadcasting by supplying alternative, progressive, informative, and community-oriented programming" ("About"). The station's mandate summarizes the unique listening experience that CiTR provides by making three key points. The first is that the station is student-run, with student executives making management decisions alongside staff members. A board of directors for a campus station is typically made up of a variety of positions held by student members, community members, and a representative from the educational institution affiliated with the station. CHMA's board, for instance, includes two students with radio experience, two students without radio experience, at least one Mount Allison faculty member, and four members from the wider community. At CiTR, the board is responsible to a student executive made up of a president, a vice-president, a business manager, a secretary, and a number of directors and coordinators. This structure facilitates student participation regardless of the volunteer base in other areas, such as programming. Second, CiTR is community-supported, which allows the station "to promote diverse cultural coverage at less than four minutes of advertising per hour." Along with musical styles of all kinds, the station broadcasts news, sports, comedy, and current issues. Third, the station is nationally recognized – fully regulated by the CRTC and an active member of the NCRA.

CiTR's published mandate is brief. Public accounts of the station's style and culture illustrate its approach to programming. In early 1990, the station came under public scrutiny for broadcasting Public Enemy's album *Fear of a Black Planet*, specifically the song "Welcome to the Terrordome." R. Gerald Hobbs, a professor of church history, wrote a letter to the station in February of that year, arguing that the university station should not be playing this album – an album, in Hobbs's words, "whose lyrics are highly objectionable for persons with a historical memory for the roots of racial injustice and persecution in our world" (Hobbs 1990). He quoted lyrics that read "Crucifixion. Ain't no fiction / So-called chosen, frozen," and he wrote that "anyone with any knowledge of the history of Christian-Jewish relations, and the origins of the Holocaust will not need lessons in identifying who is the target of this thinly veiled diatribe." A letter from the station simply titled "Welcome to the Terrordome," noted that CiTR had pulled its copy from access on 12 February 1990 following listener complaints. But a week later, on 19 February, the station's copy was made available once again. The station justified this decision by bluntly stating that "CITR uses discretion in its programming" ("Welcome …"). The station's policy stated clearly that it would not air any material that would incite hatred or discrimination against any identifiable group; that said, CiTR believed that the song's lyrics did not incite hatred against the Jewish community ("Welcome …"). CiTR ended the letter by saying it would "not remove from public contemplation and discussion an artistic work whose only offense is the fact that it is controversial."

In a *Vancouver Sun* article in September 1988, a few years before Public Enemy incited listener complaints, station manager Harry Hertscheg explained that listening to the station was not always easy or "accessible." He wrote that the station's job was to provide a challenging listen (Wong 1988). "DJs at CITR are virtually free to play anything from the station's record library or their own collections. The only restrictions include [CRTC] requirements for Canadian content and unofficial station rules against playing songs too often. No such thing as heavy rotation here." In the same article, station DJ Don Chow explained that CiTR was not just "alternative" radio – rather, the station's progamming was "more encompassing." Its programming, for example, "encompasses" a folk show, *Absolute Value of Noise* ("a program which once consisted of nothing more than the noises emanating from the broadcast studio when it was being remodeled") and heavy metal (Wong 1988).

CHMA, CKUW, and CiTR are all licensed and regulated by the CRTC, and their respective licence renewals are fairly synchronous with regard to the conditions under which they are granted at a given point in time. Also, each station has integrated CRTC regulations into its station policies and approaches to programming, although in its own distinct way. Mandates and station philosophies briefly and passionately state core values that motivate volunteers and staff members to continue broadcasting. Certain key terms connect these philosophies – for example, "alternative" viewpoints and programming, and a "community-oriented", "-based," or "-reflected" focus. Other key defining features include independent or not-for-profit status, innovative and creative programming, educational and instructive programming, and variety and diversity. Individuals are encouraged to get involved with the station regardless of experience or prior broadcast training.

A station mandate or philosophy affirms acceptance of federal broadcast regulations and at the same time expresses a level of autonomy by crafting an internal policy that governs one station and one station only. Key terms like "alternative," "community," and "independent" are significant when it comes to shaping an individual's experience with a station, whether that experience involves listening, volunteering, or being programmed or interviewed by the station. These terms also mean very different things to different groups of people or organizations. For the CRTC, the term "alternative" functions as a placeholder for a radio broadcasting sector that tailors its programming to local cultural communities, plays Canadian music, and avoids pre-packaged advertisements, and that does not program the same commercial hit songs that commercial radio stations in the same market rely on to ensure a measurable listenership to sell to advertisers. As the documents circulated by these three stations suggest, it also requires a relatively stable working culture and a certain level of organization on the part of a station's staff to ensure that mandates and philosophies are clearly communicated to volunteers (the next chapter explores what can occur if this is not the case). Independence from profit-determined programming is ensured through alternative funding models, such as student fee levies and listener donations. The funding and financial sustainability of the campus radio sector is in no way perfect. Rather, funding is one of many constant struggles and obstacles that the campus sector faces. A not-for-profit model enables campus stations to operate in a relatively diverse, varied, and autonomous manner.

A community focus manifests itself in a variety of ways, from the volunteers who host shows to the format and structure of a station's weekly programming grid. Concerning the latter, a station's program grid is a mixture of long-running schedule standards and temporary, improvised shows that fill in the programming gaps during the summer months when students are away. Some shows are hosted by community members, some by students. Others are syndicated and can also be heard on other radio stations, such as *Democracy Now*, which originates in New York City and is broadcast on many campus radio stations across Canada. A description of the programming schedules for CHMA, CKUW, and CiTR further elucidates on what exactly a community-oriented focus means for the different stations and how they envision and put into practice "alternative," "diverse," and "informative" programming.

Locality and Diversity in the Program Grid

Inside CHMA's station space is a large programming board with multicoloured squares of bristol board attached to it. The names of radio programs are written on each square. During the summer months, a large majority of the station's in-house programming is temporarily replaced with syndicated or preprogrammed shows because many student volunteers are away on break. Sandy Mackay, CHMA's programming director, explained his approach to programming at the station. Mackay had arrived in Sackville "through the secret underground tunnel from Dawson City," Yukon (more on the relationship between Dawson City and Sackville soon) (Mackay, personal interview, 3 June 2011). Mackay said that his role is to maintain a constant presence in the office. Most of this work "has to do with the training of volunteers, recruiting new volunteers, and getting programmers on the air." He added that his strategy is to get as many programmers on the air as possible, regardless of long-term commitments or skill level, and that this is what differentiates him from some past directors, who have been stricter "about things like content." Mackay provided insight into the shifts in the schedule during the summer months, which are largely due to the fact that the town is so small and that students make up so much of the population as well as the programmers at the station. "During the summer, all of the students are gone, and so my big thing is always trying to get community members out, and it's harder than you think. They've got their summers already planned out and then a radio show is more work." Many of the community members who do come out are newcomers to the town, "who don't know much about it, and might have done radio in another town and now they're here and want to get involved in something."

Pat LePoidevin, a local musician, Mount Allison graduate, and former CHMA programmer, came to Sackville six years prior to the summer of 2011 from Princeton, British Columbia. LePoidevin also described this shift in programming: in the fall and winter, there are 2,000 more people in the town, 2,000 "more young individuals who are ready to go out to shows and participate in the radio station. So, the programming board drops like, I don't know, fifty, sixty percent" (LePoidevin, personal interview, 3 June 2011). Mackay describes the student demographics as a "university full of seventeen through twenty-five year olds, and everyone's pretty segregated" (Mackay 2011). It is pretty easy to guess who the new volunteers will be on the first day of school. Volunteers are typically not "overly representative" of the entire student and community population; there is typically "at least one programmer from each demographic, but the majority of programmers and volunteers are nerdy high schoolers who are now nerdy university students." Thus, the station's program grid is influenced heavily by the fact that it is mostly students participating in the station, who more often than not are somewhat similar in their interests and style. Given that Mount Allison students make up a large proportion of Sackville's population, it is no surprise that the academic year largely shapes the station's programming grid.

Before CHMA's programming underwent its temporary summer changes, the 2010–11 schedule included twenty syndicated shows and fifty-seven local programs, covering all twenty-four hours of the day. Syndicated programs ranged from larger news and spoken-word shows like *Democracy Now*, which is played every weekday from 6:00 to 7:00 p.m., to *The Green Majority*, a program produced at the University of Toronto's campus station CIUT, which aims to raise "awareness about Canadian environmental issues, connecting listeners with their environmental communities and encouraging green values, philosophies and lifestyles." Other syndicated shows included *Footlight Parade*, which showcases Broadway and Hollywood songs "from the turn of the 20th century to today," and *This Way Out*, an "award-winning internationally distributed weekly LGBT radio program, currently airing on over 175 local community radio stations around the world" (CHMA 2010). These programs, while not produced in-house, certainly fit within a mandate that focuses on informative and diverse programming, diverse in terms of the range of topics covered by these shows.

Most of the programming produced at CHMA is music-based, which suggests that the syndicated shows serve to ensure there is enough spoken-word content to meet CRTC regulations. A few of the show descriptions offer a sense of what the local spoken-word shows focus on – generally a mix of pop culture critique and discussion. For instance, *Wasteland* challenges the idea that pop culture is a "barren wasteland" by creating "life from the nothingness." Listeners can also hear "art talk and casual conversation" (*Full of Purpose*) and "nerd-chatter" (*The Final Frontier*, "a show for those still wary of Klingons") (CHMA 2010). The range of genres and styles covered by the station's music-based programming meets the station's goal of providing educational, innovative, and community-oriented programming. The show descriptions emphasize the knowledge and expertise the programmers bring to their shows. According to those descriptions, volunteers do not aimlessly choose albums to play at random; these are intelligent, well-seasoned music fans who carefully curate their playlists. *The Massie Hour* is hosted by "Japanese exchange students," who "practice their English and *introduce us* to new music" (CHMA 2010; emphasis added). On *Hyperborean Sound*, Julie Stephenson "showcases" music that is new to her "and hopefully to you as well." The show is an "exploration through Canadian content new and old." *Sounds of the 30's, 40's and 50's* has host Alex Keeling playing the "best pre-rock recording that most radio has forgotten." Playlists are "extensively researched and prepared by Alex, one of the most knowledgeable hosts on CHMA." Meaghan Fisher, host of *Postcards from Inania*, is a "real music lover" who "attempts to provide snapshots from each different genre. Along with intelligent commentary, she is sure to be your radio hero." Commitment to local music and content is apparent throughout the program grid, especially on shows like *Songwriter Full Circle*, which brings "the best of traditional East Coast songwriters to the radio," and *A Toast to the Coast*, a "celebration" of East Coast music. Genres like bluegrass, drum and bass, and "grass-root female singer/songwriter" are mentioned across the grid, and descriptions highlight a pull towards the innovative, such as *P.H. Balance*'s commitment to "music that is anything but neutral and inert" (CHMA 2010).

The station's programmers are mostly students, and this is clearly reflected in the programming grid and in the show descriptions. A small, liberal-arts-style university on the East Coast of Canada is hardly the most diverse place in the country. Most universities are not. Thus, the shows are not all that high on the cultural diversity and community activism side. Syndicated news and talk shows do help fill in these gaps, and a campus or community station can really only be as diverse as the communities it serves, or as diverse as the ways in which it imagines the nearby communities and the volunteers who participate with the station. CHMA focuses on ensuring that programming is well researched and distinct from other programs during the week. East Coast music and culture is certainly central, as are the individual tastes and interests of the volunteers themselves. Furthermore, CHMA is the only local radio broadcaster in Sackville. Because of this, the need to diversify is much less than if the station shared the area with other local broadcasters.

CKUW in Winnipeg differs considerably from CHMA in terms of its volunteer and programmer base. Station manager Rob Schmidt commented on the station's volunteer base, noting that when the station first went on air it did not have a lot of student programmers. The station was "new," and the individuals who ran it "wanted the best of the best" (Schmidt 2011). Schmidt figured that students made up a little less than 20 percent of the participants at the time. He assumes it is closer to 30 percent now, although it "would be nice to have a 50/50 split," because "students provide a bulk of the funding." According to Schmidt, students are a bit more transient than community volunteers, and there is some turnover during the summer, but he is glad the station has never needed to go automated over the summer, like some do. "There's always been a good core of volunteers," and that is "part of the nature" of Winnipeg. "A lot of people don't leave this city for school. In Winnipeg, most people live at home and continue to go to school for much longer than what was typical for me and my friends, anyways, in Ontario." CKUW's program director Robin Eriksson became a volunteer in 2004 after moving to Winnipeg. Two years later she became the director, after filling in for a show and then taking one over as host. Eriksson said it is often hard to draw the line between "student" and "community" volunteers. Quite frequently, students enjoy their time at the station and continue their work with the station after graduating, becoming, in effect, community volunteers. "So, we haven't lost them. We've just lost that student status" (Eriksson, personal interview, 6 July 2011).

Sarah Michaelson entered the Winnipeg music community through CKUW in 2000 after her first-year orientation at the university. She has been a programmer and host of *Stylus Radio* since 2001 and is a well-known Canadian DJ performing under the name Mama Cutsworth. She has also been the news director and serves on the station's programming committee. According to Michaelson, a lot of what determines whether or not a show is accepted is that which "sets it apart from any of the shows that we already have on the air, because it's about enhancing the diversity of the program grid, more than anything … It's not about fitting in, which is kind of amazing" (Michaelson, personal interview, 7 July 2011). A pitch for a show featuring established Canadian bands like Stars and Broken Social Scene will not necessarily be accepted, because a lot of people are pitching that. "So think beyond that. And if you want to play that kind of music, what's going to make the show different?" If someone is pitching a spoken-word show, she or he should understand how to do interviews and know "how to frame a topic." CKUW also works to ensure they have enough programmers from different genders and cultural backgrounds and ages. Michaelson continues: "I love the fact that we have a nine-year-old who comes in every Saturday morning and co-hosts. And we have Bill who's in his eighties and is an amazing guy, and does a couple different programs. It's really amazing to have that." Michaelson emphasizes that programmers are "real people coming in and reflecting their interests, and serving tiny pockets of the community and celebrating the differences." She does stress, though, that this only goes so far. Because the station is funded and operates out of a university, and even though there are "tons of people who are not students," there is still

> that ivory tower issue with being based inside a university. People who maybe have never been to a university, people who are intimidated by that, or don't live downtown, being a downtown campus ... So, that has its cons, because someone's family doesn't have a history of going to university, they may never feel comfortable enough to walk on in and say they want to be a part of the station. Which, although it is *that* easy, I could see that being intimidating. We're always looking for more women programmers and more aboriginal folks. It's still my understanding of the bulk of Canadian campus and community radio that it's still pretty white. That's definitely something that I would like to change. And that's slowly shifting. (Michaelson 2011)

The station works to ensure that a range of voices are heard in its programming, keeping its downtown location in mind. Ted Turner notes that compared to nearby University of Manitoba's CJUM-FM, which went under for a while after losing some financial support, CKUW's programming has always been "a little more out there" (Turner 2011). The station definitely sounds "more like the downtown station," according to Turner, and this is reflected in its "award-winning spoken-word programming, like *Inner City Voices*, this fantastic show that really focuses on the stories of people living in this neighbourhood." Rob Schmidt connects the station's sound back to its mandate and uses the term "listener-driven radio." His favourite phrase is "participatory media," and he considers this to be the core of the station. Out of this participatory, listener-driven mandate, "you get sort of a social responsibility to get those voices on air that are marginalized, or not represented in mainstream media, or on private media or public media." Then "out of that comes the activism of getting community organizations involved, getting youth involved, getting the voices of radical movements heard, and those sorts of things" (Schmidt 2011).

CKUW's schedule lists station-produced and syndicated shows from at least 6:00 a.m. until midnight, with some shows listed infrequently during the early-morning hours. Programming is run twenty-four hours a day, though there are gaps in the late-night and early-morning time slots. Late-night and early-morning shows vary between syndicated and non-syndicated. The station's website explains that the program schedule is always changing; that said, the program descriptions illustrate the range of music and spoken-word programming, as well as the station's focus on communities in Winnipeg. As with CHMA, a variety of syndicated shows are broadcast by CKUW, although they represent a smaller percentage of total programming. *Alternative Radio* is a "weekly one-hour public affairs program offered free to all public radio stations in the U.S., Canada, Europe, South Africa, Australia, and on short-wave on Radio for Peace International" ("Programs & Archives"). The show "provides information, analyses and views that are frequently ignored or distorted in other media." *Family Matters*, produced at the University of Guelph's campus station, CFRU, discusses "supportive parenting practices, communication, and culture in the context of conventional and unconventional families." *Black Mask* and *Queer Power* are station-produced spoken-word shows. The former is "an anarchist radio show that has been broadcast since 1999"; the latter is "a weekly dose of queer news – from your community and beyond."

The range of styles and genres heard on CKUW, and its role as a downtown station, are evident in such shows as *'Peg City Groove*, which airs on Fridays from 5:00 to 6:00 p.m. and covers the "local Winnipeg music scene" ("Programs & Archives"). The show's mission is "to give local musicians a platform to promote their band, their gig, their albums; their way"; the show's hosts "want the music of the Winnipeg community to thrive." Kent Davies's *Amateur Hour* features "the best of the worst. Artists and bands that never got their fair share of airtime for how seemingly weird, awful or cheesy they are will finally get their due." *Hit the Big Wide Strum!* is hosted by Robin Eriksson and is the "only bluegrass broadcast in the province;" *Island Vibes* features soca, reggae, dance-hall, and chutney music from The Islands, plus "local Caribbean events, guest DJs and other music industry info from the Caribbean." *Rock'n'Roll Damnation* specifically plays heavy metal from 1969 until 1992, billed as "music you never hear on radio" ("Programs & Archives").

CKUW's programming is a little more "out there" than CHMA's. This is partly because it is located in a much larger city with many more people from a wider range of backgrounds and places. The station works to sustain a powerful voice in the downtown core from which it broadcasts and to transcend the boundaries between university and community. Regarding the CRTC's policies governing programming, Robin Eriksson says that "in the long run," they do not "make our programming better in any way" (Eriksson 2011). And in certain ways, they could "take away the creativity and the good judgment that volunteers could and would have on their own volition." Eriksson is confident that the station "could do just fine if we were just allowed to create programming that our community was asking for, rather than abide by things that this agency in Ottawa regulated." However, she adds, levels of regulation help ensure that the sector sounds "unlike anything on the dial." In other words, broadcasting policy ensures that campus stations do not sound like commercial or public stations. Considering CKUW's program grid, and Eriksson's confidence that the staff and volunteers will create content that reflects Winnipeg's communities, the shows and hosts are quite in sync with the station's mandate, particularly its emphasis on not sounding like other radio stations and on being an active, downtown, inner-city station.

Like CKUW, CiTR in Vancouver has more community volunteers than students. Station manager Brenda Grunau explains that CiTR is in a unique position because it has not only a board of directors but also a student executive that "isn't just a volunteer committee" (Grunau, personal interview, 11 July 2011). Because the bulk of the station's funding comes from students, and because CiTR is a student club, the board wants the station to be "student-driven and student-run." The staff and the board are responsible to the student executive. The student executive is integral to the station's structure; even so, the student programmer percentage is only about 11 percent. Grunau notes that it is "really low across the country" in general. "Even though we're really good at involving students in how the station is run, it's really hard for us to get students on air. So we've been rethinking our training process." The station has a lot of community programmers, some of whom have been around for fifteen, even twenty years. This "makes some things really rigid and then other things sort of fluid. So a balance somewhere in the middle would be preferable."

CiTR hopes to attract more student volunteers by relaxing its volunteer training process, which was once fairly difficult and rigorous. She explains that it was "a bit more like being lectured, and we're making it more interactive now." Students used to have to produce a demo, and "people would spend hours recording pieces and getting stuck and getting afraid of the equipment, and it would never get finished and then they would fall off the map." The process is now much more hands on, "where you might sit in on a show, and then program an hour. We're just shoving [new volunteers] on the air right away, so instead of doing a demo, they can do a live show with someone in the booth, watching, so it's less intimidating" (Grunau 2011). Janis McKenzie speaks to this issue, drawing from her longevity at the station and current position as a board member. She points out that the station has had consistent challenges with keeping students on the air and keeping percentages of student and women volunteers high. She adds that it requires constant work to maintain student participation (McKenzie 2011). In line with Sarah Michaelson's comments, McKenzie points to areas where representation could be better, while also highlighting an awareness of these issues and the station's efforts to increase its diversity and inclusivity.

"And that goes for other groups as well. All kinds of groups that aren't getting represented well enough on the air. So we need to do more about that. But I think there was hardly any queer programming when I started, so we've made improvements in some areas."

Nardwuar the Human Serviette has been a CiTR DJ since 1987, programming a weekly Friday afternoon show. He regularly features songs from bands in town on a given weekend and often plays his pre-recorded interviews, which he has become known for – witty and well-researched interviews in which he often surprises interviewees with albums or "gifts" from the past. Nardwuar, a Vancouver resident, began hosting a show in October 1987 after joining the station in September of the previous year. "At first, I was just happy doing public service announcements, or carts, getting the word out for different events and stuff like that. And after a while I said, 'I'd like to do a radio show.' So it took me about a year to get the courage to do a radio show" (Nardwuar, personal interview, 8 July 2011). His show is also programmed by WFMU in New Jersey, although for that broadcast, he has to spend extra time removing the swear words before it airs. He also shares his video interviews on YouTube and archives many of them on his website, Nardwuar.com. In the early 1990s, Nardwuar began conducting in-person interviews using a video camera because the audio sounded better and he could then use the video for cable access television and play the audio on CiTR. Nardwaur also plays in the bands The Evaporators and Thee Goblins.

Nardwuar explains why he is drawn to the campus radio format. "Well, you just saw exactly why I love CiTR radio. I was able to begin with dead air. What other stations are you allowed to begin with dead air? What other stations period are you allowed to have dead air?" For him, campus radio in Canada is "just so amazing," while in the United States, "you can't even say the word 'asshole.'" Although "you have to be sensitive with what you're doing, you have to worry about the time of day and you have to give warning for stuff like that, but you can still do it."

CiTR has a number of long-term programmers like Nardwuar, whose longevity is attributed to a passion for approaching radio programming in a manner that allows more freedom than would commercial radio. The station programs a range of shows that reflect its mandate to "to serve, instruct and inform the UBC and Greater Vancouver Community" by supplying alternative, informative, and community-oriented programming ("About"). CiTR's schedule runs seven days a week, with programming covering every hour, although some early-morning slots are filled by a "CiTR Ghost Mix." CiTR, like CHMA and CKUW, features a number of programs that play Canadian indie music, and a large percentage of shows in the overall schedule are station-produced. CiTR programs four syndicated shows that are produced by other campus or community radio stations. Spoken-word shows include *News 101*, "Vancouver's only live, volunteer-produced, student and community newscast," which gives listeners a "fully independent media perspective." *Prof Talk* meets the informative and educational aspect of the mandate by having UBC professors talk about current issues and events at the local and international level ("Show List"). The show offers a space for faculty and doctoral students to engage in dialogue about important events and to share their current research on the subject at hand.

Music programming on CiTR covers genres and styles from a range of musical communities and cultures represented in Vancouver and elsewhere. As well, a considerable number of shows emphasize experimental and inventive musical sounds and styles. DJ David Love Jones hosts *African Rhythms*, which has been airing for over twelve years. The show plays genres like "jazz, soul, hip-hop, Afro-Latin, funk, and eclectic Brazilian rhythms. There are also interviews with local and international artists." *Rhythms-India* is hosted by Anoop Sharma and "features a wide range of music from India. Popular music from Indian movies from 1950's to the present, Classical music, Semi-classical music (Ghazals, Bhajans, and Qawwalis), pop music and music in regional languages." Shows identifying with the "weird," the "noisy," and the "experimental" include *Misery Hour*, Hans Kloss's "sub-collection of mostly disgusting and unlistenable songs and sounds"; *Exploding Head Movies*, which "explores music from the movies, tunes from television and any other cinematic source, along with atmospheric pieces, cutting edge tracks and strange old goodies that could be used in a soundtrack to be"; *Stereoscopic Redoubt*, "experimental, radio-art, sound collage, field recordings" that are recommended "for the insane"; and *Synaptic Sandwich*, which is "full of electro bleeps, retrowave, computer generated, synthetically manipulated aural rhythms" ("Show List"). CiTR's programming features more music than spoken-word content. Much of the station's music-based programming explores sounds and styles that fall outside popular music genres, or at least land somewhere on the fringes. This hints at the station's idea of how "alternativeness" is projected through broadcasted content.

These schedules and show descriptions reveal the ways in which programming is discursively constructed and organized in line with station mandates and internal policies. Responsibility to local communities is a constant refrain, and many shows are described with colourful terms and adjectives that defy popular conceptions of how (commercial) radio is organized and programmed. Programming is created for an audience of students *and* community members, though the percentage of each is highly uncertain. This underscores the blurred function of campus stations; it also reflects the size of the university relative to to its city or town. Mandates dictate roles for both community members and students, and stations' operations and programming fluctuate in terms of serving both these constituencies. The campus station's institutional setting also contributes greatly to the programming grid and the station's sound. Mount Allison University is a major institution in a small town, and as such, the student culture and the station culture are much more prominent and present than in the larger cities where CiTR and CKUW are based. CKUW's emphasis on social justice programming has been shaped by the University of Winnipeg's location in the downtown core. Universities near urban centres attract more community members as volunteers and programmers.

There are many similarities among the three stations' programming schedules; there are also significant differences that have been shaped by location. CKUW places greater emphasis on spoken-word programming that reflects its downtown location. Each station's musical offerings are certainly shaped by its location in the vast country that is Canada. East Coast music is profiled on CHMA, while on CiTR, the weirdness and diversity that come with a large metropolis are reflected in the station's musical programming. Cultural variety depends to a large extent on location. Winnipeg and Vancouver have more cultural programming than CHMA, which is based in a very small town. Judging from programming and station policies, disconnections between the three stations are apparent, even though all share the same centralized regulations. Stations navigate and implement broadcasting policy in ways that enable them to respond to the localities they serve. A policy framework that includes central guidelines while offering the autonomy to craft internal policies specific to a locality is an effective means to ensure that campus stations operate with a specific purpose and remain distinct from commercial radio.

A program grid that positions distinct shows beside one another challenges the programming flow of commercial radio. With commercial radio programming, the listening experience is much smoother: the programs easily transition from one to the next and between commercial messages. A listener can come to predict the sound and style of a morning show format, for instance. In Raymond Williams's in-depth analysis of television broadcasting (and to a lesser extent, radio) in Britain and United States, the phenomenon of planned programming flow is said to be "the defining characteristic of broadcasting, simultaneously as a technology and as a cultural form" (1974/2003, 86). With programming flow, the notion of an interruption between programs is said to be inadequate, yet retaining "some residual force from an older model" (90). Programs are still relatively distinct from one another, in that they are different shows with different topics, narratives, or personalities, but there is a behind-the-scenes logic to the schedule that organizes content to retain viewership (or listenership) for an entire sequence. So an evening's block of television shows will include trailers for upcoming shows, and commercials are smoothly integrated between and throughout shows. By placing dramatically discrete shows side by side and accepting new shows based on novelty, campus radio stations shake up programming flow. The genres and programming styles found on a campus radio program grid do not seek to "retain" an audience in the same way that commercial or public radio might. For example, a listener who tunes in for music programming may stop listening if a spoken-word show follows. Not every program is in the same language, so listening to a campus station also requires the ability to understand multiple languages in order to fully participate as a listener.

There is much more to be said about how stations respond to the music scenes and cultural communities within their broadcast range. For instance, how do stations serve their local scenes beyond programming local music? And what other roles do station staff and volunteers play in their cultural communities and music scenes? Chapter 6 explores the relationship between a campus station and its specific locality. Surely alternativeness and community responsibility figure into the culture of campus radio beyond simply being mentioned in policy documents. Campus stations and other nodes in a music scene are connected along discursive lines, yet the links implicit in this relationship are much more dynamic than descriptions and definitions of diverse and experimental radio programming.

Besides amplifying the role of campus stations within their musical and cultural communities, the community-based mandate that accompanies FM licensing means that stations must adhere to a number of key regulations – for example, with regard to local and Canadian programming, board member structure, and advertising restrictions. The following chapter discusses the 2010 policy revision for the campus and community radio sector and discusses the licence revocation of CKLN-FM at Ryerson University. CKLN serves as an example of a station that did not meet the CRTC's requirements for a campus broadcaster, largely due to labour disputes and a negative working culture. Clearly, there are certain limits to station autonomy and broadcasting practices, and the CRTC enforces rules about how a campus station in service to the community must operate.

5

A Community-Based Mandate

Regulating the Campus Radio Sector in 2010

As discussed in the previous chapter, a community-based mandate is a key feature of licensed FM campus radio broadcasting. Before it is allowed to broadcast on the FM dial, a campus station must meet certain centralized CRTC guidelines. Besides meeting those, campus stations strive to reflect the unique localities they serve. A station's programming and operations are largely determined by its links to the nearby musical and cultural communities.

In 2010 the CRTC reviewed and revised its policy for the campus and community radio sector. This new policy once again emphasized the role and significance of campus stations for their nearby communities. Also in 2010, CKLN-FM at Ryerson University in Toronto was found to be non-compliant with CRTC regulations, in part because the station was not fulfilling its responsibility to be inclusive to both community members and students. The commission held a public hearing that considered and discussed the station's non-compliance. This led to the station losing its licence to broadcast.

These two events indicate that for campus stations, an inclusive and community-centred focus is becoming increasingly important, especially in crowded radio markets with limited spectrum availability. The new policy accounted for contemporary issues facing the sector, such as funding, sustainability, and spectrum scarcity. In some markets, the FM band had become notably competitive. This was the case in Toronto, where a commercial indie rock radio station, Indie 88, replaced CKLN on 88.1 FM. The loss of a frequency for a campus station on the FM dial raises questions about the variety and balance of Canada's single broadcasting system, especially given that the commercial station that replaced CKLN shares some programming similarities with a campus radio format (a focus on emerging artists, for instance). Campus stations, however, have an active, community-based mandate and are connected to nearby cultural and musical communities in various ways beyond simply programming local, independent, and emerging music.

Throughout the public hearings surrounding the policy decisions of 2010, proponents of campus and community radio argued the FM dial is essential for fulfilling community-based mandates both at the level of CRTC broadcasting policy and at the level of individual station principles and philosophies. An FM licence allows campus stations to establish the borders of their surrounding community through broadcast range; it also lends authority and legitimacy to the sector. Furthermore, the sound quality of FM radio compared to AM radio lends itself well to music programming. This chapter continues to focus on the importance of FM campus stations with respect to their surrounding communities by outlining the reasons why CKLN was found to be non-compliant and in disservice to its community and mandate. Campus stations are regulated in a manner that enables a certain level of autonomy in terms of how local music is reflected in programming; that said, the CRTC deems certain key characteristics essential to the local focus and community-based mandate of the campus radio sector. The commission's decision to revoke CKLN's licence implies that campus stations in urban centres may need to be particularly careful in coming years to ensure that their programming and operations meet policy requirements.

Non-Compliance at Ryerson University's CKLN-FM

In May 2008, a number of CKLN volunteers received this message by email from CKLN's interim station manager, Mike Phillips: "Please be advised that your volunteer services at CKLN Radio Inc are no longer required." *Now Magazine*, an alternative weekly publication in Toronto, profiled CKLN's ongoing organizational complications after the station's volunteers were fired. One recipient of Phillips's email was DJ Denise Benson, who was interviewed by *Now*. Benson believed that the volunteer terminations were part of an effort by newly appointed and anti-union management to "muzzle outspoken opponents" (Terefenko 2008). Benson added that the firings reflected an ideological shift at the station from political activism to mainstream commercialism. DJ David James disagreed with Benson, telling *Now*

Magazine that "talk of a philosophical shift is crap." James added that the terminated volunteers had been part of a group that "appointed their own board" (Terefenko 2008). It seems that CKLN volunteers were aligning with one of two factions at the station, each with its own divergent idea of how the station should operate. Additional ongoing issues at CKLN included an unclear mandate and a station culture that lacked inclusivity.

Earlier, in February 2008, CKLN's membership had voted to impeach most of the station's board of directors, fire Phillips, and dismiss Tony Barnes, the station's program director. According to a profile of CKLN on *Torontoist*, a Toronto-based blog, Phillips and Barnes did not consider the vote to be legitimate, so they stayed at their jobs and hired a lawyer to help them address the escalating power struggle at the station (Kupferman 2011a). In May of that year, Phillips fired more than twenty-five volunteers via email (quoted above); in July, some of the station's members elected a new board. But the old board still had not relinquished power. The new board started a blog for the purpose of claiming legitimacy and to express dissatisfaction with Phillips and Barnes and their associates (http://take backourradio.blogspot.com). On 19 June 2008 the blog distributed a press release claiming that Heather Douglas and Ron Nelson had been elected as new volunteer representatives and that Josie Miner, Tony Barnes, Mike Phillips, and Doug Barrett were "illegally controlling the space" ("Press Release" 2008). Thus, CKLN had competing boards of directors that were fighting over legitimacy and for control of the station. According to a brief history of CKLN featured in the *Toronto Star*, this period of infighting between boards also involved a police presence to keep order at membership meetings (Vukets and Infantry 2011). Between March and October 2009, the station's studios were locked, and at various times, listeners were treated to dead air and an audio loop of jazz programming. The audio loop was an obvious violation of key radio regulations such as Canadian content quotas, and it did not reflect local issues and interests. As a result of infighting at the station, CKLN was broadcasting content that violated Canadian broadcasting regulations and the station's conditions of licence. More importantly, these organizational issues were preventing the station from serving Toronto's nearby musical and cultural communities.

On 12 May 2010, to address these ongoing issues and concerns at CKLN-FM, the CRTC held a public hearing in Toronto. The purpose of the hearing was to discuss the many complaints that had been lodged against the station, including the fact that the station was having difficulties with its governance structure, daily operations, and programming consistency. Many of the complaints lodged against the station had remained unanswered since February 2008 (i.e., for the two years preceding the hearing);

the most recent complaint had been filed in November 2009 (CRTC 2010a). Of critical concern, according to the commission, was that CKLN seemed to be in non-compliance with a number of sections of the 1986 Radio Regulations. The relevant subsections included 8(4) and (6) Logs and records – Clear and intelligible tape recordings; 9(2) Requests for information – Annual returns; 9(4) Requests for information – Responding to any inquiry on a matter within the Commission's jurisdiction; 10(1) Ownership and control of equipment and facilities; and, 11(4)(a) Transfers of ownership and control. The Ryerson Student Union (RSU) had prohibited access to the CKLN transmitter site between March and September 2009, and on instructions from the RSU, Brookfield Properties (the landlord of the transmitter site) had only allowed representatives of the licensee to access the site. The RSU, however, was not the station's licensee. As well, the RSU was prohibiting access to station facilities and withholding student levies collected on behalf of the station (CRTC 2010a).

In addition to these non-compliance issues, CKLN was said to be operating in a manner that was inconsistent with the 2000 Campus Radio Policy, which had been in effect at the time the station last renewed its licence. For a number of months during the station lockout, the audio loop being broadcasted had consisted mainly of jazz music, with no volunteer involvement. During this time, "community reflection and involvement also appeared to be nonexistent." The CRTC also questioned the station's connections with Ryerson University. CKLN's by-laws were said to have made no "provision for the involvement of Ryerson's administration or other university representative on the board of directors." The commission also noted that student involvement in the board of directors was minimal (CRTC 2010a). This lack of student and university involvement was problematic, given that the boards of directors of community-based campus stations are mandated to have balanced representation.

The public hearing in May was adjourned and postponed until 8 December 2010. Reasons for the adjournment included "ongoing litigation and judicial mediation before the Ontario Superior Court of Justice concerning the governance of CKLN Radio and the legitimacy of the current board of directors" (CRTC 2010b). In advance of the December hearing, Saul Chernos, a writer for *Now Magazine* and a former programmer at the University of Toronto's CIUT, anticipated a severe decision by the commission. Chernos asked: "In the age of podcasts, blogs and tweets, would an edgy, fractious, passionate little radio outlet be missed if it were suddenly yanked from the ether?" (Chernos 2010). He added that "the regulator rarely sends a station to the gallows" but that "the formal wording of the hearing notice seems chilling."

When the hearing resumed, the onus was on CKLN to provide reasons for its non-compliance and to convince the commission that the station would comply with its regulatory obligations moving forward. Legal counsel Crystal Hulley explained that under Section 9(e) of the Broadcasting Act, the commission had the authority to suspend a licence. Hulley also referenced Section 24, which states in part that a licence will not be suspended or revoked unless "the Commission is satisfied that the licensee has contravened or failed to comply with any condition of the license" (CRTC 2010d).

Throughout the hearing, a handful of CKLN volunteers spoke to the problems and issues at the station – albeit with minimal cohesiveness and camaraderie – hoping to convince the commission of the station's improved organization moving forward. Speaking strongly in favour of CKLN was Ron Nelson, the board's chair at the time and host of CKLN radio program *Reggaemania*. Nelson told the commission that the station's volunteer base reflected Toronto's cultural diversity through genres and music from South Asia, Latin America, Africa, the Caribbean, Ireland, East Asia, and elsewhere. He added that the station had eliminated its debt. With this newfound financial stability, he was hopeful that the station could now hire a station manager and a program director within two months (CRTC 2010d). The station's goal, he added, was "to make changes to CKLN's organization structure, policies and practices to ensure organizational stability so that the governance crisis of 2008/2009 will never happen again" (CRTC 2010d). The CRTC, however, found fault with Nelson's reported timeline for implementing these initiatives. The commission was clearly looking for the station to be already in compliance, or at least much further ahead than it was at that time. Len Katz, the Vice Chairman of Telecommunications when the hearings were being conducted, asked: "Don't you think you would have advanced your position had you been able to introduce us to the new station manager, day-to-day operating manager, and sort of say we have made reparations, we have done all this, here we are, here is the guy in charge, here are the rules, he is the guy who is going to do this, rather than coming to us saying, we need time?" (CRTC 2010d).

During the hearing, commissioner Louise Poirier raised the point that CKLN was one of the campus stations in Canada that received the most listener complaints. Nelson responded by explaining that filing complaints to the CRTC was a tactic being used while the two boards of directors were competing for power. At the time of the split between the different boards at CKLN, he had been part of a board chaired by Arno Meiners that was not recognized as legitimate, and one of the board's mandates had been "to complain anytime that we saw a problem" (CRTC 2010d). Alongside Nelson, Joeita Gupta and Murphy Browne from the radio program *Frequency*

Feminisms spoke against the old board. Gupta and Browne explained that the old board members were refusing to step down despite the election of the new board. They said that Mike Phillips and Tony Barnes "undertook a campaign of intimidation and silencing of dissent within the station" (CRTC 2010d). Complaints against CKLN were also submitted to the CRTC while volunteers were locked out of the station studios by the administrator of the RSU building, the Palin Foundation.

From the old board's perspective, Nelson and the new board were working with the RSU to forcibly take over the station. Josie Miner, a member of CKLN's board in 2007 and 2008, explained that the RSU had begun running the station in July 2008 "when it withheld CKLN's funds in order to assert its will over the Board." Miner added that the new board had been put to place by the RSU and that "to allow CKLN to continue to broadcast now is to reward people who have shown that if you want a radio station you just take it over" (CRTC 2010d). A number of other interventions made during the hearing highlighted the history of disorganization at CKLN. Greg Duffell, a volunteer, co-host, and producer, traced the station's lack of leadership back to 2005, when he first became involved as a volunteer. He explained that between 2003 and 2007, the station had been without a manager. He was also critical of the relationship between the station and the RSU. Duffell claimed that when "the RSU could no longer be assured of getting their way at CKLN, they turned their attentions to fomenting and encouraging a rebellion, advanced by their loyal adherents, including CKLN paid staff, along with their dupes and cronies within the membership" (CRTC 2010d). Duffell was concerned about how Nelson was using the station for his own business enterprises and for personal profit (practices that are not in line with the mandate of community-based campus stations). *Reggaemania*, said Duffell, was not simply the name of Nelson's radio program; it was also the name of his own personal company.

Also in favour of terminating CKLN's licence was Doug Barrett, a volunteer and on-air host from 2005 until early 2009. Barrett argued that if the licence were revoked, "the precedent will be that CRTC rules and regulations apply to all campus community radio stations, and must be followed explicitly." He added that the "number of people who submitted their concerns to the Commission can be counted on one hand. That is a damning indictment of the elitist private club that CKLN has become" (CRTC 2010d). According to Barrett, Ryerson journalism professors were instructing their students to receive credit and training from CIUT at the University of Toronto, as opposed to having their students use their own campus radio station. Without the support of its institution, CKLN was in a tough situation, in that it could not clearly outline its role as a campus community radio station.

The National Campus and Community Radio Association (NCRA) expressed sympathy for the station's troubles and hoped to help the station maintain its licence. Shelley Robinson, the NCRA's executive director, recommended that the station be renewed for two years, during which the CRTC and the NCRA could help CKLN ensure compliance and help preserve "the existence of a vital and remarkable broadcasting service" (CRTC 2010d). But the station was not up for renewal; it was in the midst of a licence term that had begun in 2007 and would expire in 2014. So the CRTC responded that the licence was not renewable in the middle of the term.

December's hearing was CKLN's opportunity to explain its position for moving forward as a campus station in compliance with the Broadcasting Act and Radio Regulations. Yet throughout the hearing, it became evident that the station was also not maintaining active participation from the student body. CKLN programmer Daniel Besharat stated that training at the station had been poor or nonexistent, leading to "deteriorated" programming. David James Cooper, a former volunteer coordinator and paid employee of CKLN, said that the lack of support from Ryerson students was indicative of the station's confused mandate. Cooper told the commission "that you would have at least some students here to show support here or a petition, or you would have letters of support from Ryerson Faculty. That you do not, speaks volumes" (CRTC 2010d). In the stations profiled in Chapter 4, student involvement is central to the direction of the station even if student programmer percentages are low. The lack of student involvement at CKLN and the dismal student turnout during CKLN's public hearing were evidence that the station had lost its institutional grounding, as well as its role in Toronto's local musical and cultural communities.

A significant factor in the commission's assessment of CKLN was that the Ryerson station shared Toronto with two other campus radio stations. Therefore, a decision to suspend or revoke the station's licence would not leave the city without a campus station. As the largest city and radio market in Canada, Toronto presents an intriguing case. Besides Ryerson, both the University of Toronto and York University have FM campus stations. CKLN was the city's first, beginning as a closed-circuit station in 1971. In 1983 the station would begin broadcasting on the FM dial on 88.1 FM. CIUT-FM at the University of Toronto was licensed in 1986 as the second student FM station in Toronto. The commission claimed that the University of Toronto station "will fill a need and add significantly to the diversity and quality of programming currently available to radio listeners in Metropolitan Toronto and surrounding communities within the proposed station's service contours" (CRTC 1986). Shortly thereafter, in March 1987, a third student FM station was licensed in the Toronto radio market, CHRY at York University. The station was licensed to operate as a low-power, 50-watt station, and "would be the only station in its service area that devotes considerable amounts of its music programming to black music and folk music from different parts of the world" (CRTC 1987a). Evidently, during the mid- to late 1980s, the commission had found that the size of Toronto and the diversity of its population allowed for the licensing of three FM campus stations.

The CRTC renewed CKLN-FM's licence in 1987 for a period expiring in 1990. The renewal restricted the station's ability to program popular musical hits, down from 30 percent of all musical selections to 20 percent. The commission felt that this would result in a wider range of music programming offered to CKLN-FM listeners; this would be in line with broader FM policy objectives pertaining to musical diversity (CRTC 1987a). Efforts to enhance the station's "commercial-free access time to community groups outside of the campus" were a required component of the 1990 renewal. The station had complied by increasing community access time from two to three and a half hours per week (CRTC 1990b). The station's 1995 licence renewal raised questions about the ownership and operation of CKLN. One intervention opposed the renewal and asked about the licensee's ownership of its transmitter, which was leased to the station and located on First Canadian Place in downtown Toronto. Section 10.1 of the 1986 Radio Regulations stipulates that a licensee must own and operate its own transmitter. The commission informed CKLN that it must submit a report on the progress made to resolve this dispute within six months following the renewal (CRTC 1995b). A second intervention cited concerns about the station's broadcast policies. But the commission expressed satisfaction with CKLN's response to the intervention, including the station's "Balance in Programming Policy," and the licence was again renewed. Further licence renewals were issued in 2001 and 2007.

The fact that there were three campus stations in the Toronto market may well have contributed to CKLN's licence revocation. But even though the station shared the city with stations at York University and the University of Toronto, CKLN had carved out a distinct role in the city in terms of its programming, at least according to some of the station's programmers. During the December 2010 public hearing, CKLN's distinct role in Toronto was argued for by a few station volunteers and listeners. Allan Jones, who described himself as a "concerned citizen" and "an active Black community member in Toronto," felt that York University's CHRY was "a bit more ethnic" in its presentation, and he pointed out that the station reaches a "Jamaican-based population" (CRTC 2010d). He emphasized that CKLN meant a lot to the Black community in Toronto. In Jones's opinion, CKLN offered a service distinct from that of CHRY and CIUT. He felt that CKLN operated "with a higher level of sophistication than maybe a CHRY does. And CIUT, which is also downtown Toronto, it's very different in their presentation style and their programming from CKLN, so to remove CKLN you're really taking out a vital segment that serves my community" (CRTC 2010d). Ron Nelson has been credited with launching the first hip-hop radio show in Canada, on CKLN in 1983 – another indication of the station's groundbreaking role in Toronto radio (Infantry 2011). Jones's intervention importantly illustrates that, setting aside the disorganization and infighting at CKLN, at its best, the station had been providing a distinct service to the city.

The station's failure to respond coherently to the commission's suggestions and concerns was a common refrain during the 2010 public hearing. CKLN was without stable and organized leadership and was operating all too often without key individuals such as a station manager and program director. Competing boards of directors were struggling for power, the RSU had injected itself into the station's politics, and a number of volunteers felt that the station lacked inclusivity. The station might be serving certain communities in Toronto that were less served by CIUT and CHRY, but it was unable to strike a working balance between student and community participation and representation. Mandates and station philosophies may outline a campus station's role as a local alternative in a given radio market, but these documents are ineffective unless there is a coherent working culture at the station.

The End of CKLN-FM: An Unprecedented Decision

On 12 February 2011, the CRTC revoked CKLN's licence. The decision cited "the serious and continuous nature of the licensee's non-compliance," its "inability to institute the measures necessary to ensure ongoing compliance," and "the lack of confidence on the part of the Commission that such measures could or would be instituted within a reasonable amount of time" as reasons why the licence was revoked (CRTC 2011a). The CRTC's chairperson at the time of the revocation, Konrad W. von Finckenstein, stated bluntly in the *Toronto Star* that "CKLN Radio was given several warnings and opportunities to come into compliance. Each time, it demonstrated an inability or unwillingness to address our concerns" (Infantry 2011). The commission reiterated that CKLN was in non-compliance with the Radio Regulations and the station's conditions of licence in four main areas: non-compliance during the station's lockout period, the filing of annual returns, the provision of logs and records, and the licensee's response to the commission's requests for information.

Organizational matters such as filing returns, providing programming logs, and responding to the commission in a timely matter can be complicated daily tasks for stations that rely on modest funding, limited staff, and volunteer labour for their operations. With these issues compounded and consistent, CKLN became derailed by a lack of communication and organizational structure. Furthermore, during the lockout, the station was not fulfilling its role as a community-based campus station as determined by 2000's Campus Radio Policy. Campus stations are expected to be distinct from private and public stations by playing a valuable role for their nearby communities, by including volunteers, and by programming content that reflects the community's various groups. Former student union president Toby Whitfield sat on the station's board throughout much of its troubles. After the licence revocation, he explained that there had "been so much infighting for so many years, people lost sight of the purpose of the station. The privilege of having a license is amazing, and I think that's what was missing" (Morrow 2011). The commission determined that the station was not broadcasting with sufficient community involvement during the lockout, nor did it have sufficient volunteer participation from Ryerson University. Programming during the lockout was neither diverse nor locally relevant. Participation from both the wider community and the academic institution that houses and supports a campus station is an important characteristic of the campus sector.

Following the lockout in 2009, CKLN claimed to understand the seriousness of the situation. The station filed a report in October 2009 that responded to the commission's concerns at the time; in it, CKLN "committed to creating a stable management structure for the station, including the creation of a programming committee and hiring paid staff, both of which would be responsible for ensuring compliance and addressing complaints" (CRTC 2011a). Despite this optimism, the licensee did not implement a formalized process for dealing with complaints. No staff were hired, and the infighting persisted. The licence revocation also referenced the postponed public hearing. CKLN had been granted another chance to get things in order after the adjournment in May but had failed to do so. The commission determined CKLN's follow-up actions to be "insufficient and incomplete," and it did not have confidence that the licensee would be compliant in the future.

The move to revoke the licence was not without dissent. Commissioner Louise Poirier expressed her dissatisfaction in an amendment to the CRTC's decision. She argued that "immediate revocation, without first applying any other regulatory measure, is clearly inconsistent with the Commission's usual practice. No other licenses have been revoked in this manner in recent Commission history. Such revocations have always been preceded by either a mandatory order or a short-term license renewal" (CRTC 2011a). She also believed that CKLN had taken steps in the right direction and could have reached its goal of full compliance. She added that "despite a more problematic episode in 2009, CKLN-FM Toronto played, and up to now continued to play, a significant role in achieving" the commission's goal of providing balanced and varied programming choices (CRTC 2011a). Andrew Lehrer, a member of CKLN's board of directors, echoed Poirier's opinion. In an article about the licence revocation in the *Globe and Mail*, he disputed the CRTC's claim that the station was not addressing its concerns and explained that CKLN had worked to remedy its organizational issues by adopting new by-laws, improving equipment, and nearing the hiring of a new station manager (Melanson 2011). Poirier concluded her statement by arguing that the revocation had created a precedent she could not endorse. "Hastily revoking a campus radio station license in Toronto, Canada's biggest market," Poirier explained, "will not send a positive signal to the campus radio community, which consists of organizations comprised mainly of volunteers, who unstintingly contribute time and energy to give their community a voice" (CRTC 2011a).

Poirier's dissenting opinion raises important questions about what this licence revocation will mean for campus and community radio stations. CKLN's licence revocation may constitute a unique case, brought about by excessive and uncharacteristic non-compliance issues. At the same time, the decision suggests that campus stations in competitive radio markets are increasingly at risk of losing their frequencies in order to make room for commercial radio stations. CKLN's licence revocation is perhaps indicative of a more difficult future in which campus stations will need to continually and more aggressively justify their place on the FM dial.

CKLN was non-compliant with key regulations and conditions of licence. More importantly, it was not fulfilling its mandate as a community-based campus radio station. So there are clear limits to the freedom that community sector stations may exercise. These limits, however, ensure that community sector stations do not stray from their community-based mandates. Another question worth considering is whether CKLN would have lost its licence if it was not in Canada's biggest radio market, where FM frequencies are of notable value and where there happen to be two other campus FM stations. If CKLN was the only campus station in the area, would the CRTC have acted in accordance with Poirier's opinion on this matter? Poirier posited that the only "potential winners" of the licence revocation "could be future applicants who will have the opportunity to apply for CKLN-FM's very desirable frequency in the much sought after Toronto market" (CRTC 2011a). Shortly after the licence revocation, the CRTC began determining what would become of 88.1 FM in Toronto.

Commercial "Indie" Radio Takes Over

With CKLN off the air, the frequency of 88.1 became available in Toronto. The CRTC considered twenty-two proposals for a place on Toronto's FM radio dial. In the end, it chose the proposal by Rock 95 Broadcasting Ltd. Rock 95 was already operating two stations north of Toronto, in Barrie, Ontario, and its new Toronto station, Indie 88, would describe itself as "Toronto's first Indie station." When the commission announced that Rock 95 had won the frequency, it stated that applications had been assessed on quality of application in relation to the type of service proposed, the diversity of news voices, and the level of market impact. In the commission's opinion, "Rock 95's innovative proposal for an eclectic, Indie music format FM station focusing on emerging, independent artists from Canada and targeting a core audience of adults between the ages of 18 and 34 [would] add to the musical diversity of the market" (CRTC 2012a). The new station's condition of licence promised that 40 percent of popular music (category 2) selections would be Canadian and that 60 percent of these selections would be by emerging artists. Rock 95 also committed itself to programming 126 hours of local content per broadcast week. An emphasis on both emerging artists and local programming helped Indie 88 win the frequency. Interestingly, these are two key characteristics of campus radio programming, and Indie 88 did indeed replace a campus radio station on 88.1 FM. However, a commitment to emerging artists and local programming by a commercial radio station is rather loose in terms of how it is regulated. This vague policy framework enables commercial stations to play artists that simultaneously qualify as "emerging" and generate popular appreciation and financial success.

In 2011, the commission undertook to define "emerging artists" for both English- and French-language commercial stations. For English-language stations, an emerging artist was a Canadian artist who had never charted or reached a Top 40 position on music charts listed on "Schedule A" (popular music charts, including Canadian Music Network National Airplay, Billboard Hot 100 Singles, or Billboard Canadian Hot 100) or a Top 25 position on charts listed on "Schedule B" (country music charts, including The Record Country, RPM 100 Country Tracks, Canadian Music Network Country Top 50 Audience, Billboard Hot Country, or the Nielson BDS Country Spins). An artist would retain "Emerging Canadian Artist" status for thirty-six months from the date she or he had reached the charts. Originally, the CRTC had set a limit of twelve months after charting, but the Canadian Association of Broadcasters and the Canadian Independent Music Association argued for extending this period, thus enabling commercial stations to program a charting "emerging" artist for a longer period of time. French-language artists are considered "emerging" for six months since album sales have reached Gold Record status according to SoundScan or a period of forty-eight months has elapsed since the release of an artist's first commercially marketed album (CRTC 2011b). In terms of setting a Canadian emerging artist regulation, the commission deemed that Canadian commercial radio stations already program "a reasonable amount" of emerging music and that a "regulated minimum is not as necessary as many had once thought" (CRTC 2011b). In light of the attention given to emerging artists on commercial radio, it is no surprise that the commission was in favour of licensing a commercial music station that committed itself to programming high levels of Canadian emerging artists. Also, commercial stations are granted a lot of flexibility in terms of programming Canadian emerging artists, given that artists can retain "emerging" status for thirty-six months after charting. It is worth questioning the commercial sector's commitment to emerging Canadian artists given this policy framework, especially when considering the balance and diversity of a locality's radio stations and program offerings, as well as the overall makeup of Canada's broadcast system.

A commercial FM radio station in a market served by more than one private commercial radio station is required to devote one-third of the broadcast week to local programming. Local programming for commercial stations is defined by the CRTC as that which "includes programming that originates with the station or is produced separately and exclusively for the station" (CRTC 1993c). Local programming is not that which has been received from another station for rebroadcasting, nor is it network or syndicated programming that is five minutes or longer, unless produced by the station or by the local community in arrangement with the station. As part of a commercial station's local programming, licensees must include spoken-word content that is relevant to the community served. Examples of local spoken-word content provided by the commission include local news, weather, and sports and the promotion of local events; it does not include music produced by local artists. Also defined as local programming for commercial stations are disc jockey programs using a local announcer and assembled in the station studios; disc jockey programs using a voice-tracked announcer and assembled in station studios; brokered programs produced in the community for the station's use; programs produced outside the station studios for exclusive use by the station; and any news-cast or feature less than five minutes received from a network or syndicator (CRTC 1993c). Evidently, a commercial indie music station can promise 126 hours of local programming, but this content does not need to include musical selections by local artists.

Ryerson University also submitted a new application for the frequency to operate as a new entity, Radio Ryerson. During the public hearing that preceded the licensing of 88.1 to Rock 95, Sheldon Levy, the president of Ryerson University, told the commission that "Radio Ryerson is not just a new non-profit corporation. It is a new governance structure with an important role for volunteers from the community, from our student body and from the university administration" (CRTC 2012b). In response to Ryerson's submission, commissioner Peter Menzies questioned the need for another campus station in Toronto: "What specifically would you point to that Ryerson would introduce to the market in terms of diversity of sound experience that would add richness other than beyond an additional num-ber in a regulatory column?" (CRTC 2012b). Menzies also wondered why campus stations needed to be on the FM dial, pointing to "the democracy that takes place on the Internet" (CRTC 2012b). In Menzies's opinion, a new campus station would have little to offer beyond fulfilling the Broadcast-ing Act's requirement of having basic representation from public, private, and community elements within the overall radio broadcasting system. As long as there is one campus station in a given locality, the regulatory col-umns are sound and the radio market is "diverse." From this perspective, the not-for-profit nature of campus stations makes their presence on the valuable FM band suspect at best, especially with the opportunities offered by the Internet. However, as Shelley Robinson of the NCRA responded, the FM dial adds credibility to campus radio. Broadcasting on FM "means something. It comes along with all this training, it comes along with all this commitment and that's meaningful and people can listen to it" (CRTC 2012b). Ryerson University did not win the frequency back, but the univer-sity initiated the process of working towards establishing a new AM campus station (which it successfully accomplished by acquiring an AM licence in December 2014). An editorial in Ryerson's student newspaper, the *Ryerso-nian*, explained that the new "campus station will have students and staff on board. That alone provides enough reason to support this new venture." The new station's board will include six members from the Ryerson com-munity, including university officials and elected students, out of a total of nine seats (Smith 2013). This new broadcasting endeavour at Ryerson stems from a clear awareness of the need to maintain a balance between student and community representation in order to acquire a licence to operate.

Commissioner Menzies's comments overlook the range of musical styles and genres programmed by campus radio, as well as the varied perspectives offered through spoken-word and news programming. Indie 88 was commended by the commission because of its commitment to Canadian independent and emerging music, but the definitions of emerging and local programming for commercial radio enable stations to play "emerging" musical selections for three years after an artist reaches the charts. An "emerging" or "indie" music format that still relies on profitable and charting artists also ignores issues of range and diversity in musical selections. Rock 95's operations manager, Dave Carr, acknowledged the profitability of the artists that Indie 88 proposed to program when the company won the frequency. He claimed that "Indie artists are the industry stars of tomorrow and Indie 88.1 will simply help tomorrow come sooner" (Irish 2012). Jacky Tuinstra-Harrison, the president of Radio Ryerson in 2012, was critical of the loss of a campus radio station in Toronto and asked the commission: "If you were to license one of the triple A or Rock 95 applications, are we going to hear the hip hop, electronic, reggae, bhangra and all the other music that young people expect to hear if they are going to be drawn into a medium so many of them have abandoned? No, we aren't" (CRTC 2012b). Writing for the *Toronto Star*, Adrian Morrow recalled CKLN's history as a force of independent music and radical politics in Toronto for over three decades (Morrow 2011). A campus station in a culturally and musically diverse city offers more than just independent and emerging music; it features many other genres and styles that are not as profitable as Canadian indie rock and pop music.

A serious commitment to local culture and local music must go beyond simply programming new and emerging Canadian music – it requires the involvement of non-professionals and community members. The airwaves are a public good, as stated by the Broadcasting Act. How, then, do campus stations provide a local alternative beyond simply programming Canadian independent music? As Chapter 6 explains, campus stations extend into their localities by providing technical and informational resources to local musicians and cultural producers. There is a significant distinction between programming Canadian emerging artists and acting on a commitment to program artists from within a station's broadcast range.

The licence revocation of CKLN illustrates that campus stations must effectively implement a community-based mandate and that they must accomplish certain administrative tasks in order to maintain their licences. Leaving aside these stipulations and regulations, the specific composition of a locality factors prominently into the regulatory process, and so does the particular nature or culture of a campus station. Toronto is a diverse city, and its market is competitive and is served by a number of campus stations; these factors were cited throughout the proceeding that resulted in CKLN's licence revocation. A campus station's connection to the wider community, beyond its program offerings, is the focus of the next chapter. Exploring the place of a campus station within its locality will help us assess how the campus sector offers a local alternative that is attuned to the particularities of the localities it serves.

Campus and Community Radio Policy 2010

During the same year that CKLN-FM lost its broadcasting licence, the CRTC revised and updated its policy for the campus and community radio sector. A number of changes were implemented in the 2010 policy, including these: community and campus radio were brought together (again) under a single policy; the definitions of the campus and community sectors were revised; a new funding approach was taken, based on Canadian content development (CCD) contributions from commercial stations; and limits on advertising were eased. Representatives of the campus and community sector explained that they preferred that their stations not be defined in terms of content or as simply an "alternative" to other stations in a given market. They presented a number of defining characteristics that highlighted their sector's dynamic role in local communities. For them, programming was an important component of the sector not just because of how it sounded but also because it was a "product of the organizational structure of the stations." The sector's representatives also emphasized the "openness" of campus and community stations to community members, the training that stations made available, the volunteer component, and the sector's not-for-profit nature (CRTC 2010c).

Community representation was emphasized throughout the public hearings for the new policy. Kevin Matthews, the executive director of the NCRA, stated that the NCRA was proposing "a constructive definition and objectives for community-based campus and community radio, rather than one that is reactive." He added that campus stations define their sector in relation to community stakeholders, not to other broadcasting sectors (Matthews et al. 2010). He emphasized that community-based stations make room for community members to participate in station governance, management, operations, and programming. Most importantly, according to Matthews, the objectives of community-based stations go beyond programming. These stations provide "public access to the airwaves, skills training, a hub for community discourse, and various services to other community groups and members" (Matthews et al. 2010). By accentuating the various levels at which stations are connected to their communities – through participation, governance, and production – the NCRA argued effectively for a sector that did not simply broadcast local and Canadian music, but also enabled students and community members to share their voices and musical interests on the air.

One submission, by CKUT-FM at McGill University, stressed the importance of accessibility and training to the overall culture and operations of the sector. This submission asked the commission to consider underscoring the role that community-based campus stations play in training student and community members as radio producers and programmers (Cornell 2010). Training is essential to fulfilling a community-based mandate, the submission argued. CKUT also explained that the diversity of a station's surrounding communities must be continually emphasized by stations and by campus and community radio policy. CKUT added that it operates under the belief that diversity is a culture "and a way of operating; a value held by our institution and the people that work within it" (Cornell 2010). A number of local communities have been marginalized or ignored by mainstream media, and CKUT's submission explained that the campus and community sector must focus on issues of marginalization. The submission cited various communities for which the sector needs to provide a voice: ethnocultural minorities, Aboriginal peoples, peoples living with disabilities, working-class and poor people, LGBT people, women, youth, and elderly people (Cornell 2010). CKUT's intervention illustrated that station programming can be specifically crafted based on an awareness of marginalized groups within a station's broadcast range. With the appropriate CRTC policy, local and Canadian programming will be different and distinct within each locality, based on the needs of a given station and its communities. Thus, policy must allow for a relative level of autonomy so that each station can work with its volunteers to most effectively reflect and represent local musical and cultural activity.

The new policy grouped campus and community stations together, as did the 1992 policy, but it also acknowledged some important distinctions between the two. Campus and community stations share certain stipulations and policies: to ensure maximum use of Canadian-produced programming and local news and information, to broadcast local cultural and artistic expression, to promote emerging Canadian talent, and to broadcast local and regional content about social, economic, and community issues. Campus stations are distinguished from community stations by a number of factors: local programming is produced by student volunteers as well as by those from the broader community; the board of directors includes representatives from the campus administration, station volunteers, and the community at large; and student levies provide funding.

Instructional campus stations were abolished by the 2010 policy. At time of the new policy, only a few broadcast undertakings were licensed as such, and a new instructional station had not been licensed since 2007. According to the commission, the training provided by these stations could easily be done through unlicensed closed-circuit, carrier current, or Internet-based stations, and thus it decided to no longer license instructional stations. The submission from the University of Ottawa's CHUO had recommended removing instructional stations from the FM dial, for spectrum scarcity "is becoming a major problem in the campus and community sector" (Kepman 2010). The removal of instructional stations raises the profile of campus stations with a community mandate. For a campus station to broadcast on the FM dial, a strong community mandate was deemed essential.

Spectrum scarcity was a key issue raised by the joint submission from the NCRA/ANREC, *l'ARC du Canada*, and *l'ARC du Québec*. Their submission recommended that frequency protection be provided to low-power community stations and that commercial applications that may disrupt a low-power community station provide financial and technical assistance to that low-power station. The three organizations also suggested that FM frequencies be reserved in markets that were not adequately served by community or campus stations, so that new stations could be licensed in these areas (Matthews et al. 2010). On these matters, the commission responded that reserving frequencies fell outside its jurisdiction. However, to help low-power campus and community stations ensure that they were given notice of potential technical interference by new commercial stations, the commission would require new licence applicants to answer questions on their application forms regarding whether and how notice would be given to any low-power or community stations that might be affected (CRTC 2010c).

With respect to spectrum scarcity, the Canadian Association of Broadcasters suggested that for campus stations in the future, the AM band was viable, as was the Internet. This echoed Menzies's comments (cited earlier) in response to Ryerson's reapplication for 88.1 FM. The CAB represents private broadcasters, so clearly it favoured having commercial stations occupy valuable FM frequencies. Their submission was strongly against the recommendation that spectrum be reserved for campus and community stations: "Given the scarcity of FM spectrum, and issues related to this congestion, we consider that the use of AM frequencies or Internet radio stations for campus and community radio represents a more viable alternative" (CAB 2010). In response, Freya Zaltz, the NCRA's regulatory affairs director, raised the crucial point that the Internet is unregulated and is not based on geography. Therefore, online broadcasting undermines the social and local role of community-based campus stations (Matthews et al. 2010). This exchange between the CAB and the NCRA reflects the fact that highly valuable spectrum in competitive radio markets is assumed, by commercial radio proponents, to be less appropriate for not-for-profit, community radio.

Programming requirements were also slightly revised: the 2010 policy decreased the minimum requirement for spoken-word programming during each broadcast week to 15 percent from the previous 25 percent, which would be locally produced. Also, it was suggested that the level of Canadian content for category 2 (Popular Music) be increased from 35 to 40 percent. The commission described this suggestion as a "preliminary view" on its part and said it would issue a call for comments as to whether this would be appropriate (CRTC 2010c). An increase in Canadian content for category 3 (Specialty) musical selections was also proposed, from 12 to 15 percent.

Some parties, including CKUW at the University of Winnipeg, expressed apprehension about the requirement that 5 percent of all weekly musical selections be from category 3, arguing that this category "rarely meets the needs of the communities served." Others claimed that finding volunteers to "provide and produce such programming is problematic" (CRTC 2010c). *Association québécoise de l'industrie du disque, du spectacle et de la vidéo* (ADISQ), a not-for-profit organization that supports the music industry in Quebec, felt that campus and community radio should be offering specialty music in order to ensure diversity of music broadcasting. The commission determined that campus and community stations were regularly exceeding this requirement and that the majority of the category was being produced locally by volunteers. Thus, the commission deemed it fair to assume that communities have an interest in this content, and the 5 percent requirement remained.

Under the heading "Experimental Music," the 2010 policy stated that the commission had previously acknowledged (in Public Notice 2000-12) that turntablism and radio art are forms of artistic expression that "could be" significant parts of the programming at some stations. At that time, however, there was not enough input to "properly define those forms of artistic expression for the purpose of Canadian content requirements" (CRTC 2010c). The submission from CFRU-FM at the University of Guelph was in favour of an experimental music category and questioned the existing content categories for popular music selections. CFRU's submission read: "There is a question as to whether we are working within commercial categories, but being required to play different music than commercial broadcasters" (Ziniuk 2010). CFRU asked the commission to create a content category for experimental music that would include turntablism, sound art, and noise. Following a consultative process, the commission defined "Experimental Music" in the 2010 policy as

> the unconventional and non-traditional uses of instruments and sound equipment to create new sounds and an orchestration of these sounds. This includes audio-art, turntablism, *musique actuelle*, electro acoustic and sound ecology. While it may involve the use of previously recorded sounds to create new sounds and orchestrations, it does not include spinning or beat mixing where the alterations of previously recorded tracks are limited to mixes between two or more pieces or samples. (CRTC 2010c)

The commission explained that when measuring Canadian content for experimental music, the "artist" would be considered Canadian if the turntablist or sound artist was Canadian. If the recording was the result of collaboration, at least half the collaborators would need to be Canadian.

According to the 2010 policy revision, funding was the central concern for campus stations (CRTC 2010c). A number of financial challenges were described by the sector, including low advertising revenues, copyright tariffs, and the fact that some post-secondary institutions had removed levies on student fees to support stations. The commission fielded a number of proposals for mediating funding issues and, despite some apprehension about the commercial sector funding the campus and community sector, determined that commercial stations (including ethnic stations and spoken-word stations) earning over $1.25 million would contribute 15 percent of their basic annual Canadian Content Development contribution to the Community Radio Fund of Canada. This amount was reallocated from contributions that would normally have been made to FACTOR or MusicAction, two organizations that support Canadian recording artists (CRTC 2010c). This resolution avoided increasing the overall CCD contributions that commercial stations are responsible for; instead, it drew from two organizations that were deemed financially stable. Private broadcasters had argued against any increases to CCD contributions, as well as against setting up a "rigid funding system at the national level when community broadcasting is focused on the local level" (CAB 2010). The commission's decision to reallocate funds from within the already established CCD percentages would help to resolve the CAB's concerns. The commission also removed the four minutes of advertising per hour restriction; campus stations would be allowed to concentrate advertising during certain hours or days as long as they broadcast no more than 504 minutes of advertising per week. The CRTC's campus radio advertising policy of 1993 had stipulated that campus stations would be permitted to broadcast up to 504 minutes of advertising per week with a maximum of four minutes in any one hour

(CRTC 1993c). Within the weekly 504 minutes, a maximum of 126 minutes could be "conventional advertising"; the remainder had to conform to a definition of "restricted advertising," which prohibited statements referring to "convenience, durability and desirability or contain other comparative or competitive references" (CRTC 1993c).

During the 2010 review, the NCRA asked the CRTC to consider developing a Code of Practice for the campus and community radio sector, one that would be developed through a collaboration with the Canadian public and that would address practices for diversity, programming standards, and content guidelines. This proposed code echoed the submission made by McGill University's CKUT, which stressed that diversity was "a value held by our institution and the people that work within it. Respecting, encouraging and creating space for diverse people, ideas, music and languages should be fostered in all aspects of [campus/community] institutions" (Cornell 2010). However, the commission determined that it did not have enough information to decide whether a code for the campus and community sector was appropriate. The NCRA was directed to develop and submit the code so that the commission could issue a notice for public comment.

The 2010 policy also emphasized the significance of localism to the sector, in terms of Canadian music development as well as spoken-word programming (the overall percentage required was decreased, but locally produced content was stressed). Canadian content increases for music from both categories 2 and 3 were recommended, and new funding initiatives were acknowledged, with the funds to be rerouted from already existing funds for Canadian talent development. Although CKLN's licence revocation reminds us that campus stations in competitive radio markets need to be especially careful about meeting fundamental policy requirements, the 2010 policy revision demonstrates the campus sector's important role as a local resource for new independent artists. The sector maintains an awareness of innovative musical styles and genres, as evidenced by the inclusion of sound art and turntablism in the new policy.

The license revocation of CKLN-FM and the 2010 policy revision for the campus and community radio sector highlight the importance of a community-based mandate for campus stations. In the former instance, non-compliance and disorganization had placed CKLN's community mandate and broadcast licence in jeopardy. The licence was revoked because the station had failed to provide a timeline for compliance and to foster partnerships with the academic institution and wider community. A community-based mandate sets campus and community stations apart as a local alternative to commercial and public stations. Proponents of the sector emphasized the role of campus stations in their communities in terms of providing access to marginalized communities, offering technical training, and promoting openness. In contrast, commercial stations do not operate with a community-based mandate and they are largely moving away from local programming. Indie 88 may have replaced CKLN on 88.1, but the regulation of commercial stations enables them to program charting artists for three years as "emerging." More importantly, commercial stations do not make an effort to create content for a diverse array of communities, let alone the marginalized communities cited by CKUT in the 2010 policy revision.

A community-based mandate distinguishes the campus and community sector from the commercial sector. The previous chapter pointed out that a licence to operate on the FM band ties a campus station to a community-based mandate. As indicated by the 2010 policy renewal, this mandate remains a significant defining trait of the sector. The next chapter continues this trajectory by acknowledging the ways in which campus stations are in tune with local musical and cultural communities in more ways than through the programming of local music. Surely "alternativeness" and community responsibility figure into the culture of campus radio beyond being mentioned in policy documents and mandates to ensure difference and distinctiveness from commercial and public broadcasting. The relationship between campus stations and other nodes in a music scene is connected along discourse that strategically deploys terms and concepts such as "alternative" and "independent," yet the links implicit in this relationship are much more dynamic than descriptions and definitions of diverse and experimental radio programming.

6

Canadian Campus Radio and Local Musical Activity

Canadian campus radio stations are required to abide by key conditions and regulations that have been established and are enforced in a comprehensive policy for the sector. Non-compliance issues at Ryerson's CKLN-FM eventually resulted in the station losing its licence, in conjunction with other factors, such as the station's inability to balance student and community representation. The community-based mandate has figured prominently in the governance of the campus radio sector, for it helps distinguish campus stations from public and commercial ones. For instance, a focus on local and independent music ensures that campus stations do not program commercially successful songs of the kind that private sector radio stations rely on to secure revenue from advertisers. The community-based mandate of campus stations is interpreted and acted on in distinct ways from station to station. A locality's demographics and its cultural components significantly shape the culture of an individual station. Besides ensuring compliance with key policy stipulations, such as filing program schedules and maintaining Canadian content quotas, the CRTC regulates the campus sector in a manner that enables a campus station to tailor its policy to fit the needs of its communities.

Canadian campus stations navigate CRTC broadcasting policy through internal policies, such as a station mandate or philosophy. Internal policies and guiding philosophies shape the culture of campus stations and grant them a level of autonomy so that they can tune their programming and operations to local musical and cultural communities. The station's locality determines the diversity of its programming grid, so if some segments of a population identify with a certain cultural or ethnic group, or speak a certain language, there is a good chance that some of the station's programming will reflect this. How a locality's demographics are understood by the station's staff and volunteers does much to shape the station's programming, so it is important to understand how some communities are recognized by the station and others are not. In Chapter 4, Sarah Michaelson explained that some communities are not entirely familiar or comfortable with the university space. By her account, CKUW is aware that more effort needs to be made to represent and reflect such communities. This is a significant issue to keep in mind.

Links between a locality and a campus station are forged on both a practical level and an imagined one. Often, connections between campus radio practitioners and cultural producers fall along ideological lines – for example, through participating in an "alternative" or "independent" culture. This ideological positioning is not surprising, given that a commitment to local culture and music is a distinguishing characteristic of campus radio in Canada, especially relative to commercial radio. The connections between a campus station and its cultural communities inspire a closer look at the localities served by CHMA in Sackville, CKUW in Winnipeg, and CiTR in Vancouver, including the physical places that are described as integral to musical activity within the locality. A focus on a cultural community or locality – that is, on a geographic space that includes one or multiple musical and cultural communities, consisting of a variety of individuals with various ties and connections to the geographic space in question and to elsewhere – is an effective method for locating how the campus sector offers radio practitioners, cultural producers, and listeners a local alternative within the Canadian broadcasting system. In what ways, then, are relationships initiated and sustained between campus stations and local cultural institutions? And how do these connections circulate and promote local music and culture?

A locality is characterized by the social, cultural, and political milieu of a city or town. These factors also shape one's perceptions of a locality's music scene. A music scene is the result of the cultural and musical communities within a locality; it is a conceptual and geographic space that enters the popular imaginary through discourses and documentation, as well as through sounds that are both produced locally and from afar. Sara Cohen outlines the significant connections between place and musical activity, with a focus on popular music-making in Liverpool. She argues that the bands and the music scene those bands participate in reflect "not only characteristics of the music business in general, but those of Liverpool itself" (1991, 19). Cohen approaches her study of music-making in a locality by detailing the connections between individuals and cultural institutions, as well as the social and cultural lifestyles and practices within a music scene. These connections and practices constitute ideas about a particular scene in a given time and place. In a large country like Canada, it is productive to explore musical activity in relation to a specific city or town instead of attempting to locate a certain level of "Canadian-ness" that might be reproduced across a range of local scenes. A focus on musical activity within a given locality must also identify global musical and cultural flows, which are embedded in the connections and practices in a locality. The local is a part of the global, just as the global is involved in the local (Storey 2003, 117). However, each locality is going to negotiate the global in a different way that is determined by a variety of factors, including cultural demographics and histories and the infrastructure and support offered to local cultural and musical production and circulation. Because each locality is distinct, it is going to influence and shape the programming, operations, and culture of a campus station in its own way. At a time when the commercial broadcasting sector is increasingly consolidated in both ownership and program offerings, and because of the CBC's mandate to foster and sustain a national cultural identity, a locality's influence on a campus radio station is a key factor with regard to how the campus sector offers a local alternative.

This chapter results from campus visits to CHMA, CKUW, and CiTR in the summer of 2011. Along with each station's studio space, the corresponding city or town was explored, with close attention paid to what was happening musically. Interviews with campus radio practitioners and local music-makers are combined with analyses of cultural productions such as local magazines. All of this accompanies the discussion of policy in the previous chapters. A campus radio station's culture and operations shape and are shaped by policy, so these other realms are necessary complements when examining how the campus sector operates.

The individuals interviewed for this chapter have contributed to my project by pointing out objects and documents in an archive or in a collection of publications. Interviews with people who work in the campus sector help us understand how station mandates and philosophies are negotiated and integrated into musical and cultural practices. As well, during interviews with radio practitioners and cultural producers, a number of venues and cultural institutions became recurring points of discussion. These individuals were well versed in the city or town and in particular genres of music and culture happening in it, and they were able to locate places that maintain close connections with their local campus station. Three cultural objects are profiled toward the end of this chapter: one collaborative com-pilation album that demonstrates the partnership of CiTR and Vancouver's Mint Records; and two publications produced by CKUW and CiTR: *Stylus* and *Discorder*, respectively. When these methods are combined, a sense of each station's culture emerges and of that culture's role in shaping the sta-tion's understanding of its related music scenes and communities.

A music scene as a cultural space can be social *and* geographic, as explained by Holly Kruse, who defines independent music scenes as those that are "best understood as being constituted through the practices and relationships that are enacted within the social and geographical spaces they occupy" (2003, 1). Focus should not be placed on defining a given cultural space as belonging to this or that genre, but rather on "examining the ways in which particular musical practices 'work' to produce a sense of community within the conditions of metropolitan music scenes" (Straw 1991, 373). So one should emphasize the connections between musical sites or institutions, the people involved with them, and the resulting "work" that produces and defines a particular notion of a music scene, which may or may not be specific to one or more genres or styles.

Music scenes result from processes of documentation, such as the recording of music and the writing of articles that comment on musical activity. A number of technologies are implicit in these processes, which both sustain the circulation of music and form an idea of what a locality's music scene sounds like. In other words, a scene can refer both to lived, everyday musical practices and to the perceived sound of a city or town, a sound that is part of its popular imaginary. The place of technology has been explored in a number of studies of music scenes, such as Anthony Kwame Harrison's work on cassette tapes and DIY recording practices in the San Francisco Bay Area underground hip-hop movement, which emerged as a "response to the commercial rap music industry's unwavering commitment to gangsta rap imagery and themes" (2006, 285). Documentation through DIY recording practices helped sustain this underground movement. Simi-larly, campus radio stations are sites where technical resources are provided to scene participants with different skill levels so that they can document and record cultural expression. Scenes, then, depend not only on musical and cultural output but also on institutional spaces where individuals can converse, discover new music, and learn how to produce media. Campus radio stations help sustain local music scenes, and this is a key reason why campus radio offers a local alternative to cultural producers, musicians, and listeners.

Behind the documentation of cultural expression are participants who are central to the construction and perception of a music scene and who move in and out of prominent cultural institutions. These participants often act as cultural intermediaries or gatekeepers, in that they generate and circulate discourses that connect culture to ideas and beliefs that are caught up in concepts of value and credibility (Gendron 2002, 155). They contribute to framing not only what is heard and seen but also how culture is heard and seen. Pierre Bourdieu argued that "the sociology of art and literature has to take as its object not only the material production but also the symbolic production of the work, i.e. the production of the value of the work or, which amounts to the same thing, of belief in the value of the work" (1986/1993, 37). He wrote that artists and cultural producers must choose the most appropriate place to publish or display their work. This is of vital importance to an author or artist, because for each "production and product, there is a corresponding natural site in the field of production, and producers or products that are not in their right place are more or less bound to fail" (95). This idea is useful for thinking about how terms like "alternative" and "independent" connect campus stations to other alternative and local cultural institutions, for it foregrounds the capacity for judgments in value and taste to determine which types of music, art, and culture get labelled "alternative" or "independent" and worthy of local attention. These symbolic decisions influence and shape a music scene.

Cultural gatekeepers, and intermediaries such as radio DJs and record store employees, construct musical cultures and the scenes in which they circulate, establishing which musical forms and styles are *in* and which are *out*. This process of distinction weaves through the musical discourse and cultural and institutional sites in a music scene. The creative output of musical communities helps form a scene through the discourses of distinction and evaluation produced by cultural intermediaries. As well, the individuals involved in circulating "alternative" and "independent" culture often frame that work in opposition to, or through an understanding of, more dominant expressions of music and culture. There is an "anti-mainstream" disposition at the core of genres like alternative and independent (or indie) music. Simon Frith argues that genres like indie really only make sense within this dichotomy (1996, 87). This idea extends from similar binaries in the realm of popular music, such as "rock" versus "pop." Rock is largely perceived to be "masculine" and "authentic"; pop is considered "feminine" and "artificial" (Frith and McRobbie 1990; Coates 1997, 52). The "authentic" and the "credible" are at odds with what is popular, mainstream, commercial, or easy to digest. This is not to suggest that campus and community radio practitioners and programs fall within this idea that "authentic" equals "masculine" or "male," although Sheila Nopper, who worked at CIUT in Toronto in the mid-1990s, recounts that at that time, "there were no music programs that focused on women's music" (Nopper 2010, 56). Also, "alternativeness" is being explored here in relation to the ways in which campus radio is engaged with local musical production, and cultural practices that are distinct from the more dominant private and public radio sectors, as opposed to the ways that "alternative" has been used by various parties to define a genre of music. This chapter shows how the campus radio sector has engaged with issues of diversity and inclusivity. Simultaneously, the sector strives to realize its mandate of community representation while also realizing that some groups are still underrepresented in programming and participation. Moreover, as commercial radio becomes less relevant to localities, the musical and cultural activity of a locality can be discovered and expressed through local and independent cultural production.

Connections between campus radio stations, other cultural institutions (venues and record stores), and cultural productions (magazines, weblogs, etc.) are apparent on many interrelated levels. There are connections made within the cultural histories of the stations and in the stories recounted by radio practitioners and cultural producers. As well, the relationships between campus stations and cultural institutions are evident within the content generated by cultural productions like magazines, show posters, and promotional materials. This content circulates in print, on the Internet, throughout the town or city (a show poster on a telephone pole, for instance), and within performance and exhibition spaces. These connections demonstrate the place of campus radio stations within a broader conception of a music scene and the overall music-making taking place in a locality; they also contribute to how a music scene is constructed, sustained, and ideologically framed by notions of localness, independence, and alternativeness. Thus, interviews with station staff, volunteers, and cultural producers highlight a number of links between campus radio stations and local musical activity. These links contribute to how music scenes are imagined in both the present and the past. Some of these stories recall a particular history or story about the station's development in relation to an institution, production, or performance; others comment on the station's contemporary place in relation to its surrounding music scene. A campus station's culture is very much about its prominent role within a locality and as a communication outlet that enables community participation.

CHMA and Sackville: Music Festivals and an East Coast Cultural Hub

Sackville, New Brunswick, has a population of just over 5,500, organized more or less around one major intersection. Mount Allison University is at about the halfway point between the centre of town and the Trans-Canada Highway, a major route through the East Coast provinces. The campus is geographically and culturally central to the town, and Sackville's music venues (and the places that sometimes double as music venues) are close to one another. Ducky's is a bar just off the corner of Main and Bridge streets, the town's main intersection. CHMA's station manager Pierre Malloy described the bar as a local watering hole where people congregate for drinks on the weekend and after classes or work. The Live Bait Theatre is at the same intersection, but across the street, and is sometimes used for live music. The same intersection is also home to Thunder & Lightning Ltd., a multi-purpose arts and culture space that has become a central spot for much of Sackville's musical activity. Thunder & Lightning is the home office of the large East Coast music festival SappyFest. Though the space is not all that large, it sells records and hosts intimate live shows. The town's most active live music venue is George's Roadhouse on Lorne Street, and just north of it is Struts Gallery. Struts is an artist-run centre that is used for a variety of purposes, including art exhibitions and discussions, and it occasionally hosts live music. Essentially, all of these places are within walking distance of one another. In a short walk through the town, one can easily pass by all of these venues. Given the university's size and prominence in the town, the station easily maintains a close connection to all of these venues and bars that regularly host live music. This large number of cultural venues in such a small town justifies Sackville's 2008 designation of "cultural capital of Canada" by the Department of Canadian Heritage, as well as its role as a regional cultural hub.

Pierre Malloy emphasized the centrality of local business owner Darren Wheaton in terms of the town's local music scene. Wheaton owns George's Roadhouse, Ducky's, and the town's foundry, which according to Malloy "is like the old industry legacy of Sackville" (Malloy, personal interview, 3 June 2011). Malloy said that a lot of money used to come through Sackville, which was once famous for providing the hay that was used to feed horses during the Boer War in South Africa. Malloy expressed his admiration for the Wheaton family and the work that Darren has done in Sackville. George's was once a tavern that would have "the odd blues and/or rock band play from time to time." CHMA started to book shows at George's, which led to more touring bands inquiring about booking gigs at the tavern. Malloy explained that shortly afterwards, a man named Paul Henderson moved to town and began to book the types of bands he wanted to hear, including musicians he knew from Edmonton and Calgary. "He knew a lot of what was new and what was indie ... He started to bring people up as they were passing through and booking them tours." As interest in live music at George's increased, Darren put more money into the tavern. Darren "built a stage, lights, a smoke machine, and now it's like rock central."

Malloy's comments indicate that CHMA has a reciprocal relationship with George's and other local venues: each side benefits from the existence and operations of the other. "We have a really good relationship with George's. It's mutually beneficial. It's kind of like, we bring the party to them, and they make beer sales. And they're really nice to all of the people who come through, all of the bands. And then we hire Darren to do sound." Struts Gallery is another performance space in Sackville, described by Malloy as the local artist-run centre and gallery. "We've had a really good relationship with them over the years. It's the same group of people, basically, who are involved here and involved there." The gallery is a venue where CHMA promotes or programs all-ages shows and shows that attract a limited number of attendees. "If we're expecting a crowd of twenty-to-forty people, we'll have it at Struts, and if we're expecting a hundred or two hundred people, we'll have it at George's." Sackville is also home to a number of places that are not typical venues for live music but that have served this purpose from time to time, largely because of initiatives at CHMA. Malloy explained that during music festivals, the station "initiated the whole idea of using alternate spaces," like rock shows at the United Church during Stereophonic. "We just bring stuff and set it up, and in the last couple of years we've started using the chapel because the church is in really bad shape and we don't want the roof falling on the audience. So we're always looking for new and interesting places." The station has done shows at the old Vogue Theatre in town, which "is like a 1940s movie theatre." In a small town with only a few performance spaces suitable for live music, these "alternate spaces" enable CHMA staff and volunteers to host festivals and live events that could not be held if they relied solely on venues like George's and Struts.

Musician and former Mount Allison student Pat LePoidevin remembers his time as a student in Sackville as "almost legendary" (LePoidevin, personal interview, June 3, 2011). His experience also hints at the connections between CHMA and the surrounding music scene, which he found to be important during his time as a student. LePoidevin was in a "class with a whole bunch of peers and friends who were really gunning for the same opportunities and the same situations." On weekends, he and his friends would frequent George's Roadhouse. The venue was "an old bar/roadhouse place. A beautiful, beautiful place." His group of friends "grew" alongside the venue. He and his friends would approach bands that were travelling through town, and he would offer them a show to play and a place to stay. LePoidevin reaffirmed Malloy's comments about the prominence of alternative performance spaces in the town. He used to live with six others in a "big old Victorian mansion on Bridge Street," and they would "put on shows there all the time because it was such a show-friendly house with a big downstairs area." LePoidevin also emphasized the importance of CHMA as a production space for new and independent artists. He described himself as a folk musician who had always been involved with music, but it was coming to Mount Allison and getting connected with CHMA that really helped him establish himself as an artist. "There's been one huge thing that has made me focus on what I want to do, and that's the radio station. Actually, in the production studio here at CHMA is where I recorded my first album, called *Blue Tornadoes*, like four years ago." He was a volunteer and a programmer at the station, and he also used the station space for recording. When he toured his first album, he used the connections he had made through the campus station. A lot of campus community radio stations "work in a similar way, so they'll understand a lot more when albums are coming from a radio station directly to other campus-community stations. It's that effect of sharing, or a network that automatically occurs." Having benefited from the resources and connections that CHMA offered, LePoidevin now makes a point of advertising and mentioning the station "everywhere he goes," and he has thanked CHMA on each album he has produced.

CHMA is also central to the promotion and circulation of music and culture. Programming director Sandy Mackay said that CHMA is "integral" to the Sackville music scene and that there would not even "be a music scene without CHMA" (Mackay, personal interview, 3 June 2011). Before the annual music festival SappyFest took off and "became the entity that it is now," the station really was "the hub of everything." Now, "SappyFest has an office [at Thunder & Lightning] and it has office hours, and Paul Henderson is doing a lot more local stuff, and that sort of shifted to become more of a hub for the music scene." But CHMA is still a very important place for promoting and sustaining music in Sackville, evidenced by such initiatives as creating free posters for any show in town. Mackay explained that the show's promoter usually designs the poster and the station then prints it out for free, although the station also offers a free design service for people who need it. All of these individuals, organizations, and institutions work together, and there's a "really nice balance in town that is maintained through [the station] and SappyFest and the rabid concert-goers."

CHMA has been a strong supporter of SappyFest as the festival has grown over the years. In the festival's inaugural year, the station donated about half the cost for the festival's first paid employee. The station still helps the festival with promotions and posters, as well as ongoing on-air promotion. "Plus," Malloy added, "we often train the people they hire. The girl who's working SappyFest this summer was the Stereophonic coordinator last year." Stereophonic is a smaller festival than SappyFest and is programmed and promoted by CHMA. As Malloy explained, the "Stereophonic festival is ours. We started it in 2004. The first year I was here was the first one, January 2004. And, we've been doing it every year since." The festival originated after a lot of musicians travelling the East Coast for other festivals were looking for venues and places to play outside of the one-hundred-mile radius of Halifax. Bands playing in Halifax are often not allowed to play in nearby locations for a specific amount of time before and after their gig, as stipulated by show promoters. Similar stipulations apply to Moncton. So CHMA's music director at the time suggested hosting shows for these bands. He listed all the bands he wanted to play Sackville, and Malloy proposed having a festival so that he could program them all. Before Stereophonic, according to Malloy, CHMA was organizing "every little rock show that was coming through town and [the station] was losing money, every time." Malloy attributed this inability to break even to a lack of proper promotion and to the fact that bands often insisted on large guarantees that the station could not afford. It reached the point where the station felt it could no longer program live music, so CHMA became more of a promoter and information hub for booking agents and artists. However, the station decided to continue programming shows, but only in the context of a music festival. The first Stereophonic lasted for just two days and featured ten bands. In the festival's second and third years, it increased in size, and by the fourth year, it was featuring between twenty and thirty bands over the course of a week, a scale it has since maintained with varying levels of success each year.

The Stereophonic festival prioritizes Maritime independent music. During one year, an organizer from Ontario was really pushing to program a large percentage of bands from Ontario. Malloy had to emphasize to this person the festival's focus on "Maritime independent" music, though bringing in a band or two from Toronto that did not "require a thousand dollars for travel" was okay (Malloy 2011). They work to keep the festival local and "try to have at least one local act on every show, often two, and this then lets bands from Halifax, Cape Breton, and Prince Edward Island perform with them." The station equates "local" with "Sackville," not nearby cities like Moncton. Most of the local bands playing the festival are comprised of Mount Allison students, and Malloy figures that an increase in student bands is directly related to the fact that festivals like SappyFest and Stereophonic provide a platform for local music. "When I first arrived, and when we did the first couple of festivals, we would try to get university people, like 'do you have a band?' but nobody had bands. And now, it's like, 'How many Mount A bands *are* there?'"

Besides the many local bands that form at the university and play at Sackville's music festivals, the town attracts bands from other Canadian towns and cities. LePoidevin recalled that "there were bands that would come through Sackville and some would have a lot of hold," like the Rural Alberta Advantage. He remembers the band coming to town in their "early stages" and "a bunch of people just really loved it. So when they came back, they just *stuck* in the town. The Rural Alberta Advantage was just the band that everyone listened to in Sackville." LePoidevin would then play the band during his airtime on CHMA, further promoting the group to listeners in Sackville and to Mount Allison University students. "A lot of musicians coming through town influence what is played on the radio, I think. If you look at the charts – the weekly charts – usually you can actually line up the shows that are happening in the town to who's charting. So, if, for example, Rural Alberta Advantage was going to play a show here, they'd be charting the week before, usually." LePoidevin fondly recalled being a local artist who had the chance to open for some "really amazing" touring bands, like Toronto-based Justin Rutledge and Rock Plaza Central. For him, a key characteristic that sets Sackville apart as a live music town is that it could "never have an insular local scene that is all on its own. What's always going to happen in Sackville is that the shows are often going to be touring bands, which is so cool." This is the "great thing about living in a small town. That fear of an insular crowd that only watches local acts, that can't happen because there are just not enough people."

Sackville's modest population means that the music scene requires out-of-town bands to remain vibrant. But the students at Mount Allison play their part as well, as music fans or as musicians in local acts. Le-Poidevin's comments hint that the station depends on touring bands in terms of shaping the programming habits of radio show hosts. It is noteworthy that Sackville's connections to other cities and towns, and to the bands and artists from those places, are not randomly determined. East Coast bands often perform in Sackville, as do touring Canadian bands headed for the city of Halifax. Another interesting connection that was pointed out during the interviews at CHMA is one between Dawson City and Sackville. A former music director of CHMA is now the artistic director for the Dawson City Music Festival. Also, the station's latest music director was hired as the assistant artistic director for Dawson City's festival. Sandy Mackay noted that there is a long and storied past between the two towns. One explanation involves Shotgun Jimmie and Fred Squire from Shotgun and Jaybird, artists who became fairly prominent on the Sackville and East Coast music scenes. The two, who had been living in Dawson, went away on tour. Their van broke down in Sackville, and "they called their friends in Dawson, and people sort of went back and forth for years" (Mackay 2011). The "towns are almost identical, both small towns with seasonal populations. People go there in the summer and leave in the winter. Here, everyone comes in the winter and leaves in the summer. Similar sort of socio-economic strata I guess – artist types and people just making enough to get by."

Malloy synthesized the various connections between CHMA and local music in Sackville. CHMA has managed to "really create a sense of community, that musical community, especially with Stereophonic and SappyFest and all of the independent shows that happen in between. It's nuts here," and in the "last few years it's just been going up and getting really good." The station's role in the music scene relies on the station's volunteers and staff. "Some years we get people who are really motivated and we know it's going to be an easy year. They're going to do a lot of work and get a lot of people involved." Other years, "you might get a bunch of shy nerds, and we know this isn't going to be the year where we recruit a lot of people, but maybe we can get a bunch of technical stuff fixed. It's a balance, and very dependent on whom we have. It's the people who do it."

The interviewees at CHMA displayed ample knowledge of the interrelated cultural histories of the station and the music scene in Sackville, as demonstrated by the stories they told about the transformation of George's from a tavern to a live music venue. The station also makes use of alternative performance spaces, from old churches to large student homes that host shows. The station contributes to the production of music in Sackville by providing studio space for artists, a space seemingly appropriate for recording an album early in one's career (an opportunity that Pat LePoidevin seized). CHMA is involved in the performance of live music in Sackville through the programming and promotion of Stereophonic and by providing resources like funding and trained personnel for SappyFest. Furthermore, the station creates posters for live shows and is a hub of information and support for touring bands and artists. CHMA's programmers and hosts promote live gigs on air, and their programming practices are often inspired by the music of touring acts, as evidenced by LePoidevin playing Rural Alberta Advantage after hearing them live. Students in Sackville are central to the circulation of music in the town because their attendance at live shows is crucial for sustaining the music scene, as is their participation in the local bands that are required to provide support for touring acts. That Sackville is a small town anchors the station's strong connection to various facets of local music-making and performance, and its location – close enough to Moncton and Halifax, but distant enough for show promoters and bookers to allow a band to play the night before or after visiting these cities – makes the town an ideal spot for touring bands to stop and perform.

CKUW and Winnipeg: Isolation and Collaboration in Music Production and Mythmaking

In terms of the number of active cultural and musical institutions in the city, Winnipeg is significantly larger than Sackville. Just northeast of the University of Winnipeg is the Exchange District, an area with many small restaurants and retail stores. Into the Music, a prominent Winnipeg record store, is located in the Exchange, as is the Royal Albert, a live music venue that has had a central role in the Winnipeg punk and rock scene for decades. South of the Exchange, amid the downtown bars and clubs, is the Pyramid Cabaret, a larger music venue that hosts a variety of bands, DJs, and events. Farther south across the river is Osborne Village, a strip of Osborne Street that features shops and a number of restaurants and bars, including The Cavern, a venue under a pub. There is also Ozzy's, a basement venue located in a hotel, which features heavy metal and punk music. Of course, the city is home to many other places that feature live music, as well as to a few record stores, but during interviews with station staff and volunteers, the locations mentioned here were often cited as maintaining strong connections to CKUW. These are venues that have shaped the development of CKUW and helped the station branch out into the wider Winnipeg music scene.

CKUW is well connected to venues in the city, as well as to record stores that have been influential in the promotion and circulation of music. The station has a strong presence in cultural events and music festivals, and Winnipeg is a city where indoor music production and rehearsal occurs frequently. A notion of isolation and collaboration permeates and shapes the connections between institutional spaces, and this is evident in the city's musical mythology. In late 2012, Matt Schellenberg of the Winnipeg-based band Royal Canoe wrote an article for the *Spectator Tribune* on the "life cycle of a cool city," where something originally "real" eventually becomes "fetishized." Citing examples like Brooklyn and Portland, Schellenberg argued that Winnipeg, instead, has "what everyone is searching for. A bunch of people holed up in their basements during godforsaken cold-as-hell winter making art no-one will ever see or hear." He maintains that because the city is isolated (in his words, a "shithole"), it will never be discovered or enjoyed ironically: "It's all ours." Within the city itself, musical communities are connected to the station, and individuals with various musical tastes often collaborate with one another. Programmers at CKUW emphasized how certain radio shows are often connected to a musical community in the city or to a certain subgenre of music. The host is able to bring to the airwaves a particular understanding of a certain genre or segment of the city's music scene.

Rob Schmidt, CKUW's long-time station manager, provided an overview of the many festivals the station has been involved with. One festival in particular, the send + receive festival, began before the station received its FM licence. In the festival's early days, CKUW spent a lot of time providing promotional, logistical, and volunteer support. "Recently, we've been providing stage hosts for the Jazz Festival and we have had varying involvement in that over the years" (Schmidt, personal interview, 5 July 2011). A stage host introduces the band and converses with the crowd in between sets. In some years, the station has done the same service for the Winnipeg Folk Festival. CKUW is also connected to a variety of local arts and cultural centres and the festivals these organizations often program. "There's a community organization called Art City that is a drop-in arts centre for kids." The station "works really hard to promote the things that they do," including their various fundraising efforts. Schmidt also mentioned the Ellice Street Festival. Ellice is an avenue just north of the university that closes for the festival; "it's sort of an inner-city festival." CKUW has provided promotional and logistical support for the festival on a yearly basis. Ted Turner, the station's outreach and sponsorship coordinator, mentioned that the station often works with the Spence Neighbourhood Association. The organization is "just down the street" and "runs a lot of youth programming," including participation in CKUW's Radio Camp (Turner, personal interview, 7 July 2011). The camp runs during the summer and was described by Turner as a week-long camp for a group of children who "learn how to make radio and do interviews."

Turner emphasized the station's important relationship to local independent record stores, particularly Into the Music in the Exchange District. "In the same way that *Stylus* was the transmitter for CKUW before we went FM, there were spots like Into the Music and a skate shop called SK8 that were really important in terms of creating a sense of community and aligning certain energies that would be flowing from all these different underground points." Turner made connections between stores like Into the Music and SK8 and venues like the Royal Albert in the Exchange, claiming that all of these places eventually came together to create a sense of community around the station and the city. The Royal Albert "as a venue is really important in terms of the development of all this energy as well.

That's where these bands played, that's where local bands played, and that's where touring bands played. Along with the Spectrum, which is now The Pyramid." Thinking about the history of the station and related cultural institutions in the city, Turner said that "having a campus radio station downtown wouldn't make sense on its own. It made sense because all this other stuff was happening."

Schmidt underscored the centrality of Into the Music: "It's super important to have ties to places like that, because if there was nowhere to get the music we play on the station, it would kind of be a sterile environment." Into the Music has a ton of LPs and used CDs, and their staff are "experts." The station promotes the record store and the store sponsors many of CKUW's shows. Venues and record stores are vital to a music scene, Schmidt explained, because they are

> also social spaces where people from communities can mix and talk and share ideas. You don't really have people hanging out at Walmart talking about politics or life or things like that. Whereas record stores, or what we conceive of as a good record store, is a social place. You go there and talk to people about music and about events and about culture and politics. So it's really important to have ties like that. And a lot of those places support us financially, or they support us in other ways. So venues can support us by hosting events when we're doing our fundraising drive. And then we happily support the local bands and local music as much as we can. And not just rock music and not just pop music but cultural groups and world music.

Veteran CKUW volunteer Stu Reid explained that college radio has been a "big deal" to him since the late 1970s. He recalled first listening to music when he was fourteen or fifteen and "then all of the sudden it was the summer of 1978 and then came punk rock and new wave" (Reid, personal interview, 5 July 2011). Reid discovered CJUM at the University of Manitoba at the time and he was "reborn." He said it was great to have college radio in the city at that time, but it was only "around for about a year and a half before it died. The student union basically killed it off. And Winnipeg didn't have alternative radio for twenty years, which was insane." After losing that station, Reid vowed that if the city ever got college radio back, he would be a part of it. "And, you know, twenty years later, sure enough, we got it back." The time he spends hosting *Twang Trust* is his "favourite two hours of the week." The show started out as an alt-country show, a genre that a friend of his was particularly interested in. His friend hosted the show, with Reid as a co-host. Eventually, Reid became the show's sole host. Reid said that over time, the show started to define him. "Everything I listen to, I'm thinking about my show, like, what can I play next week?" And although his "tastes have narrowed" over time, the show is "still all over the place … I'll play weird punk stuff and somehow justify it as country music, you know, in some weird way, shape, or form. Everything I play tends to have some sort of linear flow to it, whether it's a set of live music happening soon, or whether it's based around a theme that weaves all the way through the show." Reid admitted that he has put a lot more effort into the show than he needs to but that it is a "whole lot of fun" for him.

Reid also hosts concerts at his home on a fairly regular basis. His first house show featured Jim Bryson, Mike Plume, and C.R. Avery. For his next house show, Reid would be hosting Chuck Prophet, an artist who would be playing the Winnipeg Folk Festival the following weekend. Reid is a huge fan of Prophet, and because he was worried that it might rain on the Folk Festival, he wanted to ensure he would be able to hear him in a smaller venue. A friend of Reid's from North Carolina was going to film the Prophet show and put together a package to be sold as a fundraising incentive for CKUW.

Reid has been involved in music in Winnipeg for decades. He works as a graphic artist and has created countless concert posters over the years. Before the widespread use of personal computers, he was one of the very few individuals who was creating poster art for Winnipeg shows. Reid has created posters for "just about every bar in the city" at one time or another. He has always been involved in the "local scene" in this way, and "local is a big part of [his radio show] too." One story in particular illustrates his involvement with local Winnipeg music over the past few decades. "One of my favourite bands from back in the day, local bands, is called The Fuse, who later became Jeffrey Hatcher & The Big Beat, who were slightly nota-ble." At the time, Reid was too young to get into bars and see The Fuse live, but he discovered them through college radio because the station would play the band's demos. Over the years, he got to know the band personally. During one of the station's fundraising efforts, CKUW was broadcasting live from a bar and Reid managed to get The Fuse together to perform as the house band for the night. They do not play together often but "they still keep at it to some degree." Reid then asked three different artists from dif-ferent eras "of Winnipeg live music to come up and join [him] for a couple of songs in each set." Reid's stories highlight how programmers at CKUW envision themselves as intimately connected to particular aspects of Win-nipeg's music scene, and the station facilitates these connections. Reid has made a number of personal connections with bands and artists, and this has had implications for live music in the city and for the content programmed by CKUW.

Robin Eriksson is the station's program director. She also hosts *Hit the Big Wide Strum!* – an "old-time and bluegrass music show" (Eriksson, personal interview, 6 July 2011). Old-time and bluegrass music is becoming "sort of trendy across the country right now. Old-time and roots music [are] making a comeback." Over the past seven years that she has done this show, she has noticed that more Canadian content is available. She commented on the growing number of younger musicians and female artists playing old-time and bluegrass music. "When I first started, we really had trouble finding stuff that wasn't old boys' music. And that's not the kind of stuff that I've liked in any genre. So, the longer I do my show, the more exciting it is for me in a way because I do have more options to play the sort of stuff that excites me." She does as much as possible to profile and promote old-time and bluegrass music for her listeners. She interviews artists if they are coming to town, and she challenges the restrictive boundaries that are often put around the genre:

> When I first started the show, I used to get phone calls from people who listened to the show previously and they would say, "What you're playing isn't bluegrass." And I was really self-conscious, "Oh, I'm offending the listeners." And as a young programmer I thought I was doing it all wrong. So it took me a really long time to find where my legs were in terms of doing my own thing. Because I stepped into some really big shoes from the fellow that was doing the show, and then the woman I took over from. And it's hard because those listeners expected that I was going to step in and do exactly the same thing and my taste would be exactly Bill Monroe and the Osborne Brothers. And there's this idea out there that if it's not Bill Monroe or the Osborne Brothers, then it's not bluegrass. And if you play new up-and-comers, or if you play music that takes those traditional aspects of the music and mutates it a little bit to have a fresher sound, then it's all wrong. So the longer I do my show, I feel like, if you like it, you'll listen, and if not, you'll turn it off. So I tend to promote the stuff that is exciting to me and not promote the stuff that isn't exciting to me. And some people in the bluegrass community here are offended by that. And some people aren't. And in a lot of ways it depends on their age and their gender. And that's fine.

Sarah Michaelson's relationship to music-making in Winnipeg has been greatly facilitated by the station. Michaelson, who says she entered the Winnipeg music community through CKUW, hosts *Stylus Radio*, a show that "morphed into something that became [her] DJ identity, which is looking into primarily rare soul and funk music, but also expanding into Canadian hip-hop and some contemporary stuff" (Michaelson, personal interview, 7 July 2011). For about seven years she has been performing professionally under the name Mama Cutsworth. "It was definitely *Stylus Radio* and the station as a whole that was my gateway into performing music professionally, just in terms of learning about a ton of music." Michaelson commented on the station's relationship to the music scene in Winnipeg on a more general level. "A lot of our hosts are members of a music community, whether they are DJs or musicians from different styles of music – but not just musicians, but also booking agents and whoever. There are a ton of people who are heavily invested in the community and are a big part of it." It is not really people with journalism or creative communications backgrounds who are doing shows. Programmers and hosts are often "people who are music collectors and extreme nerds about one genre. And that's why the listening is so interesting too, because obviously it's not Top 40. It's this really niche jazz programming or a whole show just dedicated to ska music." Programmers and hosts live and breathe these genres, and a lot of these programs are "anchors" for people in those music communities because it's "their only source to hear this stuff on the radio." One prospective volunteer pitched an all 8-bit music show to the station, a program that would feature only music from video games. "And there's this growing culture of 8-bit music and game culture in the city and this show has the potential to be that anchor. You kind of need to be a smart listener at a station like CKUW, where you're really engaged. We call it active listening. You know what time you want to tune in for a program and you're aware of what's happening on the schedule, which is a really different concept than just always having a station on in the background."

CKUW's awareness of musical activity in Winnipeg is a significant component of the station's culture. This relationship has become part of a larger narrative or mythology about the city's music scene. Rob Schmidt discussed the trajectories of certain Winnipeg-based bands. These artists are important in defining music in Winnipeg, and the station is aware of its role in shaping their careers. Schmidt explained that some musicians develop and get to the point where they require the station's support. "And then they get beyond that point and some of them are still really great friends." He offered the Winnipeg-based band The Weakerthans as an example. "Most or many Canadians would recognize the name of that band. They got a lot of promotion and a lot of support from CKUW in the early days. They went so far as to host fundraising events for us and things like that. So, we still play The Weakerthans, of course, but you wouldn't hear them as much as you'd hear other newer bands that are coming up." Stephen Carroll from The Weakerthans hosted a radio show at CKUW for a period of time. Schmidt said there is a "real neat organic community with that kind of stuff. And that's something that I'm pretty proud that we're able to do. Not every station has that sort of organic connection to its music community. I think with Winnipeg, just the nature of this city … That was bound to happen."

Many of the staff and volunteers at CKUW mentioned the "nature" of Winnipeg. Michaelson described the city as "small and isolated" and noted how this isolation does a "few interesting things." "You kind of know everyone in a certain genre of music. 'Oh, that's the reggae scene in town and that's the hip hop scene.' And that splinters off into a few different subgenres too." Because the city is so small, and because "each music community is so small, in terms of performers and fans," there is a lot of crossover. The city is "really a collaborative city, because it's so small and because we have long winters. Minneapolis is one of our closest cities and it's in another country and eight hours away." Different artists producing music in Winnipeg end up working together because musicians and artists from other cities are so far away. "And that's definitely happened to me," Michaelson said. "[I ended] up being a signer on an electronic music label and I had never done that before. My background was jazz or choir music. And that happens a lot in this city."

A collaborative crossover musical culture is often born out of artists and musicians working indoors. Ted Turner pinpointed the intense energy he felt in the small basement room where CKUW once operated. "The sense of the soul of the station – that is the feel of the independent music community. I mean, that's what you could feel when you walked into the room for the first time. Everyone was either in bands or about to be in bands, or [was] notorious for having a ridiculously big record collection." With regard to the city, "as much as you can kind of complain about being socially, geographically, aesthetically, and artistically isolated, there's something kind of safe and comforting in that too. This warm blanket you can just wrap up and hide in, and it is all part of the basement culture in Winnipeg." When people are indoors for such a long period of time, they are going to start making art and music. "And I think that the station has that feeling."

Schmidt viewed this notion of an indoors or basement culture as central in the mythology of Winnipeg's music scene. This basement culture is equally vital to the "musical legacy of the place" in terms of the number of successful popular music acts that started there. "Obviously, the Guess Who is still name-dropped constantly, and tons of other great bands have come from here. If you think of the '90s, there are the Watchmen and Crash Test Dummies and all of these acts went on to pretty notable success. So the mythology is that because it's so bloody miserable here for six months of the year, people stay indoors and jam, they play music. And they have house parties or basement parties." Schmidt added that there is a lot of truth to this idea, citing the fact that a lot of all-ages shows take place in basements.

He mentioned the house concerts that Stu Reid organizes. He feels it is quite strange that Winnipeg was the last major Canadian city to not have a campus station, because there has always been a strong musical community and a strong activist community in the city. "It's the same thing too, where in the winter everyone sits around drinking coffee and talking politics. Those ideas incubate and build some energy, and yeah, it's just a part of this city."

Musical activity in Winnipeg shares a notion of isolation and collaboration with the culture of CKUW. Turner recalled the "feeling" of the small basement pre-FM station, which to some degree has influenced the culture of the station as it operates today. A recurring theme throughout these conversations with individuals at CKUW was the indoor nature of cultural production in Winnipeg and how this results in people from different musical communities interacting and collaborating. Interviewees expressed awareness of the cultural institutions that are significant in their own work as radio practitioners or as cultural producers. Volunteers and staff who have been with the station for a number of years are aware of the ways in which CKUW has been implicated in the careers of local artists and musicians. Recall here Schmidt's comments about The Weakerthans. He emphasized the station's role in helping the band, much more so than the reciprocal case. One example of the reciprocal situation is LePoidevin's point about Sackville and the role of touring bands in shaping programming at CHMA. The role these bands and artists play in terms of helping the station reach a level of recognition among listeners is not as strongly articulated, but this may be the result of the difficulties that stations face in terms of measuring listenership.

The comments and stories recalled by interviewees that emphasize how connections between institutions and producers are central to the station's culture cultivate a shared history among individuals involved in various aspects of musical activity in the locality, and they help constitute the music scene in the present. Connections between individuals and institutions tend to be framed by a certain level of expertise or taste discrimination that guides listeners and the listening experience. For instance, Reid mentioned his ability to justify nearly any musical selection as "alt-country" and how he is able to do this because of his expertise in the genre and his longevity with the station. There is a tension, then, between representing a certain musical or cultural community through one's involvement with the station and passion for a certain genre or musical style, and the hierarchy of cultural value that either pre-exists or develops as one becomes more involved with the station or a musical community in the locality.

CiTR and Vancouver: Cultural Institutions and Community in a Growing City

As the biggest city of the three profiled in this chapter, Vancouver is home to many independent record stores and live music venues. It also has a large, central entertainment district in the downtown core. The campus radio station at the University of British Columbia serves as an important institutional site that helps local and independent musicians and music fans program and host live events. This is a particularly important role in Vancouver because the city has been faced with many venue closures and noise complaints due to municipal policies pertaining to noise and the sale of alcohol. As an institution with longevity and prominence in Vancouver's music scene, CiTR plays an important role in helping sustain the production and performance of local music, particularly when cultural producers have to work a little bit harder to build a sense of community. In Alan O'Connor's writing on punk music scenes, the concept of a scene is central to the "active creation of infrastructure to support punk bands and other forms of creative activity." Punk scenes share many characteristics with other underground, independent, or alternative movements. O'Connor adds that underground scenes provide local bands with "places to live, practice spaces and venues to play" (2002, 226, 233). This conceptualization of a scene as a social urban space that works to sustain itself and to ensure there are resources and places to perform is very much in line with the practices and processes of a campus station in a city like Vancouver, where venues open and close without much notice and where it can be difficult to locate live musical events. CiTR's institutional history helps the station record, document, and program live musical events, often in partnership with other cultural organizations or institutions.

The cultural institutions the station shares an affinity with include Scratch Records, which is located just east of the east–west divide on Hastings Street, right where new development had ceased at the time of this writing. A number of concerns about displacement along class lines have been raised with regard to commercial and residential development in the area because Vancouver's Downtown Eastside is the epicentre of a number of political, social, and economic issues, and an area of the city where homelessness is prominent. The new store is a small space, approximately twenty by twenty feet, and the young man working the counter said that the owner chose this spot because of the cheaper rent. Bins of vinyl records occupied the middle of the store and show posters decorated the walls. There were also listings for all the upcoming shows that had tickets for sale at Scratch Records. The employee detailed some of the new performance spaces that have been opening up in the city for live music, which are hoping to counteract the fact that the city tends to shut down live venues quickly. There is a space in an alley, he said, called 360 Glen, which is the venue's address. Naming the venue after its actual street address conveys a sense of humour (or wit's end) regarding the status of live music venues in the city – as though the locale will be shut down by the police anyways, so its location might just as well be named.

Just beyond the intersection of Main and Hastings is Rickshaw, a venue that borders on Chinatown and had been the Shaw Theatre (once a major exhibitor of Hong Kong cinema). The venue is known for hosting punk and lo-fi bands, or bands with minimal instrumentation, since the sound is not very good. The space consists of a stage enclosed by two walls of concrete blocks. Farther down Main Street, through Chinatown, is the Cobalt, a place that once often hosted punk and metal bands. Across the street from the Cobalt is a newer venue called the Electric Owl, which appears stylish and modern, dramatically different from many of the other nearby spots and indicative of the changing demographics in the area.

Closer to UBC in the Kitsilano neighbourhood is Zulu Records on West 4th Avenue, just east of Burrard Street. Zulu has been a long-time supporter of CiTR. The shop is organized in two sections. One is full of vinyl records, with local bands clearly marked; the other contains CDs, a number of books and zines, and a wall of staff recommendations. This half has a raised floor where in-store performances often take place. Another venue with a close connection to CiTR is the Biltmore Cabaret, an active venue for local music. CiTR's sibling publication *Discorder* often hosts shows at the Biltmore. The venue is on the Kingsway, not far from Main and Broadway, a major intersection in the Mount Pleasant neighbourhood. Given that venues have been coming and going quickly in Vancouver, CiTR volunteers must be aware of the intricacies of the music communities that are programmed by the station so that it can reflect and represent local music in the city.

Station manager Brenda Grunau provided an overview of some of the music promoted and programmed by CiTR, as well as the institutions supportive of the station and its music. She explained that the Biltmore Cabaret is one of the station's core advertisers and that the station promotes a lot of its live shows. Most of the bands that play in Vancouver, and that are generally representative of the styles of music heard on CiTR, are booked at the Biltmore. "We support a lot of what Mint Records does, and The Hive – the leading indie recording studio in town – is a sponsor of SHiNDiG," which is the station's annual battle of the bands that has been held at the Railway Club for "about ten years now" (Grunau, personal interview, 11 July 2011). She listed Scrape, Scratch, Red Cat, and Zulu as record stores that work closely with the station. According to Grunau, the station's sibling publication *Discorder* started because "Zulu was committed to purchasing the back page and they've been on the back page of *Discorder* since 1983, so that's why *Discorder* was able to launch, because of that ad revenue." SHiNDiG lasts for thirteen weeks; the competition takes place every Tuesday during the fall. It had been running for about fifteen years as of July 2011, with bands competing for prizes such as support from local sound production houses. Grunau mentioned a number of bands that have played SHiNDiG in the past, exemplifying the station's consciousness of its role in developing the careers of Vancouver-based artists. Bands she named included Fond of Tigers, Maow (Neko Case's first band in Vancouver), Destroyer, and They Shoot Horses, Don't They? Grunau humorously said that the first-place band often "breaks up and the second-place band goes on to do something interesting."

CiTR also works to connect with live events and festivals that reflect the diversity of the station's program grid. Board member Janis McKenzie emphasized CiTR's efforts to ensure that it is present at musical events that do not fit within "those indie rock categories," because a large percentage of the station's programming – especially long-running shows – profiles genres like folk, jazz, and bluegrass (McKenzie, personal interview, 12 July 2011). The station has a float in the Pride parade and programs music at The Pit (the Student Union pub). McKenzie said that the station has not lost its connection to the campus over the years, although it has been working hard at building connections with the wider community.

Cameron Reed has not worked or volunteered for CiTR, but his extensive experience and expertise as a producer, promoter, and performer of local music in Vancouver contributes to an overview of CiTR's relationship to local music in the city. Around 2003 or 2004, Reed was in a band and started promoting shows as an independent promoter. "Instead of waiting to be booked, we booked shows ourselves, proactively" (Reed, personal interview, 11 July 2011). "A couple of the shows that we had done went really well, especially considering that they were our first little foray into promoting." This initial experience resulted in Reed being asked to help out with the Vancouver-based music festival, Music Waste, a festival that takes place over five days and features a "half-dozen shows," including comedy and art. Reed recalled that when he first got involved with the festival, "the torch had been passed to a new group, and the people putting it on didn't really have much experience promoting." Neither did he at the time, but he took that opportunity and jumped in to help out. Over the following seven years, he began "kind of running" the festival along with some other individuals who have helped out a great deal. Sarah Cordingley is one person in particular that Reed mentioned; she helped run the festival before the partnership assembled a new group to actively organize Music Waste, while Reed took on "an overseeing position." Reed also contributed to the organization of the annual Victory Square Block Party, a free outdoor concert that features, as Reed explained, "all up-and-coming local bands." A review on *Discorder*'s website posted by Christina Gray on 9 September 2011 noted that the seventh Victory Square Block Party "took over the park at Hastings and Cambie at the edge of the Downtown Eastside. [Its] charm is that hipsters, musicians, hobos and people of all different ages come together for one afternoon to listen to local independent music on one of the last days of summer" (Gray 2011).

Reed emphasized that everything he does is very Vancouver-centric: "I'm not involved with putting on big out-of-town acts. I'm all about shows that are all local bands, all local artists, and all local comedians. No corporate sponsorship or anything like that. The idea is to make it easy for people to experience the independent local culture." The idea of treating local culture like a big festival is what motivates his work with music and culture in the city. He said that big festivals like South by Southwest (SXSW) and CMJ Music Marathon are great, "and they pull in some big acts but it really doesn't take much to take your local culture and treat it in the same way." Reed has also played in punk bands over the years, and he started an electronic project under the name of Babe Rainbow. The project was picked up by a well-known electronic label, Warp Records, which had so far released two of his EPs.

CiTR has been involved in these live music festivals in varying capacities. Reed has participated in a number of events sponsored by CiTR. Usually, the station is the title sponsor, "like 'this event is sponsored by CiTR,' and they set up a booth and they'll run PSAs for us and mention it on air" (Reed 2011). The station's involvement in the festival is helpful because "the people that are listening to the station are listening to it for the more outsider stuff, which is what we focus on." For the previous year's Victory Square Block Party, CiTR set up a booth and broadcasted live from the event. "That's the sort of thing that I like to see CiTR doing, like to really get in there and be a part of this big event. And I think they're doing this more often now. We just had to let the city know that there was going to be a table there, and we had to make sure there were enough power outlets for them. Then we just left them to do their thing for the day."

Broadcasting live from events and festivals enables the station to display and maintain a presence that communicates participation and involvement with the music scene or a particular musical community. By physically leaving the campus space and setting up a broadcast booth at a festival, stations reach out to the wider community. Conducting interviews outside the studio is another way to bring an aspect of music-making in the city into the station, and then back out into the city by broadcasting this content to listeners. For instance, Nardwuar the Human Serviette began his Friday afternoon broadcast on 8 July 2011 by talking about the Vancouver-based band Apollo Ghosts – in particular, about the upcoming release party for their newest 7-inch, "Money Has No Heart." The release party was being held at the Zoo Zhop, a record store and performance space in the city's Downtown Eastside. Nardwuar is very conscious about organizing his show around upcoming live performances in the city. This greatly influences his interview style:

> Well, for me, personally, because my show is every Friday, I'm usually scrambling for something every week. So if a band is playing in Vancouver that I'm interested in that weekend, I might talk to them. And if there's a band that I'm not interested in, I'll probably talk to them. Or I'll mention it. So I kind of do it that way. I don't really plan ahead at all. I'm thinking, "Oh this week I'll play the Apollo Ghosts and I'll play Hunx and his Punx because they came to town last week and I interviewed them." But I'm not thinking ahead, like in three weeks what I'll have on my show ... It could be anybody, I'll interview anybody. (Nardwuar 2011)

Nardwuar is known for interviewing a wide range of artists at different stages in their careers, including some of the most successful contemporary popular music artists, yet he says he always pays attention to local acts. In his early days with the station, bands would give tapes to CiTR and he would put them on 8-track cartridges so that the DJ could play them. "So there was a whole wall of local stuff. CiTR is always prided in playing local stuff. And I think people still get a kick out of hearing their music on CiTR." His interviewing and programming practices have also been greatly influenced by the station, both in terms of the resources available in the station space and in terms of a station culture that encourages discussion and the sharing of musical taste and knowledge. "When I first came to CiTR, I was only into punk rock or only into garage rock or only into 60s retro rock. That's all that I liked. My blinders were just stuck in that stuff." However, over time, he has become aware of "all the great stuff that is out there," and he has learned about new music by exploring the station's music library. Campus radio stations are much more than broadcasters or outlets for content. Stations provide technical and musical resources that influence the individuals who program and host shows.

Another example of CiTR providing resources for circulating music is its DJ training program (here, DJ refers to a performer, not a show host). According to Grunau, a number of Vancouver's night club and party DJs have shows at CiTR, and the station has all the DJ equipment needed to run a training program. "A lot of students are always asking for DJs to DJ their parties, except they have no budget. And people are always coming in here to learn how to do that. So we figured that there's a great connection there" (Grunau 2011). The station began to train DJs to then perform at club events for free, which is a "great way to promote the station and get the word out, and sort of see a need and serve it." The DJ training program is also evidence of CiTR's contribution to the cultural and musical life on campus, for it provides students and student groups with the means to host live musical events.

The programmers, staff, and technical volunteers at CiTR are both aware of and integrated with Vancouver music-making. The station is also committed to on-campus activities that are organized by student clubs or held in student spaces. The station's longevity is integral to music perfor-mance and exhibition in Vancouver, particularly because performance space in the city is often very temporary. In Vancouver, venues have had a tendency to close or change locations due to legalities pertaining to noise and the sale of alcohol, in addition to the fact that the city is quite young and currently expanding. Says Reed: "I mean we're a fairly young city, and it's being developed very quickly. You know, just the changes in my ten years in the city, you can definitely see it. I would say an obstacle, like right off the top of my mind, is having a venue that lasts a while." If a venue is around for a while, a "shitty booker" will come in, stop putting on the same sort of shows, and will eventually "have a stranglehold over that spot." Reed does not feel there is a lack of venues in the city, but "a lot of community build-ing has to do with familiarity, and if you don't have a single spot or hub to rally around, it can be difficult to build that sense of community. [The] local scene is very tight, and there are a lot of different pockets and different genres … but there's not factions like, 'You stay over there, that's your thing,' everyone's generally friendly and supportive."

One space that did have a sense of community within the music scene for a period of time was an illegal warehouse space called the Emergency Room. "It was a recording studio," says Reed, "it was a jam space, and a venue where similar bands would play. Touring bands would come in and our local bands would open up. And I feel like that's the one thing that is sort of lacking, it's hard to build that community without that one spot." It can be difficult to build and sustain a cultural core in Vancouver because of the licensing and financial barriers that face live music venues. "You can have a warehouse space, but in order to be able to make it a legitimate busi-ness, it costs one hundred thousand-some-odd dollars." He knows "there are people who would be open to running a legitimate business but they don't have that sort of money, so a lot of places have to go under the radar and have to stay illegal." These illegal venues eventually get shut down, and the community dissipates.

Nardwuar commented poignantly on performance spaces and places in the city, speaking from experience with his band The Evaporators. He said it is hard get a show booking at one of the larger, more established places like the Commodore Ballroom on Granville. It used to be possible to headline the Commodore Ballroom if you were a "really established local band," but this is not the case now. The Evaporators usually rent a hall or play an in-store gig. Nardwuar prefers playing all-ages shows because he remembers, as a kid, not being able to get into shows. Not everyone is into all-ages shows, so some people will organize "underground gigs at warehouses where they'll sell booze." There are a lot of places to play if you are "a bit creative," and this is "probably what makes bands even better in Vancouver. Because it's hard to find a place to play, when you do play, you make it really worthwhile."

Nardwuar expanded on this idea that the unpredictable location and limited temporality of venues is beneficial for the Vancouver scene. He believes it is unfortunate that venues close, but on the positive side, these closures force people to find other venues and this process of discovering new performance spaces can be exciting and rewarding. He also makes an intriguing point by connecting local "smaller" bands to certain venues, namely the illegal warehouse spaces, and larger touring bands to some of the bigger downtown venues. This idea suggests that a sustained performance space, or lack thereof, is something that affects local independent bands more than bands that have achieved recognition outside the city and that have the financial means to tour frequently. Reed echoed this point, saying there is a disjuncture between bands at different stages in their careers or with different philosophies and approaches to music-making. The more inclusive or independent cultural institutions, such as campus radio stations, are therefore more important to independent bands and artists:

> There are some bands that play the SOCAN [Society of Composers, Authors and Music Publishers of Canada] and music business game really well, and from the get-go they are applying for grants and are registered with SOCAN and playing industry events. Sometimes there's crossover. A lot of bands apply for grants, but there is a certain segment that really play up the business side, and aren't really part of the gigging community proper.

On the other hand, some bands employ an ethos of independence, and this requires a different approach to music-making. Reed continued:

And there's the other bands that are really independent, and maybe just lazy, or prefer that sort of grinding it out on the road, or sleeping on people's floors. Like "We book our own shows, we manage ourselves, we send our own press releases *if* we send out press releases." The magazine I used to work for, *Only*, and I guess before that, *Terminal City*, really had an emphasis on the more, weird, you know, I would say *punk*, DIY in its ideology, not so much in its sound, like straight-up punk music. I would say weirder stuff gets more attention from *that*, from the DIY community. A magazine like *Discorder*, also in the true college radio sense, is always focusing on the outsiders.

Both Reed and Nardwuar highlight the importance of independent and inclusive cultural institutions, particularly in a city where active and available venues and performance spaces come and go. These institutions are discussed in opposition to larger bureaucratic cultural organizations, such as SOCAN and FACTOR, which appear to favour bands that have proven their ability to garner national attention. That is, it often takes an already successful song or album to receive funding from these organizations. So we cannot overlook or understate the significance of a cultural institution like a campus radio station that has longevity in the scene and that can provide resources and promotion for new and independent artists, particularly when other forms of institutional support (including commercial radio stations) are aligned with more established artists. A campus station offers local cultural producers and promoters a space to develop their artistic personalities and technical abilities. Stations are also places where musicians and cultural producers can connect and converse, and they can use the station as an outlet for their music and their community. A campus station does not simply program local music. Rather, stations are active institutions that help foster a sense of community between cultural producers, musicians, radio hosts, and listeners.

Mint Records co-founder and former CiTR staff member Bill Baker has a rich history of participating in the circulation of music in Vancouver. His experience illustrates the station's connection to other cultural institutions in the wider Vancouver music scene. His role at CiTR and his work at Mint Records have contributed significantly to the station's legacy and to its place within the larger Vancouver music scene. Baker is the director of music licensing at Mint Records. He also works in artist relations, although the label's staff actually do "every job" (Baker, personal interview, 27 July 2011). The summer of 2011 was the label's twentieth anniversary, and "it's certainly a different story from back when the label started." Baker noted the significant differences in daily tasks between launching an independent record label and ensuring the label's sustainability. Baker and Randy Iwata started the label. The two were "real record nerds when [they] were teens and in high school." Although they did not know each other at that point, they had similar interests, including punk rock and science fiction. Iwata and Baker met later at CiTR, where Baker "became involved very quickly" at the station. Within a year or so, he was a member of the student executive. He met Iwata at a "Friday Afternoon Brewscast," which took place once every month on a Friday. The station's lounge would be closed off, station members would congregate and talk, and there was a vending machine that sold beer. As Baker explained, "Randy and I took advantage of this one Friday at about 10:30 in the morning and within about half an hour we just had this incredible rapport ... And we realized that we had been at so many of the same shows and bought so many of the same records." During their time at the station, he and Iwata "made a very good team" and "did almost every job there was to do, except engineering."

Baker contextualized the era during which he worked at CiTR, and he described the culture that would shape his future work with Mint. In the mid- to late 1980s, "what people look back on as the legitimate first wave of North American punk had totally burned out by then." Before the Internet, with its ability to connect different music scenes in Canada, the sense of the music community in Vancouver was "not Canadian so much as Vancouver, Seattle, Portland, and San Francisco." That was the geographical scene, according to Baker. "It was a lot easier to hop in a van and tour eight or ten days down the coast than it was to get eight days across Canada." The Vancouver scene was strongly influenced by the Seattle sound at that time, particularly into the early 1990s, but Baker emphasized that there came a time when there was a bit of a "gap" in the Vancouver scene, a moment when "you couldn't quite point to the hot thing at the time." This was a "really varied and unfocused time in the local music scene, but the radio station was still very well connected" to what was taking place in the city. This was the "perfect environment for a campus station like CiTR," because the diversity in the scene was well suited to the variety of the station's programming.

This sense of ambiguity and diversity in the scene became very evident to Baker and Iwata when they set out to start Mint Records. Baker recalled not feeling as though there was a certain sound that the label had to cater to or foster. He felt as though they had the opportunity to put out any sound they wanted: "I guess that was a bit of carry-over from the radio station days, just in the sense that we didn't feel that sense of 'Vancouver needs another Sub Pop or Vancouver needs another Alternative Tentacles.'" Kaitlin Fontana's *Fresh at Twenty: The Oral History of Mint Records* (2011) discusses the development of the Vancouver label in the shadow of the burgeoning grunge scene south of the border. In reference to cub, a band responsible for garnering Mint a lot of attention in its early days, Fontana writes that "if Cobain and grunge were the '90s yin, then cub's brand of pop was its yang, the echo of Sub Pop's Seattle to Mint's Vancouver" (77). But Fontana also notes that while Baker and Iwata were at CiTR, they were "on the receiving end of Sub Pop Records releases from the likes of Mudhoney and Nirvana. They looked at any and all releases that crossed their desks but they paid careful attention to Sub Pop's output" (18). Evidently, the scene south of the border served as a template for how a label operates, although there was enough diversity in the Vancouver music scene that the label had room to experiment stylistically.

The resources and experiences available to Baker and Iwata at CiTR helped establish Mint Records. Baker learned much more from the radio station than he did from his university education. At UBC, he "spent so much time at the radio station," and his experience with it provided him with "amazing insight into how the whole music business works from the other side." The station taught him how to deal with record companies, and he learned a lot about the publicity side of the music industry. By the time he and Iwata had been at the station for five years or so, "it seemed like [they] had been there forever" and they "felt that maybe it was time to find something else to do." He and Iwata spent a lot of time brainstorming for a location where they could continue their involvement with the local music scene and apply the skills they had learned, "maybe unwittingly," at the radio station. Using the collection of addresses from CiTR, the first thing that Baker and Iwata did after forming Mint was send a mail-out to all of the campus and community stations in North America. Baker and Iwata sent out a card introducing themselves, even though they had not yet signed any artists. "And in many respects," said Baker, "I'll say that I owe everything I have achieved, or everything I've done in the last twenty years is directly a result of stumbling into that station one day."

CiTR is a significant component of music-making in Vancouver, as evidenced by its centrality to the development of Mint Records and in shaping the work of established members of the Vancouver music scene, such as Nardwuar the Human Serviette. The station, as a space that facilitates the sharing of resources and musical knowledge, is a topic that recurs throughout the interviews with CiTR volunteers and staff members, whether this involves one's personal discovery of a certain record or band, or the coming together of individuals who later collaborate on future cultural work. The station's role in circulating local and independent music is a more prominent recollection than that of the role of bands and artists in helping the station, although the station has clearly benefited from having a rich musical locality to draw from. Considering the struggles that live event programmers and promoters face in sustaining performance spaces and a sense of musical community in the city, CiTR's role in the music scene is vital. By leaving campus borders to set up broadcast booths at local music festivals, the station becomes a physical presence that is able to interact with listeners and music fans. In this way, the station supports Reed's assertion that it should be easy for people to experience the city's independent local culture. Furthermore, as Reed commented, community is often built around familiarity. A station that shares a history with other prominent cultural institutions like Mint, and annual festivals like SHiNDiG and Music Waste, is perceived and recognized as a familiar node in the circulation of local music in Vancouver. The connections between campus stations and their musical communities have implications for the type of music that circulates both on air and off.

Canadian Campus Radio and Cultural Production: *Stylus*, *Discorder*, and *Pop Alliance Compilation: Vol. 2*

The stories recalled by the individuals interviewed in Sackville, Winnipeg, and Vancouver provide insight into the routes by which campus radio stations circulate and promote music in a city or town. Staff members and volunteers possess knowledge of musical communities within their broadcast range, and this contributes to constructing a notion of the city or town's music scene. This knowledge includes the history of venues and record stores and bands or artists who came up through the scene, often with strong ties to the radio station. The connections between campus stations and music scenes are found not just in the stories told by interviewees; they are also very present in cultural productions connected to campus stations, productions that both reflect and create musical activity within a local scene. A campus station provides a local alternative because of the various avenues it opens and supports between musicians, listeners, and radio practitioners. Beyond generating programming that reflects local cultural and musical communities, these three stations have contributed to the making of cultural objects that are very much products of the culture of campus radio stations as well as their surrounding musical and cultural communities. These objects further emphasize the involvement of campus stations in local cultural production, beyond the programming and broadcasting of music. They also highlight the ways in which campus radio overlaps and integrates with other media such as print, visual art, and photography.

These three cultural productions include two publications and one album. The two publications, *Stylus* and *Discorder,* are produced by CKUW and CiTR, respectively. Both magazines reflect and construct an impression of the Winnipeg or Vancouver music scene. They are the two most regularly published and widely distributed magazines associated with Canadian campus radio stations. The album is a compilation record co-produced by Mint Records and CiTR called *Pop Alliance Compilation: Vol. 2* (2011). These cultural objects are significant examples of how campus radio stations are local sources of cultural and musical production and documentation.

Stylus was CKUW's transmitter before the station went FM. Early editions of the magazine were short. Some of the first printings were essentially folded broadsheets containing the station's program grid for the following two months and a list of the top thirty-odd artists that the station was playing over the span of approximately sixty days. The tone used in early editions of the magazine is humorous and informal. For instance, Volume 2, Number 1, from October 1990 has an amusing front cover with a large "no smoking" sign and text that reads "CKUW Would Like To Thank the University For Establishing its New No Smoking Policy. Garnering Us a Great Many New Listeners" (Fig. 6.1). The university had prohibited smoking in most areas and established a smoking section near the station's on-campus speakers. This edition also included a programming guide. At this time, the station would run programming from 8:30 a.m. until 6:00 p.m., Monday

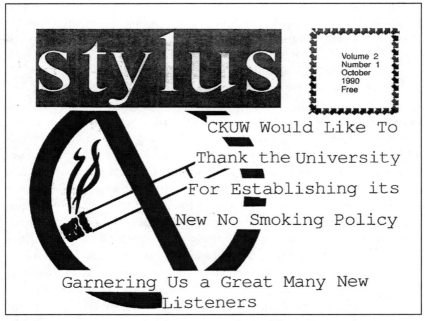

Figure 6.1 – CKUW and *Stylus* thank the university's administration for new smoking sections in close proximity to on-campus speakers. Credit: *Stylus*, reprinted with permission of Ted Turner.

to Thursday, and from 8:30 a.m. to "3:00-?" on Fridays ("Program Guide" 1990). Volume 6, Number 1, from September 1994 noted that the magazine was published monthly by the University of Winnipeg Students' Association with a circulation of 3,000 and that the "magazine's primary goal is to promote Winnipeg's local music scene and to act as a vehicle for the work of new writers" ("Advertising" 1994). According to the April 1993 edition, the magazine was published "every two months, four times per school year in order to seriously confuse our advertisers" ("Ad Sales" 1993). This irregular publishing schedule reduced the likelihood of the magazine running advertisements for large businesses with strict guidelines for advertising and marketing, while simultaneously sustaining friendly and informal relationships with smaller local businesses and student clubs, such as CKUW. The edition from September 1994 included an advertisement soliciting volunteers for the station: "CKUW Wants You! (and your musical taste)." The publication reached beyond the confines of the campus-relegated station at the time and located new volunteers and listeners. Below the ad, there is a concert calendar for shows during the month of September at the Royal Albert (CKUW 1994).

Like CKUW, *Stylus* is notably present as a component of the overall Winnipeg music scene – in terms of the objects and logos that appear and reappear as one visits cultural institutions and passes by posters advertising live events in the city – and has been since its inception. In the April 1993 edition, a short write-up by Mark Riddell in "The Open Line ..." section stated that "the Winnipeg music industry is at the very least at an exciting crossroads. To see the confidence and excitement that follows its successes is both encouraging and rewarding" (3). Riddell claimed that the city's live music patrons, "whose commitment and sophistication outweigh their relatively small numbers," deserved recognition for sustaining a vibrant music scene. He added that in conjunction with live music patrons, "a group of local professionals have developed an infrastructure of festivals, clubs, print media, radio, television, record labels, and management agencies that ... have worked within a competitive framework to promote the music industry in Winnipeg to everyone's benefit" (3). Riddell privileged the people who spend money on live music in the city over the magazine or the station, but in terms of informing these patrons about upcoming music and album releases, the role of cultural publications like *Stylus* is certainly evident in promoting live and local music.

The magazine's September–October 2000 edition included a lengthy feature on the send + receive festival. Dickson Binder wrote that "October will see the third instalment of Video Pool's send + receive: a festival of sound and as part of the festival's attempt to be a resource for local audio artists and musicians" (17). The link between *Stylus* (as the provider of this information), the festival, and CKUW is evident in a paragraph that describes one of the workshops structured around a presentation by Christophe Charles, an "internationally exhibited musician and artist," who "will present a workshop on his method of using field recordings in composition. Participants will be encouraged to contribute to a work for broadcast on CKUW 95.9 fm using field recording techniques and performance" (17).

In a section called "Indie Label Profile," the magazine reports on record labels in the city. The May 1999 edition featured the local record label Alchemy Records. The label is described in the feature as a "vehicle to promote Winnipeg DJs and live acts in an attempt to expose other markets to Winnipeg talent" (meme 1999, 24). Steve Conner wrote that the motivation behind starting the label came from the assumption that Winnipeg is a "smaller market and the music doesn't get here as quickly." By the time Winnipeg DJs received new music, it was already "three months old in some other cities and it has been played to death." Conner mentioned the prospect of CKUW acquiring an FM licence (which would indeed happen in the coming months), claiming that the exposure the station would "create for electronic music will be great" (24). He believed it would "bring new life to the scene" and "help people start to understand the music better" (24). Associations between the magazine, Alchemy Records, and the station are highlighted in this text, indicating a combined effort to promote an aspect of Winnipeg music that could certainly benefit from the added attention and promotion.

Over the years, *Stylus*'s production quality and attention to aesthetic detail have increased, as has the breadth and depth of content. The magazine is still very much involved in covering musical and cultural activity in Winnipeg. For example, the February–March 2011 edition contained a full-page advertisement for the "Twang Trust Roots-Rockin' 2011 FunDrive Spectacular," an event mentioned earlier in this chapter by *Twang Trust* host Stu Reid. The advertisement invited readers to "Be part of the LIVE Studio Audience." The June–July 2011 edition is thirty-six pages long, with full-colour front and back covers. Perhaps this increase in quality resulted in shorter print runs, for this edition notes a bimonthly release with a circulation of 2,500. It is also possible that an increased Web presence has resulted in fewer printed copies. Nevertheless, *Stylus* still describes itself as serving as "the program guide to 95.9FM CKUW" and as reflecting "the many musical communities it supports within Winnipeg and beyond." *Stylus* is also described as striving to "provide coverage of music that is not normally written about in the mainstream media" (*Stylus* 2011, 1). Content includes concert previews, interviews with both local and national artists, album reviews, and features. Advertisements found in the June–July 2011 issue include albums that were for sale at the Winnipeg Folk Festival Music Store, the Folk Festival itself, a promotion for 25 percent off all used stock at Into the Music, and upcoming concerts at the West End Cultural Centre. All of these retail outlets and organizations were mentioned during interviews by CKUW staff members and volunteers. Towards the back of the issue there are previews for the jazz and folk festivals that include paragraphs on a number of the artists playing, followed by ten pages of live show, album, and film reviews. The magazine's commitment to local artists is once again evident in the "Local Spotlight," where seven different albums by Winnipeg artists are reviewed.

There are numerous links between CKUW and *Stylus*, such as the publication's visual presentation of the station's program grid and a list of the "top artists" for the interim between current and preceding issues. The magazine profiles station DJs and provides interview space for artists that are charting on the station, giving Winnipeg music fans more information about the bands and artists that are active in the city. This connection is essential, especially given that live music patrons who listen to the station or who read *Stylus* may be making decisions on which bands to see live based on the attention given to artists featured in the magazine – bands or artists that may be touring for a first album and that may not yet have a strong fan base. The magazine also provides venues and record stores with a place to print and promote their concert calendars, upcoming sales, or featured artists. Over the years, *Stylus* has increased in size and quality, as has CKUW, and more pages mean more space for talking about music and culture in Winnipeg.

CiTR's *Discorder* has been in circulation since February 1983, when the magazine began as a guide to the station's programming. Its inaugural issue contained such items as a list of Top 30 singles and a list of Top 40 albums being played by the station. Singles ranged from prominent artists from Britain like The Jam, to demo tapes by local artists. Promotional materials for Zulu Records, upcoming UBC hockey and basketball matches, and a local hair studio were all featured in the first issue. The station's program grid and show descriptions were included, and an introductory write-up explained that "*Discorder* is not meant to be taken on its own. Chances are, that if this mag is read in its entirety by a non-listener, terrible things might happen; bewilderment, nausea, or even death. For this reason we advise that *Discorder* be cut with 100% pure CITR" ("A Guide ..." 1983). As with *Stylus*, *Discorder* emphasized its connection to its sibling radio station from the start, and the content is witty and informal. The write-up also explained that the station created the magazine in order to "improve communication, and isn't that what radio is all about?"

In 2010, *Discorder*'s media kit introduced itself as "that 28 years and running alternative music championing, local artist boosting, next latest craze spotting, just plain giving it away, sorta bad ass and definitely good-looking (free!) magazine." The media kit is written in a tone meant to entice

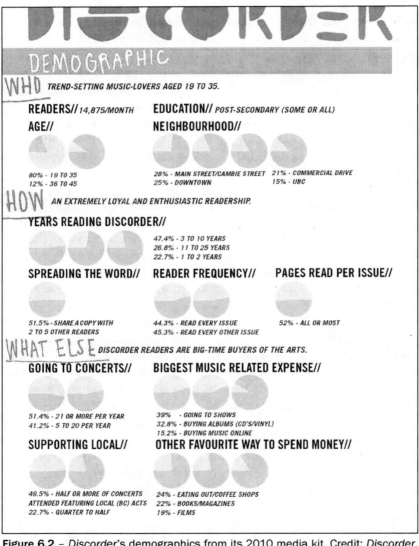

Figure 6.2 – *Discorder*'s demographics from its 2010 media kit. Credit: *Discorder*, reprinted with permission of CiTR and Brenda Grunau.

local businesses and potential sponsors. It emphasizes that *Discorder*'s writers and readers "come from within the scenes they write about, photograph and review" ("A Little About Us" 2010). Black-and-white advertisements range in price from a sixteenth of a page for $50 to a two-page spread for $600. This range gives local businesses of all sizes and budgets (including record stores and venues) an opportunity to advertise with the magazine. *Discorder* prints 8,500 copies per month and distributes to record stores, cafés, venues, and galleries throughout Vancouver and in some spots around Victoria. The media kit presents a number of statistics taken from a 2009 reader survey, including that over half its readers – 51.4 percent – attend twenty-one or more concerts a year, and that 49.5 percent attend concerts where half or more of the acts are from British Columbia (Fig. 6.2). A concert-going readership influences the magazine's content, which is heavy in show reviews and upcoming concert listings.

A flyer available at the station titled "How to Get Involved with *Discorder*" states that the free magazine is "staffed by a small group of volunteers who work like dogs to produce Canada's only monthly student radio publication" (*Discorder* 2011). The magazine "focuses on local, independent music and arts and is funded partly by advertising but mostly by CiTR." The flyer outlines a number of ways that people can get involved with *Discorder*, from writing show and album reviews to submitting art and photographs and helping with production.

Brenda Grunau noted that having a radio station and a publication working so closely together can lead to some confusion in terms of how to allocate time and resources. She emphasized that *Discorder* is the print voice of CiTR, and as station manager, she fills the role of publisher. Five part-timers produce the paper. In the past, there had been a slight cultural rift between the staff of each output, but people have worked hard to ensure integration between the two, through weekly office hours and meetings. "Part of the problem is that there are two different names, almost as though there are two different brands, and we don't want to compete with each other, so we're working on changing that over the long term." Another difference between the station and the paper, according to Grunau, is that *Discorder* only covers music, a narrower segment of music than the station represents. However, she adds, there is a lot of crossover between the two, and the station's charts and program guides are a prominent feature of *Discorder*.

At the time of this writing, issues of *Discorder* ran about forty pages. These printings of *Discorder* contained more advertisements than the *Stylus* issues published around the same time, but this should be expected with a larger city with more small and independent businesses to source from. The

// CiTR 101.9 FM CHARTS
STRICTLY THE DOPEST HITZ OF MARCH

#	ARTIST	ALBUM	LABEL	#	ARTIST	ALBUM	LABEL
1	Various*+	CiTR Pop Alliance Compilation, Vol. 2	Mint/ CiTR 101.9 FM	26	Buck 65*	20 Odd Years	Warner (WEA)
2	Colin Stetson*	New History Warfare Vol. 2: Judges	Constellation	27	The Rural Alberta Advantage*	Departing	Paper Bag
3	The Oh Wells*+	The EP That We Love	Independent	28	Yuck	s/t	Fat Possum
4	Dum Dum Girls	He Gets Me High	Sub Pop	29	The Good Lovelies*	Let the Rain Fall	Independent
5	Kurt Vile	Smoke Ring For My Halo	Matador	30	OK Vancouver OK*+	Houses	Greenbelt Collective
6	Geoff Berner*+	Victory Party	Mint	31	The Luyas*	Too Beautiful To Work	Idée Fixe
7	Destroyer*+	Kaputt	Merge	32	La Sera	s/t	Hardly Art
8	Brave Irene*+	s/t	Slumberland	33	Mogwai	Hardcore Will Never Die, But You Will	Sub Pop
9	Braids*	Native Speaker	Flemish Eye	34	The Wailin' Jennys*	Bright Morning Stars	True North
10	PJ Harvey	Let England Shake	Island	35	The Smith Westerns	Dye It Blonde	Fat Possum
11	Drive-By Truckers	Go-Go Boots	ATO	36	Eve Hell and the Razors*	When the Lights Go Out	Hell PI
12	The Babies	s/t	Shrimper	37	Deerhoof	Deerhoof vs. Evil	Polyvinyl
13	Bright Eyes	The People's Key	Saddle Creek	38	Channels 3 and 4*+	Christianity	Gilgongo
14	Beans	End It All	Anticon	39	White Suns	Walking In the Reservoir	Ug Explode
15	Wanda Jackson	The Party Ain't Over	Third Man	40	Cowpuncher*	s/t	Independent
16	Adele	21	XL Recordings	41	Ghostface Killah	Apollo Kids	Def Jam
17	Mother Mother*+	Eureka	Last Gang	42	Exene Cervenka	The Excitement of Maybe	Bloodshot
18	Esben And The Witch	Violet Cries	Matador	43	Lia Ices	Grown Unknown	Jagjaguwar
19	Iron and Wine	Kiss Each Other Clean	Warner (WEA)	44	N.213/ Reflektionss*+	Split	Needs More Ram
20	Dizzy Eyes*	Let's Break Up the Band	Hardly Art	45	Isaiah Ceccarelli*	Bréviaire d'épuisements	Ambiances Magnetiques
21	The Tranzmitors*+	It's Not Your Call b/w You Get Around	Dirtnap	46	The Radio Dept.	Passive Aggressive: Singles 2002-2010	Labrador
22	Kellarissa*+	Moon of Neptune	Mint	47	Bruce Cockburn*	Small Source of Comfort	True North
23	Joane Hétu*	Récits de Neige	Ambiances Magnetiques	48	Lykke Li	Wounded Rhymes	Atlantic
24	Miesha and the Spanks*	Gods Of Love	Transistor 66	49	Akron/Family	Akron/Family II: ... of Shinju TNT	Dead Oceans
25	Six Organs of Admittance	Asleep on the Floodplain	Drag City	50	J. Mascis	Several Shades of Why	Sub Pop

CiTR's charts reflect what's played on the air by CiTR's lovely DJs last month. Records with asterisks (*) are Canadian and those with a plus (+) are Vancouver based. Most of these excellent albums can be found at fine independent music stores across Vancouver. If you can't find them, give CiTR's music coordinator a shout at (604) 822-8733. His name is Luke Meat. If you ask nicely he'll tell you how to find them. Check out other great campus/community radio charts at www.earshot-online.com.

Figure 6.3 – CiTR's charts from the April 2011 issue of *Discorder*. The Mint/CiTR compilation album holds the top spot. Credit: *Discorder*, reprinted with permission of CiTR and Brenda Grunau.

April 2011 issue included ads from a number of venues and stores, including Red Cat Records, Sin City Fetish Night's Annual "Carnival of Kink" at Club 23 West, Scratch Records, Scrape Records, and the Emily Carr University of Art and Design. The issue contained a contents list with three sections, "Features," "Regulars," and "Reviews." The "Regulars" section included a concert calendar, charts, a program guide, and a featured "Art Project." The "Features" section was comprised of interviews with Kellarissa, "a long-time local busybody" who "dishes on her daring sophomore set Moon of Neptune, her side-gig as part of Destroyer's live band and the pros of a sunny day in the city," and other acts like Sun Wizard and Elekwent Folk ("Table of Contents" 2011). There were many illustrations in the magazine, representing a variety of styles and techniques, with a few having been submitted by readers themselves. The "Art Project" section in this issue featured the work of Andrew Pommier, a Vancouver-based artist who has spent time showing his work in the south of France (Charette 2011, 25). Three pages of the issue were devoted to his illustrations, some smaller images from his sketchbook, and two full-page images showcasing his ink and watercolour work. The issue concluded with a Top 50 albums chart from the month of March; twelve of those albums were from Vancouver, with the first spot taken by the *CiTR Pop Alliance: Vol. 2* compilation (Fig. 6.3).

The *Discorder* issue in circulation in the summer of 2011 was a "July+August" edition, with Babe Rainbow on the front cover (see Cameron Reed's electronic project, Fig. 6.4). The regular "Venews" feature in this issue profiled the "multi-purpose art centre known as the Red Gate," one of the many Vancouver venues whose future was at stake that summer (Pedri 2011, 7). The author wrote that the Red Gate "is a legitimate space for artists, musicians, photographers and filmmakers to create and display art" and that for the past seven years the space "has been a 100 per cent self-funded and self-organized cultural facility dedicated to fostering the boundary-pushing creativity for which the [Downtown Eastside] is historically known" (7). Despite the venue's successes, the city had issued a "30-day Order to Vacate," citing "'serious life and safety concerns.'" The piece informed readers that venues would continue to face such legislation unless "non-supporters voice their concerns to the City of Vancouver" (7). Clearly, *Discorder* provides a space for discussing the state of live music and performance venues in the city, one that reflects contemporary cultural and musical issues.

Cameron Reed offered some additional comments that emphasize the role of publications like *Discorder* (and *Stylus*) in influencing the listening habits of local music fans, be it in terms of acquiring albums or attending a live show. When he was younger, he was always picking up *Discorder* and "seeing what it said" (Reed 2011). "I was an insider, putting on the festivals and playing in the bands and I wasn't looking at it as just a fan. But, you see names pop up more often in a magazine like *Discorder* and all of the sudden you're thinking, 'Oh, they're a band to check out.'" This influence extends to

Figure 6.4 – Babe Rainbow on the cover of the July+August 2011 issue of *Discorder*. Credit: Robert Fougere (photo) and *Discorder*, reprinted with permission of CiTR and Brenda Grunau.

radio hosts like Nardwuar, who said he often looks to *Discorder* to see who is featured and to find potential interview subjects. He used the example of Reed's Babe Rainbow: "'Oh, Babe Rainbow is on the cover, I should do an interview with him next week" (Nardwuar … 2011). Publications like *Discorder* and *Stylus*, which share certain aspects of the mandates that drive campus stations, report on happenings within the wider music scene. This coverage is not limited to reviews and previews of live music and recorded music; it also includes articles and opinions on pressing issues that have implications for local musical activity, such as the closing of performance spaces. Campus stations can extend their mandate and local focus to related cultural productions, demonstrating the productive results of having a broadcasting sector that enables and promotes participation and inclusivity within a locality.

On 25 November 2010, Mint Records announced the release of a limited edition compilation LP with CiTR, the *CiTR Pop Alliance Compilation: Vol. 2*. The write-up, found on Mint's website, explained that "after a few Top Secret meetings at the Dairy Queen ... the news is out, we're piecing together a benefit compilation with our pals at CiTR 101.9 FM. It features 11 of our favourite Vancouver bands and only 300 waxy 180g LPs will be pressed, silkscreened and numbered by hand" (Mint Records 2010). Proceeds from the album would support the station, and each of the bands on the record had donated their songs, some of which were previously unreleased. Rain City Recorders had donated mastering time, and David Barclay of Nice Snacks had provided the artwork. Eleven different bands would be included on the record, such as Apollo Ghosts, Kellarissa, and Shane Turner Overdrive. The album release party would take place at Vancouver's Interurban Gallery, adjacent to Scratch Records, and would feature bands from the compilation, including Slam Dunk and Role Mach. A preview for the release party by *Exclaim!* called the bands on the compilation "some of the finest players in the Vancouver indie scene" (Hudson 2011).

The compilation record includes a small insert that provides information about the album, the station, the label, the artists it features, and the album's cover art. Duncan McHugh, the album's curator and host of CiTR radio show *Duncan's Donuts*, authored a brief history of the album in the insert. McHugh wrote that in 2009, before the station's annual FunDrive, he approached Becky Sandler, who was the CiTR president at the time, and told her he wanted to put a compilation together featuring local bands that could be given away during the funding drive. This initiative resulted in a twelve-song CD-R, which was the first volume under the CiTR Pop Alliance. Shena Yoshida at Mint Records heard about this compilation and approached McHugh about doing another compilation, with the aim of "raising the stakes" this time (McHugh 2010). Yoshida informed CiTR that Mint could help release the compilation on vinyl. McHugh, on his role as curator, said, "We hear a lot about bands from Brooklyn, Montreal and San Francisco, but I think Vancouver's music community is the best around ... I was hoping we could take a snapshot of Vancouver's scene in 2011. Clearly there's WAY too much great stuff to fit on a single record so the focus here is on pop."

Commenting on the compilation album from the perspective of Mint Records, Bill Baker explained that the label is happy to involve itself in any project that benefits the radio station without necessarily benefiting the label. This approach follows Baker's experience at CiTR, where there was an unwritten rule that "you don't play your own music, whether you're in a band or whether you have a label" (Baker 2011). Baker added that in the early stages of running Mint, they could have really taken advantage of their relationships with influential individuals at the station. Instead, they treated their relationship to the station "at an arm's length." Regarding the compilation record, Baker said, "Here's something where we can flip-flop and take the things that we've learned over these years and put them to some use to benefit the station, instead of the other way around." He stressed that he would "not even one one-hundredth of a percent consider that this was our way to give back, because there is no way to give back what I got out of that place." Evidently, a not-for-profit motive that is intrinsic to the community-based mandate of campus stations has remained with Baker and shapes his ongoing relationship with the station.

The artist who designed the album's cover, David Barclay, wrote a short note to include with the insert, titled "Concerning the Cover Art." It read, "CiTR 101.9FM is a college radio station situated on Musqueam land, and which through its existence has been run primarily by privileged white males" (Barclay 2010). Barclay added, "For over 50 years 'college rock' has been dominated by an elitist cultural lexicon, reinforced by the institutionalized racism of the post-secondary education system in Canada and the US." So he had designed a "Northwest Coast-style totem pole" for the front cover, made up of faces of individuals from the station and the Vancouver music communities (Fig. 6.5). The cover was "a deliberate combination of both the uneasiness and the splendour of the station's contemporary cultural history." The artists and individuals chosen for the totem pole represented CiTR's encouragement and support of "unlikely artistic voices that have become iconic local anti-corporate, anti-racist figures," like Joey Shithead of D.O.A. and "important songwriters and musical innovators," like Dan Bejar of Destroyer and the New Pornographers. As well, Barclay said that "CiTR volunteers have made music and their involvement with the station their life's passion and have become inspiring members of the local and national community," such as Nardwuar the Human Serviette and Christa Min. The note ended with instructions on how to find more information on Musqueam rights to the University Endowment Land. This note is a significant component of the compilation, for it links the station's progressive

Figure 6.5 – Shena Yoshida's show poster for the Mint Records and *CiTR Pop Alliance Compilation: Vol. 2* launch party, created from old *Discorder* magazines. Credit: Shena Yoshida, reprinted with permission from Shena Yoshida.

mandate, as well as some of its political and inclusive shortcomings, to the compilation album. The compilation is very much a product of the culture that inspires the station, and it documents a segment of Vancouver's music scene at a given time.

Support from cultural institutions helps live music circulate, especially local music that can be labelled as independent, underground, or alternative. The uneasiness around the stability of Vancouver venues and cultural institutions makes a strong argument for the importance of institutions such as campus radio stations and their related cultural productions, objects like *Discorder*, *Stylus*, and the Mint and CiTR compilation record. Campus radio stations are resourceful places with the longevity necessary to build and sustain connections between people and places. Technical and musical knowledge can in turn be shared and circulated, constructing community and a notion of a city or town's music scene. This knowledge also transfers from place to place, building musical and cultural connections between and throughout music scenes and the communities within them, as evidenced by the strong links between Dawson City and Sackville. Campus radio stations across the country facilitate the transfer and circulation of Canadian music in a manner that enables individuals at radio stations to play and promote local artists on the radio and within a locality. As Nardwuar the Human Serviette emphasized, "You mail your record to that station, somebody's going to play it, and that person might go on to be a booker at a club, that person might be in a band, that person might help you out with it" (Nardwuar ... 2011).

Stations work closely alongside other important institutional sites and cultural products within a locality. This connection is apparent in the stories recalled by station staff and volunteers, as well as by cultural producers, and it results in tangible by-products, such as magazines and records, which help document the cultural production within a locality. The combined resources of Mint and CiTR, including technical resources and musical knowledge and connections, have resulted in a compilation album and a launch party, as well as funds raised for the station by album sales. The connections between campus stations and the production, performance, and distribution of music emphasize the significant role of campus radio stations as resourceful institutions within a music scene. Campus stations do not just program local and independent music. They are places to record debut albums and to have show posters made, and they are places for out-of-town bands and artists to inquire about where to book a show. By sharing resources with other institutions and organizations, such as magazine publishers and live music festivals, campus stations help maintain the vibrancy and sustainability of live music within a locality. Moreover,

Figure 6.6 – David Barclay's artwork for the Mint Records and *CiTR Pop Alliance Compilation: Vol. 2*. Credit: David Barclay, reprinted with permission from Shena Yoshida, Duncan McHugh, and CiTR.

campus stations document moments in a city or town's musical and cultural history, and this is very central to the ways in which a station's own history and mythology are constructed and shared. The campus radio sector offers a local alternative to radio practitioners, cultural producers, listeners, and music fans through its participative and inclusive structure, through its role in documenting local cultural production, by providing amateur radio programmers with technical and musical resources, and by committing to a community-based mandate.

A key finding from this exploration of campus stations and their surrounding music scenes is that individual taste and expertise thrives and figures prominently within the campus radio sector. The ability for individual taste to play such a large role in the culture of campus radio results from the level of autonomy each station is given, in which a distinct station mandate and one's personal involvement with a given musical community come to define and shape participation. Individual perceptions regarding cultural institutions and noteworthy sites within a scene have the potential to navigate one's experience of the locality's musical activity. For instance, Rob Schmidt referenced the significance of record stores in Winnipeg, but more importantly, what the station conceives of as a "good" record store. A good record store is a place where people talk about music, events, culture, and politics. Stu Reid mentioned his ability to play music from a variety of genres and "somehow justify it as country music … in some weird way, shape or form" (Reid 2011). As an established member of the broadly defined country music community in Winnipeg, Reid is able to apply his expertise and make connections between musical styles and genres for his listeners. The prominence of expertise and experience seems to reproduce a sort of romantic idea about taste as a product of individual character, as opposed to stemming solely from social origin. Expertise and taste hierarchies are implicit in the sharing of musical knowledge. However, this production of an "alternative" music culture, where taste and expertise thrive, also tends to exclude segments of the community. It is important to keep in mind that there are those who do not find themselves on the "inside" of a particular genre or style, despite a discourse of inclusivity and diversity that is a key characteristic of the campus sector. On these issues, the campus sector is aware and reflexive of the fact that certain cultural communities are not well represented on campus radio.

But the "alternative" music culture tied to music programming on campus radio does indeed create alternative places and spaces for challenging boundaries in dominant popular musical practices, and the fact that discussions about diversity are taking place within the campus sector is evidence of this. For instance, CHMA has created innovative performance spaces in places that were previously used for non-musical purposes. The town can now sustain music festivals and offer a place for independent bands touring the East Coast to play. Recall Robin Eriksson's take on bluegrass music. When she first started the show, she had a hard time finding bands and artists that did not fall within the dominant "old boys' music" of the genre (Eriksson 2011). Over time, Eriksson has found that more women are playing old-time and bluegrass music, and this has shaped the direction of her show and her role in the Winnipeg bluegrass community. This tension between inclusion and exclusion, and the production of an "alternative" music culture within the campus radio sector, are issues taken up in the next and final chapter.

7

Campus Radio and Alternative Music Culture

Campus radio stations are cultural nodes that help constitute and shape music scenes. They do this through maintaining connections with other cultural institutions and through the sharing of musical and technical knowledge and resources. The cultural practices that are produced and performed in campus stations and by campus radio practitioners are best understood as a response to a larger problematic inherent in Canada's radio broadcasting environment, that of a decline in localism and the standardization of programming. Oppositional and alternative cultural practices that privilege local music react and respond to dominant power structures that shape the political economy of Canadian broadcasting. The market logic that increasingly motivates policy for the commercial sector, and the nationalist ideology that has shaped the public sector, are the predominant lens through which the Canadian broadcasting system is understood. The campus sector challenges and responds to these dominant ideologies, primarily through a local focus and community-based mandate. "Alternative" must not vaguely define the campus sector. Instead, the term must account for why, when, and how certain broadcasting practices, programming offerings, and station–listener relationships are decidedly distinct within Canada's broadcasting system. The campus sector is tied to larger power structures through the federal regulations that enable stations to exist on the FM dial, but beyond that, there are many ways the campus sector provides alternative methods for circulating music and culture.

A dominant understanding of broadcasting as a commercial enterprise or as a nation-binding experience shapes the specific oppositional practices that are initiated by the community and campus radio sector. This point can be understood through Raymond Williams's notions of counter and alternative hegemony. Williams expanded on Antonio Gramsci's concept of hegemony to introduce the concepts of "counter-hegemony and alternative hegemony," illustrating that dominance is neither total nor exclusive (1977). Like Gramsci, Williams challenges the notion that ideology fully permeates the superstructure as determined by an economic base. Rather, cultural and social processes are integral to the ways in which ideas and beliefs circulate, and these processes involve numerous contradictions and ·tensions. Williams argued that at all times, "forms of alternative or directly oppositional politics and culture exist as significant elements in society" (113). Alternatives are connected to and shaped by dominant ideologies (such as the the one that ties public broadcasting to nationalism in Canada, or commercial radio to capitalism), but they can be effective institutions and formations for creating spaces for alternative cultural work. Alternative practices are shaped by dominant ideologies; they also have the potential to create oppositional spaces that respond to a given problematic within society and culture.

Countercultural and alternative expressions circulate through texts that are crafted by campus stations, in station mandates and cultural publications, and in the words of the practitioners whose time and volunteerism sustain the sector's operations. A station mandate or philosophy is an internal policy document that affirms acceptance of federal broadcast regulations and simultaneously declares autonomy by crafting guidelines that govern one station and one station only. Key characteristics of the sector include independent or not-for-profit status, innovative and creative programming, educational and instructive programming, and diversity. These characteristics are missing from the dominant commercial radio sector in Canada, particularly in its relationship to Canadian localities. Within the campus sector, students and community members are encouraged to get involved with radio production regardless of their prior experience with broadcasting. Within a music scene, notions of the alternative, the local, and the independent establish ideological pathways between and throughout campus radio stations and related cultural institutions.

Emphasizing alternativeness and distinctiveness has been at the heart of the development of the campus radio sector and its expansion across the country. This has paralleled the establishment of its governing policies. The licensing of the sector followed educational radio stations and early radio experiments on university campuses. Many on-campus radio stations gradually became more ambitious, following their desire to broadcast beyond campus borders and to reflect the interests of nearby communities. The social and political activist movements that would propel community media initiatives in Canada in the 1960s and 1970s strongly influenced the campus radio sector; so did an emphasis on "high-quality" programming that reflected students' tastes and expertise. Of course, these dual characteristics were nothing new, nor were they exclusive to the countercultural and student movements of the 1960s; they were present in early educational radio as well. Stations like CKUA in Edmonton were involved in representing nearby rural and agricultural communities and social movements.

This history precedes the stories recalled by the individuals in Sackville, Winnipeg, and Vancouver who were interviewed for this book. The interviews offer insight into the routes along which campus radio stations circulate and promote music in a city or town and the ways that campus stations navigate and integrate broadcasting policy. Station staff and volunteers possess knowledge of musical communities within their broadcast range, and this knowledge helps construct a notion of the city or town's music scene. The energy or essence of the small radio clubs that existed in basements or dorm rooms before stations began broadcasting on the FM dial is remembered both negatively and positively. Some claim that a pre-FM culture set the stage for the contemporary vibe of the station, permeating the studio space. Others are proud that the campus radio sector has moved beyond insular radio clubs and into the wider community. The knowledge shared by campus radio practitioners and cultural producers in their respective localities includes stories about venues and record stores, concert programmers and promoters, and bands or artists who came up through the music scene with the station's support. These connections are also found in the cultural productions produced by campus stations, which both reflect and create musical activity within a scene. Campus stations are involved in producing, distributing, and performing music; they also maintain an institutional presence for the various musical and cultural moments that take place between and throughout these stages.

Besides conducting interviews, I have consulted and analyzed policy and archival documents from the CRTC, universities, and campus stations; listened to compilation albums; looked at station-produced magazines; examined online texts such as station mandates and philosophies; and made personal observations of musical activity in the localities surrounding campus stations. This book has brought together all of this material to paint a picture of a vibrant Canadian campus radio sector and of the musical activity that stations promote within their different broadcast ranges. However, this book reflects only part of a much larger Canadian campus and community radio sector. More research could and should be done in this area. For instance, this book does not profile the role of campus stations in delivering local news and information to listeners. Campus stations broadcast spoken-word content that caters to a variety of cultural and ethnic groups in a locality. The significant contributions of campus stations in these areas and others would make for intriguing and important research projects.

Canadian Campus Radio and Policy-Making

One question I posed at the beginning of this book concerned the significance of broadcasting policy in structuring the operations of campus stations and in shaping their various cultures. A comprehensive policy framework for the sector has been developed and revised over the years, working to match the goals and aspirations of campus radio practitioners. A single policy now governs both campus and community radio in Canada, and it emphasizes the role of stations in maintaining a level of openness to community members, the broadcasting of local cultural and artistic expression, and the promotion of emerging Canadian talent (CRTC 2010c). A shift away from the educational function of campus radio, in the instructional sense, is reflected by the fact that the commission no longer licenses instructional campus stations. According to the CRTC, broadcasters can be trained at unlicensed closed-circuit or Internet-only radio stations, or they can learn through the experience that community-based stations offer volunteers. The reiteration of community involvement is evidence of the blurred roles of community-based campus stations, and it is often difficult to discern the ratio of student to community listeners. Also, both CKUW in Winnipeg and CiTR in Vancouver have a lower percentage of student programmers to community members (although many current community programmers are former students). Both the sector and the policy that regulates it have embraced community involvement. Ultimately, a community-based mandate that is also inclusive of students has continued to be fundamental to the sector. The public hearing that preceded CKLN's licence revocation made this point very clear.

Someone who applies to program a music-based radio show at a campus station must often emphasize a "new" or diverse genre. The sector's role in developing emerging Canadian artists is also evidenced by the fact that in its 2010 policy for campus and community radio, the CRTC announced a new definition for the subcategory "Experimental music." Experimental music includes the "unconventional and non-traditional uses of instruments and sound equipment to create new sounds and an orchestration of these sounds" (CRTC 2010c). Audio-art, turntablism, *musique actuelle*, electroacoustic music, and sound ecology are all cited in this new definition. Musical communities where these sounds and styles circulate can now connect more effectively with campus stations, and experimental musical selections can contribute to Canadian content quotas for campus radio. The 2010 policy for the campus and community sector also works to ensure diversity in programming. The policy states that the "cultural diversity present in many Canadian communities places campus and community stations serving those centres in a position to make a strong contribution to the reflection of that cultural diversity, especially by providing exposure to new and emerging artists from underserved cultural groups" (CRTC 2010c).

Community representation is central to campus radio policy. A station's locality has been a key factor in determining its operations and culture. Campus stations are shaped by the cultural history of the town or city and by the students and community members who bring their individual tastes and experiences to the station. Each locality is distinct, and thus, the campus radio sector is comprised of many distinct stations, each of which has crafted its own unique style and sound. Recalling Jean McNulty's government report from 1979, local programming is best understood in relation to the society in which it developed, not just in relation to the broadcasting system itself. This assertion still holds. According to McNulty's report, three advantages of local programming are the involvement of individuals rather than "professionals," the broadcasting of local information from "alternative sources," and opportunities for artists and musicians to reach a local audience. While there are evident similarities in the way CKUW, CHMA, and CiTR structure a week of programming, there are also significant differences. CKUW puts greater emphasis on spoken-word programming, reflecting the fact that it is based at an inner-city campus. East Coast music is profiled on CHMA, the only local broadcaster in the small town of Sackville. On CiTR, "weirdness" carries throughout the station's program grid, reflecting the prominence of genres like punk and weird punk among the city's local bands and the performance spaces that quickly come and go. Each station's music programming is different, for each city or town tends to support and sustain distinct sounds and styles. Individual stations negotiate CRTC broadcasting policy through internal policies and guiding principles, and as a result, the campus radio sector is able to provide a local alternative on Canadian radio.

Complications and tensions can arise as individual stations implement broadcasting policy. Policy-making in various cultural fields is shaped by the government of the day as well as by larger trends and issues affecting other realms of cultural policy. There have been both productive and regressive moments in the history of policy-making for campus radio. Advocates for the sector have long argued for the sustainability of the sector and its place on the FM dial. Relations between the CRTC and the campus sector are not always positive, and there have certainly been tensions arising from the need for stations to continuously meet the requirements and regula- tions as set out in CRTC policy. As with many community and alterna- tive media outlets, the campus sector has limited finances and resources, so dealing with everyday administrative tasks can be taxing. Pierre Malloy shared some of his thoughts on the regulation of CHMA. His comments exemplify a disconnect between CRTC regulation and the station's inter- nal policy, which is specific to its locality. "Guidelines are great," he said in reference to Canadian content regulations, "but when it becomes the dif- ference between twenty-nine and thirty percent, that's when I'm really like, 'What's the point then? Get robots if you want that. It's ridiculous'" (Malloy, personal interview, 3 June 2011). He noted that most people who host a show at CHMA are playing a lot of Canadian music regardless of regulation, and on-air personalities are always discussing Canadian music. According to Malloy, campus radio is inherently Canadian because its programming largely comes from the surrounding locality. "And then one show happens to play a little less," said Malloy, "and then all of the sudden their numbers are off." Malloy emphasized that CHMA is more about providing people the opportunity to "talk on the radio and play songs that they want to hear on the radio." However, as Chapter 4 has illustrated, the sector was not always entirely representative of Canadian and local music. In working towards FM radio broadcasting, campus radio practitioners developed the sector alongside policy initiatives that put community representation and local musical and cultural expression at the centre of the campus sector.

Malloy also expressed concern about federal policy-making, argu- ing that the process is disconnected from the priorities and concerns of individual stations. A lot of decisions are made in "board rooms and fancy offices and in meetings with people who are used to working with people who have lots of money and resources." These decisions, then, are more in tune with "*that* environment, [but] that's not *this* environment. They're not seeing the environment they're making decisions for." The commission does not edit or censor CHMA, "but at the same time ... CHMA is very dependent on [the CRTC] for a lot of things ... so it's a weird relationship and a difficult one." Also, music rights organizations tend to treat campus stations as they would commercial ones. "They want the same money from us that they get from commercial radio, and it's hard to explain to them that we don't have revenue. There's no revenue coming in other than our mem- bership and we don't sell ads. If we do get any money it's from a grant and that's for a certain project."

At the 2011 NCRC conference, the relationship between the NCRA and the CRTC was a topic of debate during a panel that discussed compliance issues between the commission and campus stations. Ryerson's CKLN was a topic of interest, since its licence had recently been revoked for non-compliance. Some conference participants expressed concern that the NCRA was getting too close to the CRTC, arguing that the campus and community sector needed to be stronger to fight against issues like CKLN having its licence revoked; others stressed that a healthy relationship with the commission is necessary and beneficial. This book suggests that a disjuncture between the CRTC and campus stations is healthy for the circulation of local music and that the CRTC framework has appropriately provided a loose structure in which these different local music scenes and their connections to campus stations can thrive. CKLN's licence revocation is an unfortunate event that must be acknowledged as evidence of the importance of complying with basic radio regulations within the campus sector, such as Canadian content quotas, especially in competitive radio markets like Toronto, where other campus FM stations have also been licensed. Campus stations must maintain a community-based focus and be inclusive of both students and community members, and station managers and program directors must communicate station goals and guidelines to their volunteers. Beyond this, the licence renewal process for campus stations has been streamlined by the commission, and stations are able to rely on their internal policies to reflect and represent their communities.

CKUW's Sarah Michaelson highlighted the disjuncture between federal policy and the internal governance of individual stations. She claimed that CKUW broadcasts from Winnipeg in a very "proud way" regardless of CRTC regulation, hinting that the station easily meets Canadian content and local music requirements regardless of broadcasting policy. She said there have been interesting discussions between the NCRA and campus stations about the potential of "Fem-con," or a policy that ensures there is enough female content on the air. This is an important point, "because women still face a lot of challenges that men don't really face in the music industry; just *getting* recorded, let alone getting airplay" (Michaelson, personal interview, 7 July 2011). The NCRA's Resolutions from 2011 define Fem-con as "music which meets two of the following categories: music, artists, lyrics and production by women." The NCRA/ANREC recommended that all member stations implement a "percentage threshold minimum of 30% female content (fem-con) with certain genre exceptions defined and regulated by the station's programming departments" (NCRA 2011). It was then resolved that the NCRA/ANREC include this proposal in their lobbying initiatives with the CRTC. Clearly, the campus sector is aware of issues that need to figure more prominently in policy and governance decisions. Such policies can be, and are, integrated into station mandates, though it takes more work and effort to have them represented nationally in CRTC regulation.

In Canadian broadcasting today, "alternativeness" is linked to local programming practices. Campus stations emphasize localness in their mandates, in which efforts to represent communities in a station's broadcast range are recorded for volunteers and staff members to reference and use in their programming practices. Operating within "the local" also prevents campus radio stations from sounding alike. "The local" is a rallying point for asserting alternativeness, especially given broader trends toward centralization and standardization in the contemporary radio industry.

Alternative Music Culture, Cultural Capital, and the Circulation of Local Music

A key means to ensure a connection to the local community is a culture of inclusivity and diversity. The openness and relative autonomy of the campus sector allows communities to exercise a significant voice in a station's direction, especially for those individuals who program shows. Individual tastes, interests, and perceptions figure strongly in the culture of campus radio. As the previous chapter began to outline, an individual's capacity to shape the sound of a campus station through his or her musical preferences generates an alternative music culture, one that, while facilitated by a level of openness that allows volunteers to produce radio programs, is also structured in part by taste hierarchies, expertise, and, in some cases, exclusion. Music-making in a locality stems from the connections between and through people, and this invariably involves their subjective tastes and preferences, especially when it comes to selecting bands to play on air, to feature in a magazine, or to include on a compilation album. "Independent" and "alternative" cultural productions and institutions are propelled by individuals because they require inexpensive or free volunteer labour. The reward for one's volunteer labour (typically a few hours per week) is the freedom to express oneself without pressure to conform to a corporate ethos or to the standards of professional media outlets. Individuals who become central in the circulation of local and independent music become tastemakers and gatekeepers within a certain genre of music or music scene, and this can have positive and negative results.

The reflection of a locality's diversity through programming is determined by a particular impression of that city or town's demographics as understood by programmers, volunteers, and station staff. The previous chapter began to highlight a tension that emerges between individual taste and expertise and the utopian ideal of fully representing one's community. That tension is implicated in an alternative music culture, one in which the idealistic goal of total community representation is more realistically put into practice by the ways in which individuals set the terms for what community representation entails, or rather, what the limits of community representation are. Some communities are recognized and others are not, and a number of factors can contribute to this exclusion. First, there are class and cultural divisions whereby it is assumed to be the norm for some to attend university, while for others, there is no cultural or familial tradition of attending university. Sarah Michaelson explained that someone's family might not have a history of going to university, and though it does not require student status to volunteer at a campus station, a person may not feel comfortable enough to walk through the station's doors, or the university's for that matter. Also, it is her understanding that most of those involved in campus radio in Canada are white. There has been a shift toward increased diversity, but identity categories including (but not limited to) race, class, and gender are important to consider when contemplating community representation and inclusivity. The stations profiled in this book are aware that some cultural communities are not well represented on campus radio.

The "inside" can apply to physical space, as in the actual doors and walls of a campus station, as well as to the insider knowledge that allows one to participate and exert influence within a music scene. Many of the people who contributed to this work cited an initial feeling of anxiety when they first passed through the doors of their campus radio station. This suggests that some people view campus stations as exclusive places where "hip" new music that most people are unaware of thrives. Stations appear credible to listeners due to their commitment to staying on top of the genres or musical styles represented by their programs. But as both Ted Turner and Sarah Michaelson emphasized, their hesitation to get involved was essentially a result of what they thought the culture of the station *might be*. In reality, the station was a welcoming place where they were able to quickly get involved in multiple aspects of the station's operations. There is also the requirement that station volunteers learn to use the technical equipment in the studio or broadcast booth. Whether an individual wants to get involved with in-studio production, on-air programming, Web maintenance, or some other technical aspect at a station, a certain level of expertise is required. Of course, volunteer training exists so that this knowledge is passed on, and stations circulate carefully crafted training manuals for their volunteers. But this can be a significant hurdle for many volunteers. Brenda Grunau explained that CiTR has relaxed the technical components that volunteers must master before hosting a show. Prospective show hosts were once required to produce a demo tape and prove that they could use all the equipment before getting on the air. Now the emphasis is on learning about the equipment while working in the studio booth, alongside others who have already learned to use the equipment. This is an instance of a campus radio station becoming aware of a particular issue that is limiting its inclusivity and then reacting in a way that works to remedy the problem.

The level of diversity of a program grid is shaped by the level of expertise necessary to represent a niche genre or style of music. This can lead to exclusivity. Program grids are typically structured so that shows airing next to one another sound nothing alike. For instance, at CKUW, new shows must be pitched by highlighting and justifying difference. What, exactly, is a new show going to bring to the program grid in terms of diversity, and how does a potential show distinguish itself from others? The result is a commendable program schedule where one can hear a wide variety of musical styles. Programmers are also able to draw from their own personality and adopt a programming style that is decidedly unique. The hesitation that some soon-to-be volunteers have felt before entering a campus station can be attributed at least partly to the sophisticated musical knowledge that many show hosts have. If a radio program is going to be the anchor for a certain genre in a city or town's music scene, the show's host must have exceptional knowledge of that genre. This individual will likely attend shows in the city and may even organize and promote those shows or play in a band. The social theorist Pierre Bourdieu used the term "cultural capital" to highlight processes of cultural distinction that are tied in part to social origin. Society, then, is stratified not just along lines of class and education – two forms of capital required to participate in student culture – but also in terms of aesthetic discretion, that is, the ability to determine the worth of culture and exert knowledge about cultural work. "Taste classifies, and it classifies the classifier," argues Bourdieu (1984, 6). Tastes are determined by distinction and discretion, "the practical affirmation of an inevitable difference. It is no accident that, when they have to be justified, they are asserted purely negatively, by the refusal of other tastes" (56). Through the strategic collection, sharing, and distribution of cultural goods, individuals accumulate and convey cultural capital. A radio host who hopes to stay connected to a given musical community requires a high level of musical knowledge and expertise. Those who program music for and from a music community are cultural intermediaries between artists and listeners. They become critical nodes in the circulation of local and independent music; thus they are integral to an alternative music culture, in which one must have expertise and cultural capital in order to represent a genre or music community.

This book argues that the relationship between campus stations and a music scene involves much more than just programming music. Campus radio practitioners are aware of other cultural institutions and productions within a scene, and they are often involved in multiple facets of local musical activity, supporting both artists from their own locality and those touring and travelling from elsewhere. Sarah Thornton uses the term "subcultural capital" to apply Bourdieu's ideas to the study of youth club cultures in the United Kingdom. Subcultural capital is not just about conferring status and distinction through a sophisticated understanding of culture; it is also about the embedded codes and styles required to participate in a subculture. For Thornton, a form of subcultural capital is "Hipness," which "confers status on its owner in the eyes of the relevant beholder" (1996, 11). This form of capital is "embodied in the form of being 'in the know,' using (but not over-using) current slang and looking as if you were born to perform the latest dance styles" (11–12). Depending on how "underground" a particular genre or music community might be considered, a show host may need to possess subcultural capital in order to attend shows and find out about new music happening in a locality.

In Vancouver, where venues open and close on a whim, insider knowledge becomes necessary to discover live show locations, especially when an unlicensed or illegal event can be quickly shut down by the police. Thornton distinguishes subcultural from cultural capital by age: "In many ways [subcultural capital] affects the standing of the young like its adult equivalent," cultural capital (11). So there is a sense that age can also limit the inclusivity of an alternative music culture, depending on the genre. However, the range of ages of the individuals interviewed for this book challenges a complete application of this idea. A wide variety of ages are represented throughout the show hosts on a program grid. Stu Reid at CKUW has been involved with the station for decades, retaining a listenership that favours country music and his individual take on the genre. Interviewees typically referenced their youth, or their time as a student, as when they *first* became involved with a station or a show; their involvement in a music community has evolved over time, as has their show. Evidently, it requires a certain level of capital, or combinations thereof – cultural, subcultural, educational – to participate effectively in an alternative music culture. Sophisticated tastes, musical expertise, and a connection to a music community are tied to one's individual character and one's social networks. A campus radio station is a social network of students and members of the community wherein one's tastes are shaped by individual character and by connections with other cultural intermediaries – more, perhaps, than by social origin.

This emphasis on the range of programs and the diversity of sounds and styles heard on campus stations raises an issue of credibility. It appears as though a *legitimate* campus station must convincingly reflect the sounds and styles of a locality's music scene, beyond simply maintaining legitimacy through compliance with the CRTC. Moreover, programmers are responsible for developing genres or expanding a genre's boundaries. Both Reid and Eriksson at CKUW highlighted how their approach to programming has challenged their listeners' expectations about a certain genre. Over the years, Reid has justified a number of sounds as "country," and Eriksson has programmed a number of women artists on her bluegrass show. Hosts are described in program descriptions as authorities on specific genres, and this requires a certain level of work and cultural capital so that radio programs remain ahead of their listenership. This raises a further question about campus stations that may not appropriately or effectively represent their music scenes: Would such a station be thought of as inauthentic or not credible?

Promotion is central to the circulation of music. In the music industries that have developed alongside the "repeating" stage of music – an era of mass-produced music and one whereby, according to Jacques Attali, "music became an industry, and *its consumption ceased to be collective*" (1985, 88) – promotion typically involves commercial advertisements, music videos, and reviews in major commercial music magazines. Promotion, under this logic, is an economic investment that anticipates a return not just for artists but for any number of industry gatekeepers and "middlemen" once physical copies of recorded music are purchased. The alternative music culture produced in part by campus radio is not entirely disconnected from the economic logic, or capital, inherent in what promotion means for the facets of the music industries that are primarily concerned with the generation of profit; however, the circulation of music within and throughout campus radio culture is organized, much more so, by cultural capital. Despite the taste hierarchies and various instances of exclusion resulting from the individualist nature of cultural capital, there is a way in which the promotion of music by cultural status provides an alternative to the purely economic model ingrained in commercial radio. Sara Cohen, writing on music scenes, explains that people and their activities and interactions constitute a scene. Relationships are formed, some that are close, and others that are part of "looser networks or alliances." These relationships comprise an "informal economy" that involves the exchange of information, instruments, technical support, and so forth (Cohen 1999, 240). Instead of thinking of cultural capital as contributing to the systems of oppression that stratify society, the campus radio sector urges us to consider the ways in which cultural capital creates alternative values and methods for circulating music. Individuals – listeners, music fans, radio hosts – are just as much "producers" as artists are. The listening and sharing practices of those individuals who devote their time to a campus radio station organize the paths along which music and musical knowledge is shared and sustained, and this happens both inside and outside the campus station space. Campus stations remain credible through the social interactions between radio practitioners, cultural producers, and listeners. By distinguishing itself from purely economic models of circulating music, campus radio culture produces, through a variety of strategically deployed texts and practices, an alternative music culture in which local and independent music thrives. Thus, the sector is a distinct component of the Canadian broadcasting system, one that reflects a diversity of local music and culture and that demonstrates that Canadian cultural identity is much more dynamic and varied than commercial radio programming suggests.

In Kaitlin Fontana's oral history of Mint Records, the Vancouver music scene and CiTR figure prominently. She writes that "within these scenes, however, friendship is holy writ – people help each other get day jobs, trade work for album art and recording space, and generally do what they can to help a musically inclined brother or sister out" (2011, 88). This quote highlights the importance of sharing resources, new music, and technical know-how within a music community. The space of campus stations is where a lot of this dialogue and interaction takes place. These connections have implications both in terms of how music is broadcast from the station into the wider community and how the culture of the station permeates and circulates through the locality. Ted Turner shared his thoughts on why music on campus radio is much more than just broadcasted content from sender(s) to receiver(s):

> What makes campus and community radio so special is that it's really the only place where you can phone someone at two in the afternoon, after hearing something, and ask, "What is that? I have to know what that is, I love that." And that person will pick up the phone and tell you, "It's *this*. I got it *there*. Actually, there's another copy at *this* record store. It costs eight bucks. Oh, you'd probably also like *this*, thanks for calling." And you make that human connection. And that's what's really missing. You don't get that when you download something, you don't get that from a podcast. (Turner, personal interview, 7 July 2011)

He added a description of how hosts often attach their personalities to the songs they play, using the band Joy Division as an example. "There is something powerful about someone playing a Joy Division song, and you being able to call and ask that person what it is. And listen to that host tell their story about the first time they heard Joy Division on the radio ten years ago themselves, and how they came across it." Turner emphasized the importance of these points of intersection in people's lives, when songs or art becomes powerful and meaningful. The campus radio sector is distinct from commercial radio. It is not a network of stations that prescribes and promotes hit records to listeners. It is a collection of spaces that welcome the sharing of music and culture, where personalities shine through programming decisions and practices. Charles Fairchild writes that there are "specific kinds of communicative gestures involved when music is played on the radio" and these "shape how the presenter and the listener meet one another through radio" (2012, 107). He argues that this form of contact is a "specifically aesthetic encounter," one that is fully realized in community radio, where inclusion is high and individuals are able to make their own programming decisions. And this encounter extends beyond the playing of music on the radio and into the cities, towns, and cultural spaces that influence and shape these communicative gestures.

Beyond the station space, connections are apparent between campus stations and other cultural institutions in a locality. Campus radio stations are resourceful places with the longevity necessary to build connections between people and places such as venues and record labels, and this is particularly significant in places where a reliable cultural institution is pivotal for building a sense of community and for circulating independent and local music. Vancouver with its issues over sustaining live performance spaces, and Sackville with its need to appropriate alternative spaces to accommodate a music festival, are examples of how campus stations have been particularly resourceful. By making performance spaces out of taverns, churches, and theatres, CHMA has helped Sackville become a place where bands and artists can play a show on their way to Halifax or while touring the East Coast. A local music scene does not just include local bands and artists. It also involves connections to other spaces and places. As Cohen explains, "scenes are lived, experienced, and imagined by particular groups within particular situations" and include local, national, and transnational connections (1999, 249). So while local identities and "relations of similarity and difference" on a local scale are important, so too are connections and relationships "within a system of translocality" (Kruse 2010, 637). These connections also produce cultural objects, like magazines and records. Within the broadcast range of a given campus radio station, these connections provide alternative methods for circulating and experiencing music for listeners, radio practitioners, and musicians. Furthermore, these connections document moments in a city or town's musical and cultural history, contributing to the ways that a station's own history and mythology are constructed and shared.

For a campus station to be able to reflect and represent each and every community in its broadcast range is an idealistic goal, one that is difficult to fully achieve and measure. There are notable limitations in terms of how fully integrated a station can be with the community. Campus radio stations are mostly volunteer-run, and the amount of time spent at a station by personnel fluctuates. There are also limits to financial and technical resources. As Turner explained, CKUW is "running radio camps, and has a news department, and ... [is] completely happening on the largest scale possible within this community, for what we can do." Community representation, then, falls somewhere between the ways in which a community-based mandate is outlined in internal policy and the various ways that musical and cultural communities are imagined by, and connected to, radio practitioners and programmers. Radio has the ability to constitute communities of listeners and multiple listening publics (Lacey 2013, 14–18), where significant connections are made through the act of listening. Alexander Russo argues that alongside the narrative of radio constituting a national imagined community, where listeners experience a shared sense of belonging to the nation (see Anderson 1936/1991), it has also "constructed smaller regional and local ones that were linked to the larger community in some ways and independent of it in others" (2010, 4). It is on this local level that campus radio constructs *imagined* community representation. Each member of every local community may not have a voice on air, but radio hosts are connected to a segment of a music scene through a shared taste culture for which musical selections are programmed. "Imagined-community radio" is still very much tied to segments of the local music scene in important ways that facilitate the documentation and sharing of local music. Furthermore, campus stations are predominately inclusive and accessible spaces that enable one to participate in producing radio. In Sackville, students comprise nearly half of the town's population, and thus, CHMA's programmers are predominantly students. By contrast, in Vancouver and Winnipeg, student programmer percentages are relatively low in relation to community member participation. This means that many community members are participating in campus radio, particularly in cities, building connections between the campus and its locality. The participation of community members is an essential component of "community" broadcasting, one that distinguishes the sector from private and public radio. Recall as well the significantly disconnected nature of unlicensed, closed-circuit campus radio stations. Radio clubs that included engineering students and professors, or basement and dorm room spaces described as boys' clubs, have been regarded as former practices that campus stations have left behind.

Community representation and program diversity have improved over time, and there is hope that this trend will continue.

Exclusivity within campus radio and alternative music is something the sector is aware of, and interviewees stated their desire to devote further time and effort to this important issue. The "future of the sector" is a topic that many of participants in this work discussed, with regard to both their home station and the sector as a whole. The following comments reflect both hopeful and apprehensive projections for the space and place of the campus radio sector within the larger Canadian media environment and cultural industries.

The Future of the Canadian Campus Radio Sector

Participants mentioned the future relevance of campus and community radio. They were concerned about radio listenership at a time when digital and online music services are increasing in popularity. Sarah Michaelson is nervous about losing community radio: "The value of radio has gone down for the average listener, but we move with the times, in terms of being able to download the shows after they've been recorded." She worried that "we'd be losing a certain way of relating and connecting to people" if campus and community radio were to disappear (Michaelson, personal interview, 7 July 2011). She related some of this nervousness to fundraising pledges over the past few years. CKUW's main measure of success is how many pledges they receive during their "Fundrive." A slight plateau over the past few years has made the station a little anxious. For her, this does not necessarily mean that listenership is decreasing for the station, just that the landscape is changing in general. She drew upon her experience working at the CBC, where the trend of cutting funding to television and radio has been apparent. "Radio had really been lashed a couple of years ago, and I don't know if it will make a comeback. And they call it radio, but it's really just websites and blog posts, or basically playing an iPod shuffle overnight." Michaelson's comments highlight the prominence of personality and individuality in campus radio programming, especially the presence of a live voice, recalling also Fairchild's notion of the aesthetic encounter that can occur between the person programming the music and the listener. Michaelson distinguished campus radio operations from some of the initiatives that radio services provided by the CBC, such as Radio 2 and Radio 3, have implemented, where online content has become much more prominent. "I love that we have *live* radio at three in the morning at our station. There are people who are night owls, playing music for other night owls." In the face of this changing radio landscape, CKUW's programming committee has adopted the strategy of serving the community "as much as possible, because there will be no other, with the Internet and other things that are so global, there will barely be anything that is local anymore. And that may be our key to surviving as a station ... because people will start yearning for local again."

Program director Robin Eriksson believes that CKUW is losing students' interest on a grand scale and that this is a trend across the country. She said that young people do not listen to or discover music the same way she did as a teenager. But many people, both young and old, are still interested in "local content, local news, and the local music scene, and they still tune into campus radio" (Eriksson, personal interview, 6 July 2011). At CiTR, redefining what it means to "reach" listeners is an ongoing discussion. Janis McKenzie explained that "we have to deal with a lot of technological change. What does it mean to expand our reach? We used to be concerned with whether our transmitter could reach people ... and whether people could hear us in their houses or in their cars. And now we still are, but that's only a percentage of how we reach our listeners" (McKenzie, personal interview, 12 July 2011). For McKenzie, this is both an exciting and a difficult time for campus and community radio, but stations do not have large budgets to throw at these issues. "For the most part, we're finding that our old models don't really hold true. Just knowing about 'cool music' isn't going to help us compete in this current marketplace where people can listen to other campus and community radio stations from around the world. I don't think we used to really think in terms of competition."

Out of these concerns, a number of innovative approaches to programming and methods for engaging with listeners are being tested by campus stations. Campus radio stations, because of their close ties to music scenes and emerging cultural practices, generally have inventive ideas for sustaining relevance in a changing landscape. Ted Turner discussed CKUW's digital archive, where all programming is archived for a month after it has been broadcasted. Listeners can download or stream a program if they miss it in real time. Eriksson added that when the station's archived content "goes down, and when our stream goes down and our podcasts don't record, there is an influx of calls, so we know it's being used. And some shows, when you trace their history of how many [gigabytes] are downloaded, it's huge" (Eriksson, personal interview, 6 July 2011). A novel idea that Turner mentioned was a potential partnership between *Stylus* magazine and the station, where old archived issues of the magazine would be redistributed with newly released editions, and old copies of recorded local music could be recirculated in a digital format. Turner gave the example of CKUW digitizing old cassettes and vinyl recordings of local bands, especially those that are just sitting "buried at the back of the station or in a box in someone's basement." The station would then write about the process of recovering this music in *Stylus*, telling readers the story behind the band and the original recording. For Turner, these potential collaborations and different ideas demonstrate that campus radio is "definitely not getting stale." CKUW is "coming up with new ideas all the time."

At CiTR, station manager Brenda Grunau believes that online music streaming channels would be great for the sector. "Say we have a bluegrass channel and it RSS-feeds all the bluegrass shows from across the country. Because what we're best at is our niche programming … we could easily beat the quality and the range and the amount of music showcased, we could easily beat any satellite channel" (Grunau, personal interview, 11 July 2011). Making innovative music accessible across the country is something the campus sector could attempt in this changing landscape, according to Grunau. In an article profiling CiTR and the station's seventy-five-year anniversary, new digital practices are mentioned alongside fresh ideas for older formats. CiTR arts director Maegan Thomas explained that the station is perfecting its online listening app while also curating a local jukebox with 7-inch records and working on the third volume of the Mint Records/CiTR compilation (Thomas 2012).

These innovative ideas are paired with a certain confidence throughout the sector, in which cultural institutions and shared resources will always be central in the circulation of local and independent music, as will the cultural labour of individuals who devote their time in exchange for the ability to put their passion for music to use. As Nardwuar said, "I think what makes college radio or campus/community radio better than anybody doing their YouTubing or podcasting is *that*, look at that library we have there. Look at all the resources and look at all the people hanging out here … Let's say we were hanging out, I could ask you about that [recent] gig" (Nardwuar the Human Serviette, personal interview, 8 July 2011). He believes that a collection of resources, and the discussions and shared experiences that take place within the station space, grant campus radio a certain level of legitimacy that may not be as present elsewhere. "Be part of a group and an organization that has some history behind it. They can help you get an interview with bands. It also treats people with respect. It isn't racist, sexist, or homophobic." The fact that campus stations are tied to a larger academic institution is another important point to consider with respect to a station's legitimacy. Campus stations often rely on funding from students and the university, and this adds another layer of responsibility that stations must be aware of. Throughout this book, varying relationships between campus stations and their home institutions have been profiled. CiTR has been able to increase its funding from the student body and has worked hard to maintain a positive relationship with UBC. By contrast, CKLN's licence revocation highlights an instance where the station had become removed from the institution and the student body.

Concern, innovation, and optimism all stem from the passion exuded by campus radio advocates and practitioners. "We're just really passionate about campus radio," McKenzie said. "It's harder for me to put my finger on what campus radio is now compared to what it was twenty-five years ago." She continued:

> But I still believe independent voices in media are really, really important, perhaps more important than ever. I feel good every single day that I'm involved with CiTR, and to give different groups a voice ... We've seen some pretty scary things happen, with stations being sold or licences disappearing. We have to continue to fight really hard for what we do. It's a challenge because we have to be all things to all people. We have to provide a way for students to have fun and get training and get hooked, because they're our supporters now and for the future. And we have to continue to provide the really excellent community programming that we do. And sometimes all of that can be a lot to keep in our mind at once, and it can be a tough thing to be fighting on all these fronts.

Bill Baker echoed McKenzie's comments, drawing from the past to comment on the future:

> I came to university ... I didn't really know what exactly I wanted to do. And I like to imagine that my experience with CiTR was kind of that old-fashioned version where the extracurricular aspect, the university experience, is actually what informed my life later on. So I think it's a tremendously valuable institution, something like a campus radio station or a film society, and, we've just recently, or they at CiTR just recently, went through a funding challenge where they were very close to being in financial trouble. I guess it's similar to how people on a federal level look at arts organizations. (Baker, personal interview, 27 July 2011)

Baker ended by connecting his current work at Mint back to his days at the station to stress the importance of the experiences one can gain while spending time in a cultural institution like a campus station:

> I don't mean to suggest that I'm anybody particularly important, but when I think of all the people that have been positively affected by all of the various artists that we were able to work with, and all the things we've been able to do over the twenty years because there was this kooky, weird, cliquey, gothy radio station that was financed by the student body. I think it's something very precious and something very easy to lose sight of. So, maybe that is my closer for you.

The passion of the individuals involved with cultural production and music circulation on a local level is a significant distinguishing factor in campus radio culture, one that does much to convey its alternativeness and to distinguish it from other radio sectors. This passion also figures into the discussion of cultural capital above, in that it motivates the collecting, sharing, and creating of music and drives the circulation of local and independent music. While most campus radio practitioners are volunteers, their work helps increase the value and prominence of local and independent music. Grunau explained: "One thing we have that a lot of other places don't is a community of people that is locally oriented. And since we're connected to all the local bands and local venues, we've got this local foothold. So it's a greater reach than say just a blogger. Because essentially, we've got one hundred bloggers, right, they're just on the radio." The force of a campus radio station as a cultural intermediary is strong according to this logic, because it is collective and more diverse than someone operating alone or for a company with a much more limited vision. Grunau explained that because of initiatives to branch out into online spaces, she would translate this collective cultural force into an online platform. "We have a lot of our programmers blogging, and a lot of them have websites and their own Twitter and Facebook. So it's almost like we have a hundred networkers all doing their own thing in their respective community. And we might be a bit more unwieldy of an organization, but at least we can provide a licence for the community to use."

Individual taste is a significant factor in determining the range and scope of sounds heard on campus radio. The campus sector is a network of stations where community representation takes place along the lines of participation in music scenes and shared preferences for certain musical styles and sounds. Nevertheless, the collective work of the individuals who produce and program campus radio facilitates the distribution, circulation, and promotion of music, in a way that is not determined by a purely economic logic. Rather, passion, taste, and cultural capital are the driving forces in supporting and sharing music that is often independent and local, or representative of some notion of the "independent" and "local." And while the merits of a system that circulates music based on status and expertise within a certain music scene are certainly up for debate, it is clear from the stations profiled in this book that the relationship between campus radio and local music-making provides listeners, radio practitioners, and cultural producers with a local alternative to commercial radio. Moreover, individual taste and the sharing of musical preferences are only becoming more prominent as the flow of digital formats reshapes the music industries and the emergent cultural process of quickly and easily sharing music challenges the dominant industry model that has thrived alongside mass-produced music. As campus radio looks to the future, tensions and overlaps between the digital and non-digital, and the local and translocal, both in definition and operation, will be more pronounced. The 2010 policy that governs campus stations notes that "campus and community radio has always played a pivotal role in the development of new and emerging Canadian talent" (CRTC 2010c). Campus radio stations, as places where the sharing of musical knowledge, experience, and expertise has always been central to their function, within the studio space, over the air, and in the wider surrounding alternative music culture, are arguably more important than ever. In an increasingly global and digital society, the campus radio sector poses a significant challenge to the increasingly centralized and homogenous cultural offerings of the commercial radio sector. More importantly, the social relations that unfold on a local level, between campus stations, musicians, volunteers, and those who have a passion for radio, are an incredibly strong force for sustaining innovative sounds and styles that, to the best of their ability, reflect and represent the actual lived realities and intricacies of the many diverse musical communities of Canada.

List of Participants

CHMA/Sackville

Pierre Malloy, station manager at CHMA

Malloy became involved with CHMA in spring of 1995 after moving to Sackville the previous year. He moved to the town to pursue a job at one of the local newspapers. When it was announced that the company was going to be sold to a larger company, he left, citing the fact that he really likes independent media and has a problem with the corporatization of media. He took the job of station manager in 2003. Prior to this, he worked at CHSR in Fredericton, New Brunswick in the early 1980s, and he had a radio show in the Northwest Territories during the late 1980s and early 1990s. He has been involved with campus–community radio since 1982. He also ran a video store in Sackville, which gave him some business training in terms of handling staff.

Sandy Mackay, program director at CHMA

Mackay says that as much as he's not directly responsible for what's on the air, he is at the station listening all the time, maintaining a constant presence in the space. He is from Whitehorse, Yukon, and he came to Sackville to attend Mount Allison University. One show that he has programmed at the station is called *Working Fulltime*, a rock 'n' roll show that broadcasts in the morning to "get people out of bed."

Pat LePoidevin, folk musician, former Mount Allison student, and CHMA Programmer

LePoidevin had been a folk musician for about four years as of the time of my visit to Sackville. He recorded his first album, *Blue Tornadoes*, in the production studio at CHMA. He is from Princeton, British Columbia, and he came to Sackville to attend Mount Allison.

Steve Ridlington, founding member of CHMA

Arrived at Mount Allison University in 1972 and was involved with the station when it circulated via carrier current. Currently, he does live sports reporting for CHMA from time to time.

CKUW/Winnipeg

Rob Schmidt, station manager at CKUW

Schmidt has been at CKUW since 1996. He was integral in taking the station to the FM dial in 1999, writing also for *Stylus* magazine. He moved to Winnipeg after attending McMaster University in Hamilton, Ontario. Before that, he grew up in northeastern Ontario.

Robin Eriksson, program director at CKUW

Eriksson became a volunteer at CKUW in 2004, after feeling as though she needed to get more involved with the station than just donating money annually. When summer came, a number of hosts went on holidays and Eriksson found herself filling in on air. She remained on the air and still hosts *Hit the Big Wide Strum!*, an old-time and bluegrass music show. When the program director position opened in 2006, she applied and got the job. She is also currently on the board of the NCRA.

Ted Turner, outreach and sponsorship coordinator at CKUW

Turner first got involved with CKUW in 1990, during his second year at the University of Winnipeg. He started hosting a radio show and then became involved in many aspects of the station, quickly becoming the station manager. He has also been the program director and operations manager. He is now the outreach and sponsorship coordinator and the advertising manager at *Stylus*.

Sarah Michaelson, host of Stylus Radio and DJ (Mama Cutsworth)

Michaelson became involved with CKUW in 2000 during her first year at the University of Winnipeg. She had been hosting *Stylus Radio* for just over ten years at the time of my visit. She DJs as Mama Cutsworth and has been for over seven years, playing rare soul and funk music. She also sits on the programming committee for the station and produces *Garageland*, a show that runs every Saturday in June that broadcasts from garage sales in the city. She has also been a producer for CBC Radio One and Two.

Stu Reid, host of Twang Trust

Reid has been a fan of college radio since the late 1970s. After CJUM at the University of Manitoba stopped broadcasting, he vowed to get involved with campus radio if the city ever got it back. He hosts *Twang Trust*, a country music show, and is involved with the West End Cultural Centre, volunteering also at the city's Jazz Festival. He also works as a graphic designer in the city, producing posters for countless bands.

CiTR/Vancouver

Brenda Grunau, station manager at CiTR

Grunau attended university in Winnipeg, then moved to Toronto to do a master's in Business with an Arts and Media specialization. She ended up in Vancouver after travelling for a while. She came across the job posting for station manager and thought it would be a good fit, given her prior experience. Since taking the position, she has been rethinking the volunteer training process and improving communications between the station and *Discorder*.

Nardwuar the Human Serviette, host of Nardwuar the Human Serviette Presents ...

Nardwuar has hosted his radio show since October 1987 while a student at the University of British Columbia. His show is now also broadcast on WFMU in New Jersey. A native of Vancouver, Nardwuar also plays in the bands the Evaporators and Thee Goblins. He also puts out records on Nardwuar Records about once a year. He began doing interviews in the early 1990s, and is now well known internationally for this after being involved with Much Music for a while. He now hosts his interviews on YouTube and on his personal website, http://nardwuar.com.

Janis McKenzie, chair of the CiTR Board

McKenzie joined CiTR in 1984 or 1985 while an undergraduate student at UBC. She began hosting a show shortly after joining and became a writer for *Discorder*. She returned to the university for a graduate degree in the 1990s and ended up hosting another show for a few years. McKenzie has been involved with the administrative side of the station, sitting on the board for eight years and chairing for three.

Bill Baker, Mint Records co-founder

Baker formed Mint Records about twenty years prior to my visit, with friend Randy Iwata. He is now the director of music licensing for the label. He got involved with CiTR in the early 1980s, and between he and Iwata, the two have done almost every job at the station. He stresses that he got more out of the station than he did his undergraduate education at UBC, and still works closely with CiTR.

Cameron Reed, musician and promoter

Reed began promoting shows in 2004 while playing in a punk band based in Vancouver. He has been involved with promoting Music Waste and the Victory Square Block Party. His current musical project, Babe Rainbow, is represented by the prominent electronic music label, Warp Records.

References

Personal Interviews

Baker, Bill. 27 July 2011, via Skype.
Eriksson, Robin. 6 July 2011, Winnipeg, MB.
Grunau, Brenda. 11 July 2011, Vancouver, BC.
LePoidevin, Pat. 3 June 2011, Sackville, NB.
Mackay, Sandy. 3 June 2011, Sackville, NB.
Malloy, Pierre. 3 June 2011, Sackville, NB.
McKenzie, Janis. 12 July 2011, via Skype.
Michaelson, Sarah. 7 July 2011, Winnipeg, MB.
Nardwuar the Human Serviette. 8 July 2011, Vancouver, BC.
Reed, Cameron. 11 July 2011, Vancouver, BC.
Reid, Stu. 5 July 2011, Winnipeg, MB.
Ridlington, Steve. 4 December 2012, via email.
Schmidt, Rob. 5 July 2011, Winnipeg, MB.
Turner, Ted. 7 July 2011, Winnipeg, MB.

Printed Works and Online Sources

"About." *CiTR 101.9 FM*. 25 August 2011. http://www.citr.ca/index.php/about/about.
"About CKUW." *CKUW 95.9 FM*. 25 August 2011. http://ckuw.ca/about.
"About Us." *CHMA 106.9 FM*. 10 September 2011. http://chmafm.wordpress.com/about.
Adorno, Theodor. 1938/1991. "On the Fetishistic Character in Music and the Regression of Listening." In *The Culture Industry: Selected Essays on Mass Culture*, 26–52. New York: Routledge.
"Ad Sales." *Stylus*, April 1993, 2.
"Advertising." *Stylus*, September 1994, 3.
"A Guide to CITR fm 102." *Discorder*, February 1983.
Albert, Michael. 1997. "What Makes Alternative Media Alternative? Toward a Federation of Alternative Media Activists and Supporters." *Zmag*, 28 August 2011. http://www.zmag.org/whatmakesalti.htm.

"A Little About Us," *Discorder Media Kit 2010*, PDF.

Anderson, Benedict. 1936/1991. *Imagined Communities: Reflections on the Origin and Spread of Nationalism*. New York: Verso.

Armstrong, Robert. 2010. *Broadcasting Policy in Canada*. Toronto: University of Toronto Press.

Arpin, Michel. 2010. "Opening Remarks." CRTC Public Hearing. Gatineau, Québec. 18 January 2010.

Attali, Jacques. 1985. *Noise: The Political Economy of Music*. Translated by Brian Massumi. Minneapolis: University of Minnesota Press.

Atton, Chris, and Nick Couldry. 2003. "Introduction." *Media, Culture, and Society* 25.5: 579–86.

Barclay, David. 2010. "Concerning the Cover Art." *CiTR Pop Alliance Compilation: Vol. 2*. Insert. Vancouver: Mint Records.

Barnett, Kyle. 2013. "On Radio: Holding on to Localism in Internet Radio." *Antenna*, 3 January 2014. http://blog.commarts.wisc.edu/2013/02/05/on-radio-holding-on -to-localism-in-internet-radio.

Barney, Darin. 2005. *Communication Technology*. Vancouver: UBC Press.

Barrett, Jessica. "Is Vancouver Still the No Fun City?" *Vancouver Sun*, 16 November 2012. http://www.vancouversun.com/Vancouver+still+City/7561307/story.html#ixzz 2Hhyc5qOX.

Bennett, Tony, Simon Frith, Lawrence Grossberg, John Shepherd, and Graeme Turner. 1993. "Introduction" to Part 2. In *Rock and Popular Music: Politics, Policies, Institutions*. Edited by Tony Bennett, Simon Frith, Lawrence Grossberg, John Shepherd, and Graeme Turner. 99–103. New York: Routledge.

Berland, Jody. 2009. *North of Empire: Essays on the Cultural Technologies of Space*. Durham: Duke University Press.

———. 1993. "Radio Space and Industrial Time: The Case of Music Formats." In *Rock and Popular Music: Politics, Policies, Institutions*, edited by Tony Bennett, Simon Frith, Lawrence Grossberg, John Shepherd, and Graeme Turner. 104–18. New York: Routledge.

Binder, Dickson, "send + receive <003> profile." *Stylus*, September–October 2000, 17.

Bourdieu, Pierre. 1984. *Distinction: A Social Critique of the Judgement of Taste*. Translated by Richard Nice. Cambridge, MA: Harvard University Press.

———. 1986/1993. *The Field of Cultural Production: Essays on Art and Literature*. Edited by Randal Johnson. New York: Columbia University Press.

Bredin, Marian. 2012. "Indigenous Media as Alternative Media: Participation and Cultural Production." In *Alternative Media in Canada*. Edited by Kirsten Kozolenko, Patricia Mazepa, and David Skinner, 184–204. Vancouver: UBC Press.

Burnett, Robert. 1996. *The Global Jukebox: The International Music Industry*. New York: Routledge.

CAB. 2010. "Broadcasting Notice of Consultation CRTC 2009-418: Review of Campus and Community Radio." Canadian Association of Broadcasters Oral Presentation – January 19, 2010." Ottawa: CRTC.

CAB Radio Board. 1999. "A Submission to the Canadian Radio-television and Telecommunications Commission with Respect to: Public Notice CRTC 1999-30." Ottawa: CRTC.

Caldwell, John Thornton. 2008. *Production Culture: Industrial Reflexivity and Critical Practice in Film and Television*. Durham: Duke University Press.

Cameron, David, and Janice Gross Stein. 2002. "The State as Place amid Shifting Spaces." In *Street Protests and Fantasy Parks: Globalization, Culture, and the State*. Edited by David Cameron and Janice Gross Stein. 141–59. Vancouver: UBC Press.

Campbell, Charles. 1985. Letter to Secretary General of the CRTC, Ferdinand Belisle. Ottawa: CRTC.

Canada. 1991. *Broadcasting Act*.

———. Committee on Broadcasting (Fowler 2 Committee). 1965. *Report of the Committee on Broadcasting*. Ottawa: Queen's Printer.

———. Minister of Supply and Services Canada. 1986. *Report of the Task Force on Broadcasting Policy*. Ottawa: Canadian Government Publishing Centre.

———. Standing Committee on Canadian Heritage. 2003. *Our Cultural Sovereignty: The Second Century of Canadian Broadcasting*. Ottawa.

Charette, Brie. "Art Project // Andrew Pommier." *Discorder*, 25 April 2011.

Chernos, Saul. 2010. "CKLN Picks up Static." *Now Magazine*, 5 December 2014. https://nowtoronto.com/news/ckln-picks-up-static.

CHMA. 2005a. "CHMA Training Manual Session 1: Orientation & Station Tour." *CHMA 106.9 FM*. 10 September 2011. http://www.mta.ca/chma/content/orientation.pdf.

———. 2005b. "CHMA Training Manual Session 2: Rules and Regulations." *CHMA 106.9 FM*. 10 September 2011. http://www.mta.ca/chma/content/rulesregs.pdf.

———. 2005c. "CHMA Training Manual Session 3: Technical Training." *CHMA 106.9 FM*. 10 September 2011. http://www.mta.ca/chma/content/session3.pdf.

———. 2005d. "CHMA Training Manual Session 4: Your First Show." *CHMA 106.9 FM*. 10 September 2011. http://www.mta.ca/chma/content/session4.pdf.

———. 2010. "Program Descriptions: CHMA 106.9 FM Campus & Community Radio." *MTA.ca*. 20 August 2011. http://www.mta.ca/chma/content/program_descriptions_2010.pdf.

CiTR. 1985. "FM Application: High Power FM." Submitted to CRTC. Vancouver: UBC Archives.

"CJLO Fee Levy—CSU Elections 2011." *CJLO.com*. 19 December 2011. http://www.cjlo.com/feelevy.

CKUW, Advertisement. *Stylus*, September 1994, 12.

———. 2008. "The Winnipeg Campus / Community Radio Society By-Laws." *CKUW 95.9 FM*. 24 August 2011. http://ckuw.ca/images/uploads/by-laws_revised_march08.pdf.

Coates, Norma. 1997. "(R)evolution Now? Rock and the Political Potential of Gender." In *Sexing the Groove: Popular Music and Gender*. Edited by Sheila Whiteley. 50–64. New York: Routledge.

Cohen, Sara. 1991. *Rock Culture in Liverpool: Popular Music in the Making*. Oxford: Oxford University Press.

———. 1999. "Scenes." In *Key Terms in Popular Music and Culture*. Edited by Bruce Horner and Thomas Swiss. 239–50. Malden: Blackwell.

Cornell, Andrea-Jane. 2010. "Radio CKUT Inc." Letter to the Secretary General of the CRTC. Gatineau: CRTC.

Cote, Carolyn. 1999. "Re: Public Notice CRTC 1999-30." Email to CRTC Secretary General. Ottawa: CRTC.

Croteau, David, and William Hoynes. 2001. *The Business of Media: Corporate Media and the Public Interest*. Thousand Oaks: Pine Forge Press.

CRTC. 1975a. Decision CRTC 75-102. Ottawa: CRTC.

———. 1975b. Decision CRTC 75-247. Ottawa: CRTC.

———. 1975c. *FM Radio in Canada: A Policy to Ensure a Varied and Comprehensive Radio Service*. Ottawa: CRTC.

———. 1981a. Decision CRTC 81-661. Ottawa: CRTC.

———. 1981b. Public Hearing for CITR. 29 April 1981. Vancouver: CRTC.

———. 1983. Public Notice CRTC 1983-43. Policy Statement on the Review of Radio. Ottawa: CRTC.

———. 1984. Decision CRTC 84-10. Ottawa: CRTC.

———. 1985a. Decision CRTC 85-664. Ottawa: CRTC.

———. 1985b. Decision CRTC 85-1122. Ottawa: CRTC.

———. 1985c. Public Notice CRTC 1985-194. The Review of Community Radio. Ottawa: CRTC.

———. 1986. Decision CRTC 86-237. Ottawa: CRTC.

———. 1987a. Decision CRTC 87-505. Ottawa: CRTC.

———. 1987b. Public Notice CRTC 1987-255. Educational and Institutional Radio. Ottawa: CRTC.

———. 1988. Decision CRTC 88-590. Ottawa: CRTC.

———. 1990a. Decision CRTC 90-379. Ottawa: CRTC.

———. 1990b. Decision CRTC 90-620. Ottawa: CRTC.

———. 1990c. Decision CRTC 90-664. Ottawa: CRTC.

———. 1990d. Public Notice CRTC 1990-111. An FM Policy for the Nineties. Ottawa: CRTC.

———. 1992a. Public Notice CRTC 1992-38. Policies for Community and Campus Radio. Ottawa: CRTC.

———. 1992b. Public Notice CRTC 1992-59. Implementation of an employment equity policy. Ottawa: CRTC.

———. 1993a. Decision CRTC 93-169. Ottawa: CRTC.

———. 1993b. Decision CRTC 93-169-1. Ottawa: CRTC.

———. 1993c. Public Notice CRTC 1993-38. Policies for Local Programming on Commercial Radio Stations and Advertising on Campus Stations. Ottawa: CRTC.

———. 1995a. Decision CRTC 95-527. Ottawa: CRTC.

———. 1995b. Decision CRTC 95-867. Ottawa: CRTC.

———. 1996. Public Notice CRTC 1996-116. Amendments to the Radio Regulations, 1986—Simulcasting, Canadian Content, Ownership, Definitions of a 'Commercial Message' and an 'Associate.' Ottawa: CRTC.

———. 1997. Public Notice CRTC 1997-105. An Agenda for Reviewing the Commission's Policies for Radio. Ottawa: CRTC.

———. 1998a. Decision CRTC 98-476. Ottawa: CRTC.

———. 1998b. Public Notice CRTC 1998-41. Commercial Radio Policy 1998. Ottawa: CRTC.

———. 1999. Public Notice CRTC 1999-30. Call for Comments on a Proposed New Policy for Campus Radio. Ottawa: CRTC.

———. 2000a. Decision CRTC 2000-1. Ottawa: CRTC.

———. 2000b. Public Notice CRTC 2000-1. A Distinctive Voice for All Canadians: Renewal of the Canadian Broadcasting Corporation's Licences. Ottawa: CRTC.

———. 2000c. Public Notice CRTC 2000-12. Campus Radio Policy. Ottawa: CRTC.

———. 2000d. Public Notice CRTC 2000-156. New Licence Form for Campus Radio Stations. Ottawa: CRTC.

———. 2001. Decision CRTC 2001-114. Ottawa: CRTC.

———. 2006a. Broadcasting Decision CRTC 2006-137. Ottawa: CRTC.

———. 2006b. Public Notice CRTC 2006-158. Commercial Radio Policy 2006. Ottawa: CRTC.

———. 2007. Broadcasting Decision CRTC 2007-149. Ottawa: CRTC.

———. 2008. Broadcasting Public Notice CRTC 2008-4. Diversity of Voices. Ottawa: CRTC.

———. 2010a. Broadcasting Notice of Consultation CRTC 2010-146. Ottawa: CRTC.

———. 2010b. Broadcasting Notice of Consultation CRTC 2010-146-4. Ottawa: CRTC.

———. 2010c. Broadcasting Regulatory Policy CRTC 2010-499. Campus and Community Radio Policy. Ottawa, CRTC.

———. 2010d. Transcript of Proceedings before the Canadian Radio-television and Telecommunications Commission: To Consider the Broadcasting Applications Listed in Broadcasting Notice of Consulation CRTC 2010-146. 8 December 2010. Toronto: CRTC.

———. 2011a. Broadcasting Decision CRTC 2011-56. CKLN-FM Toronto – Revocation of Licence. Ottawa: CRTC.

———. 2011b. Broadcasting Regulatory Policy CRTC 2011-316. Definition of Emerging Canadian Artists on Commercial Radio. Ottawa: CRTC.

———. 2012a. Broadcasting Decision CRTC 2012-485. Licensing of a New Radio Station to Serve Toronto. Ottawa: CRTC.

———. 2012b. Transcript of Proceedings before the Canadian Radio-television and Telecommunications Commission: To Consider the Broadcasting Applications Listed in Broadcasting Notice of Consultation CRTC 2012-126, 2012-126-1, 2012-126-2, and 2012-126-3. May 14, 2012. Toronto: CRTC.

———. 2013. Broadcasting Decision CRTC 2013-263 and Broadcasting Orders CRTC 2013-264 and 2013-265. Ottawa: CRTC.

Davies, Kent, "Narwhals Are Gnarly! An Interview with The Blowholes." *Stylus*, June–July 2011, 7.

Delanty, Gerard. 2003. *Community*. New York: Routledge.

"Demographic," *Discorder Media Kit 2010. Discorder.ca.* 21 April 2010. PDF.

Discorder. *How to Get Involved with Discorder*. Vancouver, 2011.

Douglas, Susan. 1999. *Listening In: Radio and the American Imagination, from Amos 'n Andy and Edward R. Murrow to Wolfman Jack and Howard Stern*. New York: Times Books.

Downing, John. 2003. "Audiences and Readers of Alternative Media: The Absent Lure of the Virtually Unknown." *Media, Culture, and Society* 25.5: 625–45.

Downing, John. 2001. *Radical Media: Rebellious Communication and Social Movements*. With Tamara Villarreal Ford, Genève Gil, and Laura Stein. Thousand Oaks: Sage.

Edwardson, Ryan. 2009. *Canuck Rock: A History of Canadian Popular Music*. Toronto: University of Toronto Press.

Fabrikant, Geraldine. "Radio Giant Faces Crisis in Cash Flow." *New York Times*, 29 April 2009. http://www.nytimes.com/2009/04/30/business/media/30clear.html.

Fairchild, Charles. 2001. *Community Radio and Public Culture*. New York: Hampton Press.

———. 2012. *Music, Radio, and the Public Sphere: The Aesthetics of Democracy*. New York: Palgrave Macmillan.

Faris, Ron. 1975. *The Passionate Educators: Voluntary Associations and the Struggles for Control of Adult Educational Broadcasting in Canada, 1919–52*. Toronto: Peter Martin Associates.

Fauteux, Brian. 2008. "Campus Frequencies: The 'Alternativeness' of Campus Radio." M.A. thesis, Concordia University, Montreal.

FCC (Federal Communications Commission). 2013. "Low Power FM Broadcast Radio Stations (LPFM)." *FCC Encyclopedia*, 20 August 2013. http://www.fcc.gov/encyclopedia/low-power-fm-broadcast-radio-stations-lpfm.

Filion, Michel. 1996. "Radio." In *The Cultural Industries in Canada: Problems, Policies, and Prospects*. Edited by Michael Dorland. 118–41. Toronto: James Lorimer.

Finnegan, Ruth H. 1989. *The Hidden Musicians: Music-Making in an English Town*. Cambridge: Cambridge University Press.

Fisher, Marc. 2007. *Something in the Air: Radio, Rock, and the Revolution That Shaped a Generation*. New York: Random House.

Fontana, Kaitlin. 2011. *Fresh at Twenty: The Oral History of Mint Records*. Toronto: ECW Press.

Fortner, Robert S. 2005. *Radio, Morality, and Culture: Britain, Canada, and the United States, 1919–1945*. Carbondale: Southern Illinois University Press.

Frith, Simon. 1996. *Performing Rites: On the Value of Popular Music*. Cambridge: Oxford University Press.

———. 1993. "Popular Music and the Local State." In *Rock and Popular Music: Politics, Policies, Institutions*. Edited by Tony Bennett, Simon Frith, Lawrence Grossberg, John Shepherd, and Graeme Turner. 14–24. New York: Routledge.

Frith, Simon, and Angela McRobbie. 1990. "Rock and Sexuality." In *On Record: Rock, Pop, and the Written Word*. Edited by Simon Frith and Andrew Goodwin. 371–89. New York: Routledge.

Gainor, Chris. "Squabble Splits CITR Hacks." *The Ubyssey*, 4 March 1976, 1–2.

Gendron, Bernard. 2002. *Between Montmartre and the Mudd Club: Popular Music and the Avant-Garde*. Chicago: University of Chicago Press.

Gilfillan, Anna, "CKUW 95.9 FM," *Stylus*, Oct. 1998, 9.

Gitelman, Lisa. 2008. *Always Already New: Media, History, and the Data of Culture.* Cambridge, MA: MIT Press.

Gordon, Janey, ed. 2012. *Community Radio in the Twenty-First Century.* New York: Peter Lang.

Gradin, Justin. "Releases." *Nominal Records,* 20 September, 2011. http://www.records nominal.com/er.php.

Gray, Christina. 2011. "Victory Square Block Party." *Discorder.ca,* 19 November 2011. http://htl.li/6CiwR.

Hall, Stuart. 1981. "Notes on Deconstructing the Popular." In *People's History and Socialist Theory.* Edited by Raphael Samuel and Kegan Paul. 227–40. London: Routledge.

Hamilton, James. 2000. "Alternative Media: Conceptual Difficulties, Critical Possibilities." *Journal of Communication Inquiry* 24.4: 357–78.

———. 2008. *Democratic Communications: Formations, Projects, Possibilities.* Lanham: Rowman & Littlefield.

Hanomansing, Ian. 1982. "To All SAC Members." Letter to Students' Administrative Council members. Sackville: CHMA Records.

Harrison, Anthony Kwame. 2006. "'Cheaper Than a CD, Plus We Really Mean It': Bay Area Underground Hip Hop Tapes as Subcultural Artifacts." *Popular Music* 25.2: 283–301.

Hartley, John. 2000. "Radiocracy: Sound and Citizenship." *International Journal of Cultural Studies* 3.2: 153–59.

Henderson, Ralph. Letter to the Editor. *The Ubyssey,* 3 November 1959.

Hesmondhalgh, David. 2002. *The Cultural Industries.* Thousand Oaks: Sage.

Hilliard, Robert L., and Michael C. Keith. 2005. *The Quieted Voice: The Rise and Demise of Localism in American Radio.* Carbondale: Southern Illinois University Press.

Hilmes, Michele. 1997. *Radio Voices: American Broadcasting, 1922–1952.* Minneapolis: University of Minnesota Press.

———. 2013. "The New Materiality of Radio." In *Radio's New Wave: Global Sound in the Digital Age.* Edited by Jason Loviglio and Michele Hilmes. 43–61. New York: Routledge.

Hilmes, Michele, and Jason Loviglio, eds. 2002. *Radio Reader: Essays in the Cultural History of Radio.* New York: Routledge.

Hobbs, R. Gerald. Letter to Chris Buchanan. 22 February 1990.

Hudson, Alex. 2011. "Mint Records and CiTR's *Pop Alliance Compilation* Gets Release Show with Slam Dunk, Fanshaw, Role March." *Exclaim.ca,* 17 September 2011. http://exclaim.ca/News/mint_records_citrs_pop_alliance_compilation_lines_up_ release_show_with_slam_dunk_fanshaw_role_march.

Hughes, Josiah. 2008. "Strange Brew: Vancouver's Weird Punk Scene Invents Itself." *Exclaim.ca,* 20 September 2011. http://exclaim.ca/Features/Research/strange_ brew-vancouver.

Huntemann, Nina. 2003. "A Promise Diminished: The Politics of Low-Powered Radio." In *Communities of the Air: Radio Century, Radio Culture.* Edited by Susan Merrill Squier. 76–90. Durham, NC: Duke University Press.

Infantry, Ashante. 2011. "CKLN Board 'Not Going to Lie Down' after Licence Revoked." *Toronto Star*, 5 November 2014. http://www.thestar.com/news/gta/2011/01/28/ckln_board_not_going_to_lie_down_after_licence_revoked.html#.

Irish, Paul. 2012. "Indie-Rock Station Coming to Toronto." *Toronto Star*, 6 January 2015. http://www.thestar.com/entertainment/music/2012/09/11/indierock_station_coming_to_toronto.html.

Jenkins, Henry. 2006. *Convergence Culture: Where Old and New Media Collide*. New York: NYU Press.

Kaestner, Melissa. 2008. "Community Radio Fund of Canada to Support Local Grassroots Media." Email notice. Ottawa: CRFC.

Kepman, Stephanie. 2010. "RE: Broadcasting Notice of Consultation CRTC 2009-418." Letter to Secretary General of the CRTC. Ottawa: CRTC.

Kidd, Dorothy. 1999. "The Value of Alternative Media." *Peace Review* 11.1: 113.

Kidd, Dorothy, Francisco McGee, and Danielle Fairburn. 2007. "Clear Channel: The Poster Child for Everything That's Wrong with Consolidation." In *Converging Media, Diverging Politics: A Political Economy of News Media in the United States and Canada*. Edited by David Skinner, James R. Compton, and Michael Gasher. 77–100. Lanham: Lexington Books.

Kozolenko, Kirsten, Patricia Mazepa, and David Skinner. 2012. "Considering Alternative Media in Canada: Structure, Participation, Activism." In *Alternative Media in Canada*. Edited by Kozolenko, Mazepa, and Skinner. 1–22. Toronto: UBC Press.

Kozolenko, Kirsten, Patricia Mazepa and David Skinner, eds. 2012. *Alternative Media in Canada*. Toronto: UBC Press.

Kruse, Holly. 2010. "Local Identity and Independent Music Scenes." *Poplar Music and Society* 33.5: 625–39.

———. 2003. *Site and Sound: Understanding Independent Music Scenes*. New York: Peter Lang.

Kupferman, Steve. 2011a. "CKLN Will Remain on the Air, For Now." *Torontoist*, 5 December 2013. http://torontoist.com/2011/02/ckln_will_remain_on_the_air_for_now.

———. 2011b. "Timeline: Why CKLN Radio's Broadcast License Was Revoked." *Torontoist*, 18 November 2011. http://torontoist.com/2011/01/timeline_why_ckln_radios_broadcast_was_revoked.

Lacey, Kate. 2002. "Radio in the Great Depression: Promotional Culture, Public Service, and Propaganda." In *Radio Reader: Essays in the Cultural History of Radio*. Edited by Michele Hilmes and Jason Loviglio. 21–40. New York: Routledge.

Lacey, Kate. 2013. *Listening Publics: The Politics and Experience of Listening in the Media Age*. Malden: Polity Press.

L'Allier, Jean-Paul. 1971. "Toward a Quebec Communications Policy." Quebec: Ministry of Communications.

Land, Jeff. 1999. *Active Radio: Pacifica's Brash Experiment*. Minneapolis: University of Minnesota Press.

Langlois, Andrea, Ron Sakolsky, and Marian van der Zon, eds. 2010. *Islands of Resistance: Pirate Radio in Canada*. Vancouver: New Star Books.

Lenthall, Bruce. 2002. "Critical Reception: Public Intellectuals Decry Depression-Era Radio, Mass Culture, and Modern America." In *Radio Reader: Essays in the Cultural History of Radio*. Edited by Michele Hilmes and Jason Loviglio. 41–62. New York: Routledge.

Lewis, Peter M., and Jerry Booth. 1989. *The Invisible Medium: Public, Commercial, and Community Radio*. London: Macmillan Education.

Lewis, Peter M., and Susan Jones, eds. 2006. *From the Margins to the Cutting Edge: Community Media and Empowerment*. New York: Hampton Press.

Light, Evan. 2012. "Public Participation and Community Radio in Quebec." In *Alternative Media in Canada*. Edited by Kirsten Kozolanka, Patricia Mazepa, and David Skinner. 145–64. Vancouver: UBC Press.

Longford, Graham, Marita Moll, and Leslie Regan Shade. 2008. "From the 'Right to Communication' to the 'Consumer Right of Access': Telecom Policy Visions 1970–2007." In *For Sale to the Highest Bidder: Telecom Policy in Canada*. Edited by Marita Moll and Leslie Regan Shade. 3–16. Ottawa: Canadian Centre for Policy Alternatives.

MacDonald, Andrew. 1984. Letter to Mr. G. Harvey Gilmour, Secretary to the Executive Committee of the Board of Regents, Mount Allison University.

Matthews, Kevin, Freya Zaltz, François Coté, Michèle Leblanc, Martin Bougie, and Lise Morisette. 2010. "Présentation au CRTC du 18 janvier 2010 Audiences CRTC 2009-418." Letter to Secretary General of the CRTC. Gatineau: CRTC.

McChesney, Robert W. 2005. "Foreword." In Robert L. Hilliard and Michael C. Keith, *The Quieted Voice: The Rise and Demise of Localism in American Radio*. ix–xi. Carbondale: Southern Illinois University Press.

———. 2004. "The Political Economy of International Communications." In *Who Owns the Media? Global Trends and Local Resistances*. Edited by Pradip N. Thomas and Zaharom Nain. 1–22. New York: Zed Books.

———. 1999. *Rich Media, Poor Democracy: Communication Politics in Dubious Times*. Urbana: University of Illinois Press.

McChesney, Robert W., and Dan Schiller. 2003. *Political Economy of International Communications: Foundations for the Emerging Global Debate about Media Ownership and Regulation*. Geneva: UNRISD, Technology, Business and Society Programme Paper no. 11.

McClure, Steve, "CITR Spreads Waves over Public," *The Ubyssey*, 25 January 1980, 4.

McCourt, Tom. 1999. *Conflicting Communication Interests in America: The Case of National Public Radio*. Westport: Praeger.

McHugh, Duncan. 2010. "A Bit of History." *CiTR Pop Alliance Compilation: Vol. 2*. Insert. Vancouver: Mint Records.

McLeod, Kembrew. 2005. "MP3s Are Killing Home Taping: The Rise of Internet Distribution and Its Challenge to the Major Label Music Monopoly." *Popular Music and Society* 28.4: 521–31.

McNulty, Jean. 1979. *Other Voices in Broadcasting: The Evolution of New Forms of Local Programming in Canada*. Simon Fraser University, Burnaby, BC, Telecommunications Research Group.

Melanson, Trevor. 2011. "CRTC Yanks Licence of Ryerson's CKLN Radio." *Globe and Mail*, 1 December 2014. http://www.theglobeandmail.com/news/toronto/crtc-yanks-licence-of-ryersons-ckln-radio/article1886385.

meme. "Indie Label Profile ... Alchemy." *Stylus*, May 1999, 24.

Miller, Lorey. 2011. "Dear Editor." *The Argosy*, 25 August 2012. http://argosy.mta.ca/?q=article/dear-editor-23.

Mint Records. 2010. "Mint and CiTR release Limited Edition Vancouver Compilation LP!!" *Mint Records*, 20 September 2011). http://www.mintrecs.com/index.php?component=news&id=109.

Monk, Lisa. 1997. "Beyond Polarity: Campus–Community Radio and New Relations of Power in Radio Broadcasting Policy in Canada." M.A. thesis, Concordia University, Montreal.

Morrow, Adrian. 2011. "CKLN: From Revolution to Radio Silence." *Globe and Mail*, 12 December 2014. http://www.theglobeandmail.com/news/toronto/ckln-from-revolution-to-radio-silence/article580933.

Nakamura, Lisa. 2009. "Digital Media in *Cinema Journal*, 1995–2008." *Cinema Journal* 49.1: 154–60.

NCRA/ANREC. 2011. "Resolutions: Updated 2011." *NCRA/ANREC*, 10 June 2010. www.ncra.ca/resolutions2011.pdf.

Nopper, Sheila. 2010. "Freedom Soundz: A Programmer's Journey Beyond Licensed Community Radio." In *Islands of Resistance: Pirate Radio in Canada*. Edited by Andrea Langlois, Ron Sakolsky, and Marian van der Zon. 51–69. Vancouver: New Star Books.

O'Connell, Freddie. 2011. "The Day the Music Died." *New York Times*, 10 December 2011. http://www.nytimes.com/2011/06/12/opinion/12oconnell.html?_r=1.

O'Connor, Alan. 2002. "Local Scenes and Dangerous Crossroads: Punk and Theories of Cultural Hybridity." *Popular Music* 21.2: 225–36.

Ogilvie, Jean. 1983. "Community Radio in Quebec: Perspectives in Conflict." M.A. thesis, McGill University, Montreal.

Opel, Andy. 2004. *Micro Radio and the FCC: Media Activism and the Struggle over Broadcast Policy*. Westport: Praeger.

Peers, Frank W. 1969. *The Politics of Canadian Broadcasting, 1920–1951*. Toronto: University of Toronto Press.

———. 1979. *The Public Eye: Television and the Politics of Canadian Broadcasting, 1952–1968*. Toronto: University of Toronto Press.

Pedri, Jennesia, "Venews // Save the Red Gate." *Discorder*, July–August 2011, 7.

Peterson, Richard A., and Andy Bennett. 2004. "Introducing Music Scenes." In *Music Scenes: Local, Translocal, and Virtual*. Edited by Richard A. Peterson and Andy Bennett. 1–23. Nashville: Vanderbilt University Press.

"Press Release: Volunteers Locked Out of CKLN Without Explanation." 2008. *Take Back Our Radio Station*, 6 December 2013. http://takebackourradio.blogspot.ca/2008/06/volunteers-locked-out-of-ckln-without.html.

"Program Guide." *Stylus*, October 1990.

"Programs & Archives." *CKUW 95.9 FM*. 12 September 2011. http://ckuw.ca/programs.

Raboy, Marc. 1990. *Missed Opportunities: The Story of Canada's Broadcasting Policy.* Montreal and Kingston: McGill–Queen's University Press.

Radio Centre-Ville. 1992. "Inventing and Experimenting." In *A Passion for Radio.* Edited by Bruce Girard. 49–58. Montreal: Black Rose Books.

Riddell, Mark. "Co-operation Fuels Local Muzak Scene." *Stylus*, April 1993, 3.

Ritcey, Geoff. 1980. "Report on the Viability of a CHMA FM Transmitter." Letter to CHMA membership. Sackville: CHMA Records.

Rock, Michael. 1999. "Re: Public Notice CRTC 1999-30: Proposed New Policy for Campus Radio." Letter to the Secretary General of the CRTC.

Russo, Alexander. 2010. *Points on the Dial: Golden Age Radio Beyond the Networks.* Durham: Duke University Press.

Russo, Alexander, and Bill Kirkpatrick. "Beyond the Terrestrial?: Networked Distribution, Multimodal Media, and the Place of the Local in Satellite Radio." In *Down to Earth: Satellite Technologies, Industries, and Cultures.* Edited by Lisa Parks and James Schwoch. 156–76. Piscataway, NJ: Rutgers University Press.

Sauls, Samuel J. 2000. *The Culture of American College Radio.* Ames: Iowa State University Press.

Saunders, Chad. 2007. "Re: Broadcasting Public Notice CRTC 2007-23 (PN 2007-23) Renewals for Radio Programming Undertaking Licences Due to Expire in 2007." Letter on behalf of NCRA/ANREC, submitted as intervention to CRTC.

Schellenberg, Matt. "What Everyone Is Searching For." *Spectator Tribune*, 11 December 2012. http://www.spectatortribune.com/article/what-everyone-is-searching-for.

Schmidt, Rob. "Launching an FM Radio Station Isn't as Easy as You Might Imagine." *Stylus*, December 1998, 7.

Shade, Leslie Regan. 2007. "Aspergate: Concentration, Convergence, and Censorship in Canadian Media." In *Converging Media, Diverging Politics: A Political Economy of News Media in the United States and Canada.* Edited by David Skinner, James R. Compton, and Michael Gasher. 101–16. Lanham: Lexington Books.

———. 2011. "Media Reform in the United States and Canada: Activism and Advocacy for Media Policies in the Public Interest." In *The Handbook of Global Media and Communication Policy.* Edited by Robin Mansell and Marc Raboy. 147–65. Malden: Blackwell.

Shade, Leslie Regan, and Michael Lithgow. 2010. "The Cultures of Democracy: How Ownership and Public Participation Shape Canada's Media Systems." In *Mediascapes: New Patterns in Canadian Communication*, 3rd ed. Edited by Leslie Regan Shade. 200–20. Toronto: Nelson Education.

———. 2013. "Media Ownership, Public Participation, and Democracy in the Canadian Mediascape." In *Mediascapes: New Patterns in Canadian Communication*, 4th ed. Edited by Leslie Regan Shade. 174–203. Toronto: Nelson Education.

Sherbert, Erin. 2011. "USF Sells Off KUSF, Its College Radio Station, Escorts Staff Out." *SF Weekly*, 15 December 2011. http://blogs.sfweekly.com/thesnitch/2011/01/usf_sells_off_kusf_its_college_radio_st.php.

"Show List." *CiTR 101.9 FM.* 15 August 2011. http://www.citr.ca/index.php/shows/profiles.

Skinner, David. 2010. "Minding the Growing Gaps: Alternative Media in Canada." In *Mediascapes: New Patterns in Canadian Communication,* 3rd ed. Edited by Leslie Regan Shade. 221–36. Toronto: Nelson Education.

Skinner, David, James R. Compton, and Mike Gasher. 2007. "Mapping the Threads." In *Converging Media, Diverging Politics: A Political Economy of News Media in the United States and Canada.* Edited by David Skinner, James R. Compton, and Michael Gasher. 7–23. Lanham: Lexington Books.

Skinner, David, and Mike Gasher. 2007. "So Much by So Few: Media Policy and Ownership in Canada." In *Converging Media, Diverging Politics: A Political Economy of News Media in the United States and Canada.* Edited by David Skinner, James R. Compton, and Michael Gasher. 51–76. Lanham: Lexington Books.

Smith, Lindsay. 2013. "Welcome Back Radio Ryerson." *Ryersonian,* 1 February 2013. http://www.ryersonian.ca/?p=177.

"Sound Off." *Stylus,* June–July 2011, 17.

Spencer, Kyle. 2011. "College Radio Heads: Off the Dial." *New York Times,* 2 December 2013. http://www.nytimes.com/2011/11/06/education/edlife/college-radio-heads-off -the-dial.html?pagewanted=all&_r=0.

Stahl, Geoff. 2003. "Crisis? What Crisis? Anglophone Musicmaking in Montreal." Ph.D. diss., McGill University, Montreal.

Sterling, Christopher H., and Michael C. Keith. 2008. *Sounds of Change: A History of FM Broadcasting in America.* Chapel Hill: University of North Carolina Press.

Stiles, Mark J., and Jacques Lachance. 1988. "History and Present Status of Community Radio in Quebec." Toronto: Ontario Ministry of Culture and Communications.

Storey, John. 2003. *Inventing Popular Culture: From Folklore to Globalization.* Malden: Blackwell.

Stout, Hilary, "Students Own Secret CITR." *The Ubyssey,* 11 September 1980.

Straw, Will. 1997. "Sizing Up Record Collections: Gender and Connoisseurship in Rock Music Culture." In *Sexing the Groove: Popular Music and Gender.* Edited by Sheila Whiteley. 3–16. New York: Routledge.

———. 1996. "Sound Recording." In *The Cultural Industries in Canada: Problems, Policies, and Prospects,* Edited by Michael Dorland. 95-117. Toronto: James Lorimer.

———. 1991. "Systems of Articulation, Logics of Change: Communities and Scenes in Popular Music." *Cultural Studies* 5.3: 368–88.

Stuart, Alec. "Catching a Radio Wave." *Stylus,* September 1994, 5.

Stylus, October 1990.

Stylus, June–July 2011, 1.

"Table of Contents." *Discorder,* April 2011, 3.

Terefenko, Paul. 2008. "Out of Tune at CKLN: Cops Are Becoming a Sad Fixture at Ryerson Radio Station as Labour Dispute Drags On." *NOW Magazine,* 2 December 2013. http://www.nowtoronto.com/news/story.cfm?content=164676.

Thomas, Eric. 1992. "Canadian Broadcasting and Multiculturalism: Attempts to Accommodate Ethnic Minorities." *Canadian Journal of Communication* 17.3. http://cjc -online.ca/printarticle.php?id=99&layout=html.

Thomas, Maegan. "CiTR: Ruling Campus Airwaves for 75 Years." *The Tyee*, 17 November 2012. http://thetyee.ca/ArtsAndCulture/2012/11/17/CiTR-Birthday.

Thornton, Sarah. 1996. *Club Cultures: Music, Media, and Subcultural Capital*. Hanover: University Press of New England.

Troop, Don. "What's Eating College Radio?" *Huffington Post*, 23 June 2011. http://www.huffingtonpost.com/2011/06/23/whats-eating-college-radi_n_882876.html?

Twang Trust Fundraiser. Advertisement. *Stylus*, February–March 2011.

"Two Hopeful Students." Letter to the Editor. *The Ubyssey*, 10 November 1959.

Vipond, Mary. 1992. *Listening In: The First Decade of Canadian Broadcasting, 1922–1932*. Montreal and Kingston: McGill–Queen's University Press.

Vorwald, John. 2010. "Waning Support for College Radio Sets Off a Debate." *New York Times*, 6 December 2011. http://www.nytimes.com/2010/12/06/business/media/06stations.html?_r=1&partner=rss&emc=rss.

Vukets, Cynthia, and Ashante Infantry. 2011. "Dead Air for Ryerson Community Station." *Toronto Star*, 1 December 2014. http://www.thestar.com/news/gta/2011/04/16/dead_air_for_ryerson_community_station.html.

Wagman, Ira. 2006. "From Spiritual Matters to Economic Facts: Recounting Problems of Knowledge in the History of Canadian Audiovisual Policy, 1928–61." Ph.D. diss., McGill University, Montreal.

Waits, Jennifer. 2013. "Former KTRU Frequency, Classical 91.7, Cuts Local Hosts." *Radio Survivor*, 6 December 2013. http://radiosurvivor.com/2013/11/10/former-ktru-frequency-classical-91-7-cuts-local-hosts.

Wallis, Roger, and Krister Malm. 1993. "From State Monopoly to Commercial Oligopoly. European Broadcasting Policies and Popular Music Output over the Airwaves." In *Rock and Popular Music: Politics, Policies, Institutions*. Edited by Tony Bennett, Simon Frith, Lawrence Grossberg, John Shepherd, and Graeme Turner. 156–68. New York: Routledge.

Walters, Marylu. 2002. *CKUA: Radio Worth Fighting For*. Edmonton: University of Alberta Press.

Weisz, Iolanda, and Harry Hertscheg. 1987. "Fifty Years of UBC Radio: 1937–1987." Vancouver: Alma Mater Society and Student Radio Society of the University of British Columbia.

"Welcome to the Terrordome." Letter from CiTR to listeners, 23 February 1990.

Wiener-Bronner, Danielle. 2010. "The 9 Best College Radio Stations." *Huffington Post*, 8 November 2010. http://www.huffingtonpost.com/2010/10/26/9-best-college-radio-stat_n_773720.html#s164554&title=CJLO_Concordia_University.

Wilkinson, Kealy, and Associates. 1988. *Community Radio in Ontario: A Dynamic Resource—An Uncertain Future*. Toronto: Ontario Ministry of Culture and Communications.

Williams, Raymond. 1980/2005. *Culture and Materialism*. New York: Verso.

———. 1977. *Marxism and Literature*. New York: Oxford University Press.

———. 1974/2003. *Television: Technology and Cultural Form*. New York: Routledge.

Wilson, Jill. "Mouthpiece." *Stylus*, September 1994, 3.

Wong, Chris. 1988. "Student Radio: It's a Wild, Wacky World." *Vancouver Sun*, 10 September, , E2.

Zimmerman, Arthur Eric. 1991. *In the Shadow of the Shield: The Development of Wireless Telegraphy and Radio Broadcasting in Kingston and at Queen's University: An Oral and Documentary History, 1902–1957*. Kingston: A.E. Zimmerman.

Ziniuk, Tara-Michelle. 2010. "CRTC Hearing on Campus–Community Radio Policy." Letter to Secretary General of the CRTC. Gatineau: CRTC.

Index

Books in the Film+Media Studies Series
Published by Wilfrid Laurier University Press